TAKE THE JOURNEY

JAMES A. PERCOCO

FOREWORD BY MILTON CHEN / AFTERWORD BY CATHY GORN

For Matt Dymek —

Enjoy the journey!

STENHOUSE PUBLISHERS
PORTLAND, MAINE

Stenhouse Publishers
www.stenhouse.com

Credits
Figure 1.1: Courtesy of the Eugenics Archives, University of Virginia
Figure 1.2: Courtesy of Library of Virginia Education and Outreach Division (www.virginiamemory.com/shaping)
Pages 33–35: Excerpts from *Beyond Jamestown: Virginia Indians Past and Present*, eds. Melanie R. Brimhall, Carole Nash, and Karenne Wood. Copyright © 2006, Virginia Foundation for the Humanities.
Figures 4.1–4.7: Courtesy of the Civil War Trust (www.civilwar.org)
Figure 4.9: Image owner Michael J. McAfee; courtesy of Irving D. Moy
Figure 5.2: Courtesy of the Dwight D. Eisenhower Presidential Library and Museum
Appendix 1.2: From *"Why Won't You Just Tell Us the Answer?" Teaching Historical Thinking in Grades 7–12* by Bruce Lesh, copyright © 2010. Reproduced with permission of Stenhouse Publishers. www.stenhouse.com
Appendixes 2.2, 2.3, and 4.3: Used with permission from Teacher Created Materials

Library of Congress Cataloging-in-Publication Data

Names: Percoco, James A., author.
Title: Take the journey : teaching American history through place-based
  learning / James A. Percoco.
Description: Portland, Maine : Stenhouse Publishers, [2016] | Includes
  bibliographical references and index.
Identifiers: LCCN 2017011539 (print) | LCCN 2016047552 (ebook) | ISBN
  9781625311436 (pbk. : alk. paper) | ISBN 9781625311443 (ebook)
Subjects: LCSH: United States--History--Study and teaching. | Place-based
  education--United States.
Classification: LCC E175.8 .P473 2016 (ebook) | LCC E175.8 (print) | DDC
  973.007--dc23
LC record available at https://lccn.loc.gov/2017011539

Cover and interior design by Blue Design, Portland, Maine (www.bluedes.com)

Manufactured in the United States of America

PRINTED ON 30% PCW
RECYCLED PAPER

23 22 21 20 19 18 17   9 8 7 6 5 4 3 2 1

In Memory of **Ronald C. Maggiano**

1952–2014

Beloved Colleague and Friend

May Those Whose Lives You Touched Live Long and Prosper

CONTENTS

Foreword

For many years, Jim Percoco, an award-winning teacher, has been inspiring students to a deeper understanding of American history by taking them to our nation's most important places. His book *Take the Journey* will now inspire teachers to embrace place-based learning, the best path to creating more engaged citizens and, ultimately, a stronger democracy.

Take the Journey could not appear at a more propitious time as the nation celebrates the centennial of what author Wallace Stegner called "America's best idea," the National Park Service. For many years Percoco has been an advocate and champion of using national parks to teach history, either by bringing his students to a variety of these places or taking his students there virtually by working with educational specialists at each site. Over the course of his classroom career, thirty-six of Percoco's students joined the National Park Service as rangers, a living testimony to what the power of place can do in transforming young people.

In this book he takes place-based learning to a new level by highlighting the educational work of the many partners within the Journey Through Hallowed Ground National Heritage Area—the stretch of land that connects the battlefield at Gettysburg in Pennsylvania to the home of Thomas Jefferson, Monticello, in Charlottesville, Virginia.

Reading as if it were itself a travelogue, *Take the Journey* presents a myriad of rich and diverse lessons from which teachers can choose that reflect the complexity of the American dream while honoring the diversity of the nation. The material herein covers, like the Journey itself, the breadth and depth of American history; the lessons presented span the founding of the nation through the twentieth century. Robust and rich, these lessons are easily replicated in any classroom in any school in the United States. Whether you are teaching about the founders, examining the Civil War, comparing or contrasting the views of African American leaders, learning about the treatment of Eastern Indian tribes, or studying the Cold War, it's all here.

Teachers west of the Mississippi often feel at a disadvantage when it comes to teaching the history of the United States, as it can seem as if most of American history took place east of the "Father of Waters." *Take the Journey* solves that problem by bringing historical sites into the classroom and offering teachers and students a window into America from any distance. In an age of fighting cultural illiteracy, *Take the Journey* will help you to see how place-based learning can unfold in your lessons without having to leave the classroom.

Percoco does not shy away from the difficult topics in American history, and he shows you how to avoid pitfalls when teaching difficult topics, such as race relations. These lessons are prescient and will give your students a balanced view of the American past without making anyone feel guilty. The author also provides many practical tips that can be used to enhance your current instruction.

Much of this material easily fits into the Common Core quite naturally since it is rooted principally in primary sources. Whether or not teachers and students are discussing the nation's formative documents composed by Jefferson and Madison, such as the Declaration of Independence and the Constitution; letters from Civil War soldiers sent home to family members; or speeches by social justice advocates Frederick Douglass or W. E. B. Du Bois, the educational material developed by the staffs of the many organizations that compose the Journey Through Hallowed Ground partnership will help you with your curricular focus. The multiple service-learning projects discussed in this book expose students to the kinds of work they will perform in colleges and universities as well as to all kinds of career possibilities and choices.

Take the Journey will benefit veteran teachers and new teachers alike, breathing life into instruction that may have fallen flat and inspiring teachers to think and teach not only outside of the box but also outside of the classroom. It is a book that is tailor-made for our times whose material will prove usable decades hence. I encourage you to wrap yourself up in this user- and teacher-friendly book: follow Jim Percoco—the Pied Piper of American history teachers—and take the journey. The price of admission is well worth it.

Milton Chen
Senior fellow, Edutopia, George Lucas Educational Foundation

Acknowledgments

I t goes without saying that writing a book requires investing more than just the soul of the author. Writing *Take the Journey* has been no exception.

I am indebted to a fair number of people who helped in myriad ways as this project was shepherded forward. First and foremost to my wife, Gina, who understands my need to write and always provides the space for me to do so. My daughters, Stephanie and Claire, were also enthusiasts of this book as they have been for my others. Collectively these three essential women in my life give me the gift of their lives every day, whether they are near or far. My mom and dad and siblings also provided support and the joy that comes when talking with one's family about one's life work.

Karenne Wood of the Monacan was helpful in providing me with resources related to the history of the Monacan people, and to her I am thankful for putting me in touch with Dr. Jeffrey Hantman at the University of Virginia, who has devoted his life to studying the indigenous people of Virginia. Jeff also provided cogent critiques of Chapter 1 to make sure that it was accurate and appropriate with regard to all the journalists, anthropologists, and historians who have labored to bring the struggle of the Monacan and other groups and their stories to the forefront. Staff members of the Albert and Shirley Small Special Collections Library at the University of Virginia were also helpful as my former student Priya Chhaya and colleague Amy Trenkle spent a day combing through the papers of Walter Plecker. Hats off to Priya and Amy for joining me on this aspect of my writing and this part of the Journey and to Amy for allowing me to field-test lessons at Alice Deal Middle School in Washington, DC. In a crowded curriculum that increasingly constrains teacher creativity, Amy was more than happy to give up two valuable instructional days to help me out. Friends and activists Kim and Reggie Harris provided the inspiration I needed in using their music to help solve a literary difficulty as did a one-on-one conversation with Reggie with regard to the role that race plays not just in American history but in our current national life as well.

Friend and biographer James McGrath Morris played an instrumental role in helping to shape my chapter on Jefferson and Madison, particularly when it came to working out how best to explain Madison and his work and writings to students. When he was my colleague in the classroom, he had that gift of being able to take difficult topics and make them digestible for his government students. Thus a debt of gratitude is owed for helping me visualize his teaching and putting it into words. At Montpelier, the home of James Madison, I am indebted to staff educators Christian Cotz, Emily Voss, and Kyle Stetz, who met with me on a lovely spring day to talk about the resources they had developed to teach about him. Their suggestions, as well as those of Madison scholar Philip Bigler, helped shape a chapter that proved in its initial stages to be cumbersome. All of them helped me get out of the weeds. At Monticello I received a warm welcome from Linnea Grimm and Melanie Bower, who put me on to Dan Korn's eminently teachable video, *We Won't Apologize,* as well as helped me work through the various materials their education department has developed relating to our third president and one of American history's more controversial and enigmatic characters.

Whether he is in the Eternal City, Rome, or at home in Fort Payne, Alabama, author Jerry Ellis, a writer not unfamiliar with journeys, has been an ardent supporter of my writing for close to two decades.

At Harpers Ferry National Historical Park I owe a big thanks to Dennis Frye, chief of Interpretation and Educational Partnerships, for putting me in touch with former students of the Journey's Of the Student, By the Student, For the Student project who became National Park Service rangers. Additionally he reviewed Chapter 3 and provided suggestions on content to include what Harpers Ferry National Historical Park would like to see teachers use in the classroom. Thanks also to Autumn Cook for providing the image of the Heyward Shepherd Memorial on such short notice.

In the chapter on the Civil War, Peter Maugle, National Park Service ranger and historian at Fredericksburg & Spotsylvania National Military Park, helped me understand the power of their Community at War online instructional materials. Also helping was Rebecca Capobianco, Teacher-Ranger-Teacher. Readers should consider applying to this marvelous National Park Service program where a teacher works in a national park during the summer as a park ranger and then returns to the classroom ready to teach from a unique perspective. Barbara Sanders, education specialist at Gettysburg National Military Park, spent time with me in her office detailing the multitude of teacher and student programs offered by the park as well as read and commented on my drafts of

Chapter 4. My colleagues at the Civil War Trust, Garry Adelman, director of history and education, and Sam Smith, education program manager, provided collegiality and a flexible schedule when needed to address my writing. Veteran teachers Joe Foster, David Kendrick, and Bob Rinehart, who do so much for Civil War battlefield preservation with their respective students, also pitched in when asked for ideas, as did Phil Caskey, who put me on to the essential idea of using board games to teach American history.

At Eisenhower National Historic Site, site manager Ahna Wilson was very accommodating to my needs as I worked on Chapter 5. I'd like to thank Elwood "Woody" Strait, principal of Gettysburg Area Middle School, and his staff members Jennifer Riddlemoser and Karen Briant, two teachers who worked to see that the Of the Student, By the Student, For the Student project on Eisenhower became a reality. Michael Birkner, Eisenhower Scholar at Gettysburg College, provided counsel and suggested potential topics for students to pursue with regard to the Eisenhower National Historic Site vodcast.

Thanks also should go to Corrine Burton, president and CEO of Teacher Created Materials, for permission to reprint the three reader's theaters in the appendix.

At LSG, founder Deep Sran discovered my interest in what his students were doing compelling enough to provide counsel, as did the Old Ashburn School project manager, Sharon Knipmeyer.

My colleagues at the Journey Through Hallowed Ground Partnership have been faithful to this book as supporters and friends. I am particularly indebted to Cate Magennis Wyatt, founder and president emeritus, who enthusiastically supported the book from the moment I raised it as an idea, and to William Sellers, the current chief executive officer and president, who embraced it once he took the helm from Cate. Board member Stuart Haney also played a significant role in helping to see the project shepherded along. Michelle Burrelli, chief operating officer, supported the project, as did Ashley Abruzzi and Shaun Butcher, director of the National Scenic Byway, who gladly gave of his time in shooting some of the photographs that illustrate *Take the Journey* as well as selecting other related images. A huge supporter of this effort was Dan Jordan, president emeritus of the Thomas Jefferson Foundation and former member of the board of the Journey Through Hallowed Ground. Dan understands the need for strong teaching of American history and has always enthusiastically embraced my myriad teaching efforts. Finally at JTHG a big hug goes to Jessie Aucoin, former director of educational programs, who worked very closely with me on this project, from dealing with my sometimes run-on sentences to lifting my spirits when the writing got tough and providing sterling feedback where needed on the manuscripts direction and development. There is no way this book would be in your hands were it not for Jessie.

I'd like to thank National Archives and Records Administration archivist Rick Blondo, my colleague and friend, for leading me to some important federal records for Chapter 1, and Pam Sanfilippo, education specialist at the Eisenhower Library in Abilene, Kansas, who helped with federal records related to the Eisenhower presidency for Chapter 6.

At Stenhouse it has been a pleasure to work once again with editor and friend William Varner. I am so gratified he saw the value of this book and the resources created by JTHG and our partners. The fifteen-year wait to work with Bill on another book project has been well worth it.

Many thanks to Milton Chen, senior fellow at Edutopia—the educational arm of the George Lucas Foundation—for the stirring foreword. Milton, who chairs the National Park Service Advisory Board's Education Committee, took time from a busy year helping to shepherd the National Park Service through its centennial celebration. I'd like to thank Cathy Gorn, National History Day executive director, for providing the afterword. A big thanks also goes to Julie Washburn, the National Park Service's associate director for interpretation, who supports not only my work as a teacher but also the important work of JTHG.

I'd also like to extend my gratitude to documentary filmmaker Ken Burns; Brent Glass, the Smithsonian Institution's National Museum of American History director emeritus; and Dr. Yohuru Williams, professor of history and dean of the College of Arts and Sciences at Fairfield University for their sterling jacket blurbs.

At West Springfield High School in Springfield, Virginia, where I taught for thirty-two years, I tip my hat to former colleagues Brad Swain, Brian Heintz, and Tim Spicer, with whom I remain connected and to whom, when solicited, I have offered any sort of sage advice that is possible.

Finally, to Neal Adams, my high school teacher during the mid-1970s who is now a beloved and good friend and to whom I still turn to talk about history and current events. In my work, I help pass on Neal's history teacher DNA to those I encounter either in person or on the written page.

Those who benefit from this book will upon completion owe thanks to all the good, kind, gracious, generous people mentioned above. They too will be with them as they "take the journey."

Invoking the Spirit of History

t is mid-November. Thanksgiving break is a week away. Students and teachers alike are longing for the days off. The first quarter has come to a rapid close, and everyone at school is now in "full year" mode. I have dozed off on the charter bus, having met it at 6:00 a.m. with my thirty students; now, ninety minutes after departing from the school, I look through the haze of my sleep-laden eyes and can see we are approaching our destination, Gettysburg National Military Park. I rouse myself and look down the aisle of the bus. Students doze, earbuds dangling from many heads. Pillows are propped along breath-steamed windows with heads tilted against them. Blankets cover many of those snoozing. Adult chaperones, too, are sleeping. I sidle up to the driver, giving him directions as we make our way through the south end of the battlefield, through the town of Gettysburg, and head west on the Chambersburg Pike. As we near the crest of McPherson Ridge, I direct the driver to pull off to the right, near the statues of the Battle of Gettysburg Day 1 heroes, General John Buford and General John Reynolds. I pick up the microphone and announce that we have arrived. A collective groan emanates.

I pull on my wool Civil War colonel's jacket that I have borrowed from the prop shop at Arlington House National Historic Site. Its feel awakens me even further. The students and adult chaperones assemble. Vapor clouds form in front of everyone as they speak and yawn. The driver cuts the engine off. Now my head is clear and I am ready for the day. I huddle everyone over toward the statue of Buford. As I wait for the noisy traffic to subside, I reach into my pocket and pull out a set of Tibetan bells. The students see them and know what is coming. I ask everyone to face west as the sun begins to rise behind us. After a few remarks about where we are standing and why, I turn to face the assembly, bring the bells to front and center, and invoke the mantra that I have been doing for the last couple of years in the classroom. Some of the students chime in: "It's that time, in moment and space, when we bring the bells together and invoke the spirit of history." The bells meet each other in a gentle clang. In a non-creepy way the spirits and energy of Gettysburg, and all that it means in American memory, rise up to greet us. The sky is clear. The sun is now up and warming us. I know it is going to be a good day!

We are standing not only near the northern end of Gettysburg National Military Park, but at the northern terminus of the Journey Through Hallowed Ground, a 180-mile National Heritage Area. It is a corridor that runs from Gettysburg south to Thomas Jefferson's mountaintop home—Monticello—in Charlottesville, Virginia. The Journey cuts through four states—Pennsylvania, Maryland, West Virginia, and Virginia—yet you can make the drive from Gettysburg to Monticello in just over two hours, heading down Routes 15 and 29 (see Figure 1). Along this swath of land are nine presidential sites, including the homes of not only Jefferson, but also James Madison, James Monroe, and Dwight D. Eisenhower. It is the land of literally hundreds of Civil War battle sites, many of them locations of small skirmishes but others with national significance, including Antietam, Spotsylvania, the Wilderness, and Gettysburg. There are places where America's first residents, American Indians of the Susquehannock, Piscataway, and Iroquois tribes, left their footprints, sites from the American Revolution and War of 1812, and Underground Railroad sites, such as Harpers Ferry, where John Brown and his band of raiders set in motion actions that led to the Civil War. Within its boundaries are thirteen National Park units, numerous scenic rivers, roads, farms, and small towns, all from a time before the Internet, smartphones, and electronic tablets.

Calling this "Where America Happened" is the Journey Through Hallowed Ground (JTHG) Partnership, an affiliation of organizations that seek, by working together, to preserve the beauty and historical integrity, and to educate people—particularly the young—about the richness of this seminal parcel of America.

Pulitzer Prize–winning author Geraldine Brooks told me in a phone interview, "This remarkable region tells the story of how and where America happened. It has the power

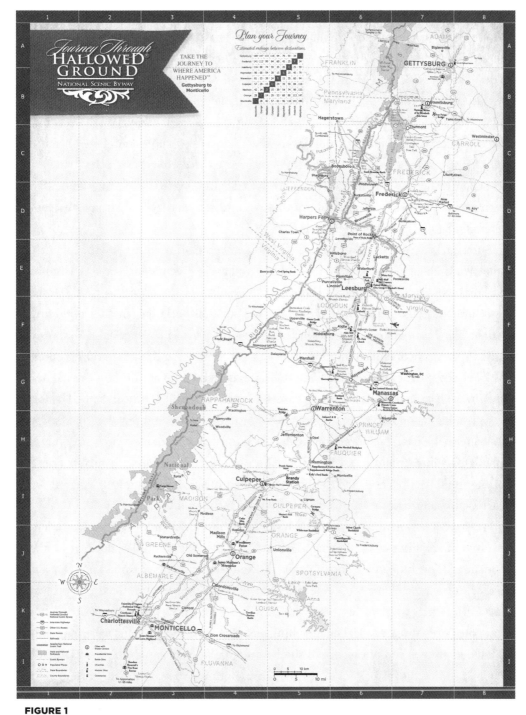

FIGURE 1

Map of the Journey Through Hallowed Ground

to transport us on the greatest journey of all: the journey of empathy and imagination into the lives of the people—famous and unknown, humble and distinguished—who shaped this country and made us who we are." I first encountered the Journey in an article in the *Washington Post*. Always looking for new ideas to employ in my classroom instruction, I knew from what I was reading that it offered a cornucopia of ways for me to engage my students. The forthcoming school year was on the horizon, too, so the timing was exceptional. The following Monday, I called the Journey's president, Cate Magennis Wyatt, introducing myself as a high school history teacher from West Springfield High School. I told her I was an advocate of place-based learning and expected my students to learn much more from the physical world around them than they could from a textbook. I abandoned using textbooks years ago.

Informal place-based learning was part of my education as a student. I went to elementary school in Concord, Massachusetts, and have very fond memories of climbing over rocks and walking along trails the minutemen traveled on April 19, 1775. Minute Man National Historical Park is where I figured out at an early age what I wanted to do with my life. I wanted to be a storyteller of history, preferably in a National Park ranger's uniform, but as I got older, I migrated to being a schoolteacher. I get to live my National Park Service ranger alter ego through the thirty-six students of mine who went on to work in the National Park Service as rangers. My teaching philosophy of applied history, an active, hands-on, integrated approach to the subject, which many described as my passion for the past, had a real influence on many of my students who went on after college to be history and social studies teachers or public historians. If you, too, seek to inspire students, then applying this approach of enthusiasm with a joy for learning and teaching to your instruction can produce similar results for you.

When we finally met, Wyatt and I brainstormed some ideas for how to get my students involved in activities of the Journey Through Hallowed Ground. We decided to have students adopt some of the locations in the Journey and create some kind of visual related to their visit. They could be videos or PowerPoint presentations. The projects had a direct link to historic preservation, too; each project needed to address how these sites were threatened by encroaching development, and students were to include a detailed connection of the site to the National Historic Preservation Act of 1966. Students visited the historic town of Waterford, Virginia, where the headquarters of the Journey is located. Some went to Monocacy National Battlefield, site of an important 1864 Civil War engagement that blunted a Confederate attack on Washington, DC. One student went to Oatlands Historic House & Gardens, a property of the National Trust for Historic Preservation, and another visited Dodana Manor, the home of George C. Marshall. I gave the students two months to complete the assignment.

All the sites were ninety minutes away or less from school. I made sure that students called ahead to make arrangements with site staff, as this needed to be more than a photo opportunity. They framed their final visual results and their visit within historical context, being certain to have the project reflect the provisions of the United States Historic Preservation Act of 1966. Students also needed to demonstrate how this local site was tied to the bigger national narrative of American history.

A project such as the one I developed with Cate Magennis Wyatt is possible to implement in any classroom, in any part of the country. Every community has a history. Every community has a story, and those stories are invariably connected to that national narrative of American history. For example, civil rights sites in the South are not just places like Selma, Montgomery, and Birmingham, Alabama. African American communities throughout the South galvanized during this period to gain access to public libraries and all schools. Sites in southern Virginia address African American agency during massive resistance, the political movement led by Virginia to resist the decision of school integration in the *Brown v. Board of Education* case of 1954. In Alaska, the Klondike Gold Rush sites provide fodder for a different kind of frontier and are filled with stories of economic and social expansion in Alaska after the purchase made by Secretary of State William Seward in 1867. Utah has a rich history, too, of which its Mormon residents are fiercely proud. The story of the Mormon migration is deeply part of the American tale, as it is about prejudice in America. Teachers can employ with the same success these best practices at schools from the Canadian border to the Rio Grande.

One of the really engaging projects conducted by schools inside the Journey is to create vodcasts or mini-movies for historic sites, as part of an initiative called Of the Student, By the Student, For the Student. This is an immersive middle school service-learning project in which students become the actual historians. Shortly after the Journey Through Hallowed Ground Partnership was formed, Wyatt and the National Park staff of Harpers Ferry National Historical Park put their heads together. The park was looking for a primary source–based hands-on project that would engage middle schools more effectively within the park. What was born out of that meeting was an award-winning, student-produced video project, called a vodcast, under the moniker Of the Student, By the Student, For the Student. The project has been so successful and the outcomes have been so strong, including an increase across the board in student standardized testing scores, that the vodcasts are endorsed by school administrators, state board of education specialists, and parents alike. The work that students create ultimately becomes part of the official interpretive material of places such as Manassas National Battlefield, Fredericksburg & Spotsylvania National Military Park, and Monticello, among dozens of other places inside the Journey.

And the sites within the Journey offer many educational activities, lesson plans, and strategies for teachers to use easily within a K–12 curriculum. The Civil War Trust, one of the Journey's partners, has countless free digital educational tools to bring places such as Gettysburg to your classroom in Nevada—and it's providing much more interaction for your students than a virtual field trip! By the time I left the classroom, I was doing all kinds of activities with my students using their digital devices. We were having fun doing it, too! Speaking of the Civil War, how would you like to have your students engage in a research project that honors each one of the 620,000 Americans who died in that conflict? The Living Legacy Tree Planting Project does just that. I'll talk about this remarkable project in the forthcoming pages, too. Want to teach about James Madison? Come to the Journey! Want to engage students in women's history? Stop by the Journey! When you commemorate Black History Month, the Journey is there for you, too!

It is nice when your professional life brings you full circle, particularly when you come to realize that you are part of a much larger whole. In my post-classroom life, I have discovered I can still inspire other teachers and students in my work as teacher-in-residence at the Journey Through Hallowed Ground Partnership. Using this great outdoor classroom you could teach most everything you need to have your students connect with our shared American history.

Since the Journey covers the span of American history, you can frame your entire course around the region, especially since a map comes with this book. I suggest that you post the map in your classroom adjacent to a map of the United States on which you have highlighted the Journey Through Hallowed Ground National Heritage Area. Each time you teach an activity, look for ways that you can connect the Journey to the larger narrative of American history. I detail this more specifically in Chapter 4.

I also suggest that you secure a copy of David Edwin Lillard's *The Journey Through Hallowed Ground: The Official Guide to Where America Happened*, Deborah Lee's *Honoring Their Paths: African American Contributions Along the Journey Through Hallowed Ground*, and National Geographic's *Journey Through Hallowed Ground:*

Birthplace of the American Ideal by Andrew Cockburn. These books will augment your reading of this one and each in their own unique way inspire you as well.

As I write this, the National Park Service centennial is upon us. The National Park Service centennial goals, like those of the Journey, are to connect with and create the next generation of park visitors, supporters, and advocates. What is so wonderful about the centennial is that the Park Service is embracing all kinds of parks, including state and local parks, as part of its celebration. The Journey, and all that has developed under Wyatt's leadership, has a huge role to play with regard to the educational purpose of parks and how they can be incorporated into the classroom. Even celebrated filmmaker Ken Burns recognized the value of what author Wallace Stegner called "America's Best Idea" and made a masterful film series about our national parks.

Bring your students with you along the Journey. Like history itself the Journey is full of surprises. Let yourself and your students have one of those spontaneous "aha moments" without ever having to leave the classroom—though, of course there is always summer vacation and winter and spring break, when the actual Journey will always welcome you.

In this book I bring the Journey to you with the hopes that you will be able to tap into the rich repository of resources produced by and for the Journey and available to teachers nationwide. Some chapters look at specific partners with whom the Journey works such as the Civil War Trust or Thomas Jefferson's Monticello. Other chapters are more topical and deal with lesson materials related to themes, ideas, or people who lived inside the Journey.

Jon Jarvis, the director of the National Park Service, said in a meeting on the cusp of the 2016 National Park Service centennial celebration, "Our first century was about bringing people to the parks, but the next century will be about bringing parks to the people." In many ways that is what this book is all about: bringing the Journey Through Hallowed Ground National Heritage Area to you, your students, and your classroom. Come, take the Journey and enjoy the ride.

CHAPTER 1

We Are Still Here—The Research Road Trip

t's early, and my former student Priya Chhaya, public historian for the National Trust for Historic Preservation, is annoyed with me. I've dragged her out of bed on a Monday holiday, the birthday of Dr. Martin Luther King Jr. Also joining me at this Northern Virginia shopping center parking lot is Amy Trenkle, who teaches eighth-grade United States history at Alice Deal Middle School in Washington, DC. I met her a decade ago when she was a participant in a Teaching American History Grant project sponsored by American University and the District of Columbia Public Schools. She started her career in 1998, became Nationally Board Certified in early adolescent social studies/history in 2005, and was recertified in 2015. We immediately connected over our shared deep commitment to teaching history more effectively. Amy also participated in the National Park Service Teacher-Ranger-Teacher summer program, working in 2009 as a National Park Service ranger at Chickasaw National Recreation Area. We are equally enthusiastic about our national parks being outdoor classrooms.

Priya understands what it takes to achieve the best learning and teaching about history. She also recognizes the value of place-based learning in teaching American history. Priya maintains a public history blog called *This Is What Comes Next*, an excellent resource for teachers because she brings a great deal of thought to her posts and almost always brings the past into our present. One of her posts is titled "*Hamilton* and Public History:

Who Lives, Who Dies, Who Tells Your Story" about the blockbuster Broadway show by Lin-Manuel Miranda. This seems really relevant today, because much about our work is about recovering lost voices from the past.

As we pile into the car on this holiday, the three of us are on a mission. Having learned about the Virginia Racial Integrity Act of 1924 and its effect on Virginia Indian tribes and African Americans living in Virginia, we are searching for primary document materials that can be developed into lesson plans and added to the repository of educational materials offered to teachers by the Journey Through Hallowed Ground Partnership. The Monacan lived in the Virginia Piedmont and thus inside the borders of the National Heritage Area, and they were one of the tribes at the center of resistance to the law, offering a perfect case study about the value and importance of agency. This story really matters, because although academic historians have rooted the tale out, there is still very little discussion in American schools about this law and the effect of the eugenics movement in the United States. It is one of those stories that reflects the dark underbelly of America and needs to be taught to students if we are going to continue moving toward becoming a more equitable and just society. (See Appendix 1.1.)

Fortified with caffeine we head out to the Albert and Shirley Small Special Collections Library at the University of Virginia in Charlottesville. Thomas Jefferson's university is at the southern end of the Journey Through Hallowed Ground National Heritage Area, a two-and-a-half-hour drive from the Northern Virginia suburbs. We are going to look through the correspondence of Walter Ashby Plecker, the head of the Virginia Bureau of Vital Statistics, and his compatriot John Powell, the American composer and music historian. Both men were unequivocal white supremacists and proponents of eugenics. Both men were enthusiasts for Virginia's Racial Integrity Act of 1924, which wreaked havoc on people of color throughout the state until it was finally struck down once and for all in the landmark 1967 US Supreme Court decision of *Loving v. Virginia*, in which the court ruled in favor of an interracial couple's decision to marry.

In all of my thirty-two years of teaching United States history to eleventh and twelfth graders, I had never heard of this law. Had I known of it, I am sure I would have found a way to incorporate it into my teaching, and in some ways I want to make up for what I missed by crafting lessons for the Journey Through Hallowed Ground Partnership that will help other teachers get their students to study this topic and all its sordid aspects, through an inquiry-based approach. The law basically said that if you had one drop of "negro" blood in you, you were black, and it became known as "the one drop rule." That it was passed in the 1920s should have come to me as no surprise, as that was a grim decade for people of color, particularly right after World War I. There was a spike in the number of lynchings, race riots took place in several major cities, the African American community in Rosewood, Florida, was razed and burned to the ground in 1922 by a hate-filled white mob, and the Ku Klux Klan held sway in state and national politics, even holding a massive demonstration down Pennsylvania Avenue in Washington, DC, an event I knew of and had taught my students about.

My first encounter with the Racial Integrity Act of 1924 came out of two conversations I had in early 2016. The first was with Karenne Wood, a member of the Monacan tribe, and the second was with Dr. Jeffrey Hantman, an anthropologist at the University of Virginia who specializes in the native peoples of Virginia. There are nine Indian tribes in Virginia that are not recognized by the federal government, and the Monacan—who lived for at least ten thousand years on the Virginia Piedmont and inside the Journey Through Hallowed Ground National Heritage Area—are one of those indigenous peoples. These Indian people are not recognized because of the Racial Integrity Act of 1924 and the vigor with which Plecker bullied people into enforcing the letter of the law, including the altering of both birth and school records. Any living Monacan, or other Virginia Indian for that matter, had to be legally declared a "negro." Thus there is no paper trail that provides the evidence they need regarding their ancestry to secure federal recognition.

I learned this, and more, when I met with Wood and Hantman while looking for teaching materials to develop in my role as teacher-in-residence for the Journey. Still not knowing about the Racial Integrity Act, I explained to Wood from the get-go that I was a white guy coming onto their turf and wanted to get it right. She said nothing, but smiled pleasantly. As our meeting ended, she handed me a number of materials to examine, and suggested I reach out to Hantman at the university. "We are still here!" she said as I prepared to go, shaking my hand. "We want our story told."

Little did I know where this initial conversation would lead me. In my stereotypic mind-set, I had hoped that the lessons I was going to develop would be about how indigenous people lived and thrived centuries ago as well as their interactions with the early European settlers of Virginia. But it was clear now that knowing about the "three sisters"—beans, corn, and squash, the staple food of Virginia Indians, duly noted as a benchmark of learning on the Virginia Standards of Learning—was going to have to be pushed aside. I'm not dismissing the need for students to know about the early lives of native people, but somehow this story about the Virginia Racial Integrity Act really tugged at me and seemed just as important, if not more so, for teachers to teach and for students to know.

Today the population of the Monacan numbers more than 1,400 people. The Monacan continue to preserve their heritage, customs, cultural traditions, and language, and have kept their memory alive by building a museum near the spiritual center of their community at Bear Mountain, Virginia. Also at Bear Mountain is an Episcopal mission church, constructed for them in 1908, and an old log cabin schoolhouse, the site where many Monacan children were educated after having been denied access to Virginia public schools. The locals in and around Bear Mountain during the first half of the last century referred to the Monacan as the "issues."

One week after meeting with Wood, I found myself back in Charlottesville, this time in Hantman's office. He was very encouraging about my efforts and directed me to a number of strong sources where I could pursue information about the Virginia Racial Integrity Act. Hantman suggested that a way to think of it was to ask, "If the law was undone by the United States Supreme Court in *Loving v. Virginia* forty-five years ago, why is there only one tribe with federal recognition in Virginia?" Current state and congressional representatives support the federal recognition effort, for the most part. The Monacan fought against an unceasing din of opposition to establish their own voice and promote agency. In particular they waged war against their oppressors in the courts and were able to persuade major newspapers in Virginia to report the story to readers. They even played a role in drafting text for a related historic marker on the Monacan village just outside Charlottesville.

Despite all this public coverage, I kept bumping into my own ignorance on the topic, and I found that frustrating, mostly because I view myself as a teacher who generally puts these kinds of topics on my radar screen. As much as I wanted to develop good lesson plans for teachers to use, I began to see this as more of a story of personal discovery than an unearthing of history never reported or written about before. I think that when teaching difficult or controversial topics such as this, history and social studies teachers need to ask themselves some questions: What is their own personal interest in the topic? What does the way they handle teaching it say about them? In the classroom I never shied away from controversial topics, and I always encouraged teachers I met and worked with to do the same. It is important that students see teachers as role models in teaching about such difficult topics. Never preach to students, and always let oppressors hang themselves with their own words when using material aimed at pointing out a social wrong.

My personal interest in stories of social injustices committed in the United States is probably rooted in the fact that when I was a young child, the civil rights movement was always at the forefront of the news. Some of the best field trips I took with students were to sites in the Deep South connected to the civil rights movement. If students see you, their teacher, become passionate about a topic, there is a good chance that they too will become passionate about it, and that pays out in dividends in educational capital.

Hantman told me, "When I first heard about Plecker, I was told by Indian people not to speak about him. Leave him dead and buried in the ground. That has changed, clearly. It's easy to hate Plecker, it's important to know about eugenics, but take it to the present, and why is there still a battle over federal recognition?" That is a good question to raise with your students, because we are still wrestling with matters that are close to a century old. As William Faulkner famously wrote in his novel *Requiem for a Nun*, "The past is never dead. It's not even past." Historian David McCullough always points out that what is the past to us was someone else's present and that if issues from those moments are not resolved, then we must take up the mantle of folks who went before us and work for change. You can do that when your approach to teaching is rich in both content and presentation.

Continuing my research, I discovered that Plecker's correspondence and other related documents were housed in the Albert and Shirley Small Special Collections Library at the University of Virginia. I have always been a strong advocate for the model of the "teacher-scholar." Teachers need to view themselves as more than just dispensers of information and practitioners of pedagogy, and should embrace themselves as scholars with genuine intellectual curiosity. And there is an element of fun in digging through old records. Teachers should have fun not only in their teaching, but also in pulling together the materials they teach.

We hear a great deal about top-down creation of professional learning communities. The problem with this top-down approach is that it is so inorganic. If you want a real professional learning community, get a bunch of like-minded, interested teachers and visit historic sites together, go through archives searching for "good stuff" to teach, and let the conversation flow naturally.

I continued to scour the Internet for both primary and secondary sources to start wrapping my head around the Virginia Racial Integrity Act and its effect on not only the Monacan, but other Virginia tribes as well. The more I dug, the more I learned, particularly about Powell and his leading role in establishing Anglo-Saxon Clubs in the United States. Powell was also instrumental in organizing the White Top Mountain Festival, an annual folk music festival held in Virginia between 1931 and 1939. Not surprisingly, African Americans were prohibited from performing and attending. Though I tracked down the Virginia state historical marker at White Top Mountain that explains the purpose of the festival and why it was important, it bears no discussion of the racial dimensions of the annual event.

Anglo-Saxon Clubs were social clubs across the United States organized by white adult males to promote their belief in white supremacy through public programs and lectures. They were not vigilante groups like the KKK, but more like the White Citizens Councils of the Deep South in the 1950s and 1960s. Clubs of upstanding community members pledged to keep the races separate, in this case under the guise of programs that supported intellectual discourse about the races. For Powell, whose first love was music and who used music as a means to separate whites and blacks, it was the perfect cover. Under Powell's leadership, the capital of the former Confederate States of America, Richmond, Virginia, became the hub of the Anglo-Saxon Club movement when it was launched in 1922. The club was political in nature, and members enthusiastically endorsed miscegenation laws and racial integrity acts, which became law in Virginia and were proposed in a number of other states. A year after its founding, its membership had risen from just a few members to more than four hundred men, and by 1925 there were thirty-two posts across the United States.

Through all of my digging I felt like I was having a personal Indiana Jones moment. Why had I never known about this sordid story? Like Lin-Manuel Miranda I kept asking myself, *What did I miss? And why did I not know about this?* Before much time passed, I longed to be back in the classroom. I would have been all over this tale and the many things it offered a teacher. Thus my outreach to Amy and Priya. I knew that with their companionship and assistance, I could pull together awesome teaching materials on the legacy of the Virginia Racial Integrity Act of 1924. We would examine the Plecker-Powell correspondence to see what documents we could use in conjunction with the records I received from the National Archives to craft meaningful lessons. Amy was particularly thrilled when I asked her if we could try out the lessons in her eighth-grade class. However, given the constraints placed on teachers today in our standards-based, data-driven climate, we knew we would have to be creative. The more Amy and I talked about it over the phone, the clearer it became that by the time we assembled all of the material after our research, this would be more than just a one-day lesson.

I met with Amy at Deal Middle School to pass off the National Archives materials and some other eugenics-related documents that I had found on the website of the American Philosophical Society, in Philadelphia. One of those documents was an application to join Powell's Anglo-Saxon Club. As we considered the documents we had on hand, we knew we would find more on our road trip and that the relevance of the Virginia Racial Integrity Act would not be lost on her students. Given the tenor of the times in which the Virginia Racial Integrity Act was passed, students would be able to see correlations to their own times, particularly within the context of the likes of the Black Lives Matter movement. As teachers you can ask students to consider whether much, if anything, has changed in America since 1924 or, as the Bible says, "There is nothing new under the sun." If the latter is the case, then what is the point of studying history? Ask your students to consider whether they think the study of history should be some form of social engineering. Have your students debate the premise in class or respond in a free-verse journal entry.

With wide-eyed wonder, Amy looked through the documents I had brought with me. She had never heard this story either and immediately recognized how powerful a primary source–based lesson could be with this material. I wanted to be respectful of Amy's teaching responsibilities. An option we explored was to teach the lesson in an extracurricular fashion to the history club at Deal, which she sponsors.

History clubs are popping up in schools all over the United States. Some at the high school level are known as history honor societies and even provide cords at graduation for students who meet certain criteria. History clubs and their proliferation are living proof that young people do indeed "like" history; what students don't like is how it is sometimes taught in school, as a litany of unconnected names and dates with little context. What really "hooks" students are the stories of the past. If you can bring those stories to life in a creative way, you will have a classroom in which students not only like history, but thrive as people. If you don't have a history club in your school, you should seriously consider sponsoring one. In this informal learning environment there is no one looking over your shoulder telling you what, when, and how to teach, so you are free to become the teacher that your aspirations call you to be.

In my classroom, I focused a lot of time on teaching about the civil rights movement. I used everything at my disposal: primary source documents, music of the period, audio recordings of Dr. King's speeches well beyond his iconic "I Have a Dream" speech, and video footage of protests and marches. My students read John Lewis's civil rights memoir, *Walking with the Wind*, a hefty but highly accessible tome. Over the years I had many students tell me it was the only book in high school that they read cover to cover. We even trekked into the US Capitol to meet with Congressman Lewis and have the students get their books signed. After our visit, one of my students wrote a letter to Lewis, and in return was invited to meet and speak with the congressman one-on-one. For five years I led a civil rights pilgrimage to Birmingham, Selma, and Montgomery, and in 2005, on the fortieth anniversary of Bloody Sunday, my students and I walked across the Edmund Pettus Bridge along with forty to fifty thousand other people. That moment remains a highlight of my tenure in the classroom. I know it was a day that changed many of my students' lives.

Stumbling across this story of the Virginia Racial Integrity Act has in some way jump-started me. And so, we head down Route 15/29 to Charlottesville, listening to the original cast recording from *Hamilton* along the way. Priya has been on my case about not listening to it and is taking this opportunity to make it happen. I feel an old familiar energy rekindled. As we near Charlottesville, we pass a state historical marker that indicates the location of the Monacan village. It's a great omen, and we note its location so we can take pictures of it on our return trip. My hope is that what we uncover and develop to teach will find merit and value in any seventh- to twelfth-grade history classroom in the United States.

Although this is in many ways a piece of local history, it has national implications, and I encourage you to follow the same formula when you work with your students. Thomas "Tip" O'Neill, former Speaker of the United States House of Representatives, once famously said, "All politics is local." The same can be said of history.

The first thing you need to do is look right outside your school's front door. What local history do you see? Consider your school's age—every school has a record in its collection of yearbooks and archives of school newspapers. Find a tale that tantalizes you and that you think you want to use to make history come alive for your students. The US escalation in Vietnam in the late 1960s was a rather tumultuous time in America. I remember being in junior high and high school with many students demonstrating their opposition to the war either by holding rallies or wearing those ubiquitous antiwar buttons. Look through back issues of your school newspaper and old yearbooks to see what students in your school were doing during the turbulent 1960s and early 1970s.

You need to do your homework. Learn as much as you can before you head out to dig through your school or local archives, be they in a public library, a university library, or a historical society. Find out at the repositories who you need to speak to and if they have online finding aids, which will help you refine your search. Pick up the phone, or e-mail the people who can help you, and share with them your enthusiasm to get researching. I know that seems like the most obvious step, but it's the one that holds teachers up the most. You have to take the leap, and the phone call or first contact e-mail is where it begins. Don't let the process intimidate you, either. Embrace it! It's part of your unique journey as a teacher. Just like you have rules for students to follow in your classroom, the repositories that hold primary source documents have rules, too. You have to follow them when you do your research, and they vary from repository to repository. Don't look at the rules of researching as an impediment. All the while, engage with your students; tell them about your research process. For example, when I wrote my Lincoln sculpture road trip book, *Summers with Lincoln: Looking for the Man in the Monuments* (2008), I made sure I shared all of my research adventures with my students. I kept them abreast of where I was going, what I was doing, and how I was doing it. It helped me to let my students know that I lived by the maxim I repeated at the beginning of each school year: "There is nothing I ask of you that I don't ask of myself." This was not about boasting, but rather about building credibility with my students. I wanted them to see Jim Percoco the teacher-scholar/historian at work. My approach paid off, because my students saw that I was willing to go the extra mile for my own personal edification, and it modeled for them what I expected them to do in the classroom—not necessarily write a book, but rather, bring excellence to their work.

As our research at the Albert and Shirley Small Special Collections Library on the University of Virginia campus would soon uncover, the eugenics laws of the time were on a national level. Plecker and his cohorts, leading the fray, urged other states across the nation to pass similar laws. In 1974 the Virginia General Assembly repealed the Sterilization Act and paid reparations of $25,000 to each survivor who was still alive at the time. Sitting in the reading room waiting for the Hollinger boxes to arrive, I am struck by how this one piece of local history had such national implications.

At last the moment arrives; as I see the boxes on the cart coming through the reading room doors, I feel I am having my Indiana Jones moment. I have these moments a great deal when working in archives. There's a certain mystique and aura surrounding primary records. The doors open automatically, the cart moves through them, and a sense of "here it comes" courses through my body. For the next four hours the three of us carefully go through the files in each box, looking for documents we could use to create our lesson. We religiously cross-reference what we had indicated that might be of interest. Priya and I go through the boxes of Plecker's correspondence while Amy looks through the box loaded with newspaper articles and opinion pieces of the time period. It is both heartening and sickening at the same time.

Much of what Priya and I encounter are letters of Plecker's that supported the proposed passing of similar legislation in states such as North Carolina, Ohio, Massachusetts, Arkansas, Texas, Oklahoma, Georgia, Tennessee, and Mississippi, and the District of Columbia. Many of the letters were responses to families making inquiries about birth and marriage record status. In most of them Plecker denied anyone who requested an identity change. He was a cagey old fox, too, obsessively researching family names long before people had written to him. If they had surnames that he had researched and deemed "Indian," requestors never had a chance to get the identity change to the "white" status they desired. To Plecker all Virginia Indians were black; he called them "Negros in feathers." Plecker pursued deep research into family names just to make certain no Indian could "sneak" into being white. He looked as far back as a century to secure names of family members who were born as Indians. In most of these letters he offered to refund the one-dollar application fee submitters had supplied. I keep thinking, tongue in cheek, *Gee, what a nice guy!* After making this gesture, Plecker would follow up by saying all correspondence would be kept on file to make sure this individual knew that he or she would never secure the status of being white. In fact, the only way one could be classified as white was by proving direct lineage to Pocahontas, since she had married Englishman John Rolfe and was, in some bizarre way, then identified as Virginia "royalty."

Plecker was ruthless to a fault, and his use of the term *issues* to identify the Monacan is replete. Many of the letters in the University of Virginia holdings are to state registrars, indicating that if they tried to circumvent the law, the wrath of Plecker would descend upon them with not just with a threat of a fine, but incarceration in a state penitentiary. Plecker was one of the most important and pernicious factors underlying failed efforts to gain federal recognition.

More famous Americans supported the white supremacy values of eugenics, too, including Alexander Graham Bell; Lawrence Lowell, president of Harvard University; and David Starr Jordan, president of Stanford University. Folks like these gave legitimacy to the idea of white supremacy.

Hantman had advised me, though, "not to simply focus on this one man, as that may oversimplify multiple issues in the historic and contemporary fight for federal recognition. "By solely blaming Plecker," he told me during our conversation, "it takes the state and Congress, especially the Senate, off the hook for so many other unfair policies not tied to the 1924 Act. Colonial policies and racism and local myths of legitimacy and invented fears of casinos and other sources of economic power for Indians play a role too." Frederick Douglass once wrote, "Power concedes nothing lightly. It never has and it never will." Those words continue to ring true in twenty-first-century America.

We continue to pore over the documents, and Amy stumbles upon the letters to editors of various newspapers across the United States that endorse Plecker and his work. Then she hits a jackpot: a political cartoon from *The Chicago Defender*, one of the nation's preeminent black newspapers. When she shows it to me, I say, "Wow! We have to get that document into the lesson." It's a cartoon of a dog labeled Virginia howling at the moon and is labeled "Virginia Racial Integrity Act." Once finished going through the boxes we begin the process of photographing the items we think will be useful in the classroom. There is so much "good stuff" to use that at times it appears as though we will be overwhelmed.

After an exhilarating, long, and exhausting day, we begin the road trip home. In the car we not only talk about the content but also brainstorm how we can use it in the classroom and whose voice we want to reflect in the lesson plan. I think of it as a "mobile professional learning community." Along the way, we stop to take a selfie at the Monacan Indian Village state historical marker alongside Routes 29/15, which leads to banter about having the students create some kind of historical marker or wayside exhibit that explains the Virginia Racial Integrity Act, as seen from the perspective of the Monacan and not some white state historian or bureaucrat. Much later I learn that this particular historical marker was written by Wood and Hantman, not some state bureaucrat, as we had assumed at the time. The process was apparently rather contentious as well, which gives insight into the use of agency of oppressed people when trying to distill a difficult story into one hundred words or less. But ultimate control of the text—which is quite political and radical for such signs if you study those one hundred words—went to Wood and Deanna Beacham of the Virginia Council of Indians. The sign was part of an effort to add about two dozen historical signs written by Virginia Indians, coordinated by the Virginia Council on Indians. What you might want to have your students consider is why creation of such signs can be so contentious and why people in power often are reactive to such efforts of agency on the part of the oppressed.

Ironically, we are listening to act 2 of *Hamilton,* which includes a song near the end about the role of legacy building. Given the hip-hop nature of *Hamilton* I suggested we incorporate that song into the lesson somehow. Legacy is identified with identity, and the Monacan and other Virginia Indians had their identity ripped out from beneath them. Voice is the predominant theme of our conversation for the remainder of the ride home.

I want to be clear about something: in this book I deal frequently with race. This is not about bashing white people or a reaction to white guilt. Rather it is an exercise in getting students to see how history is constructed and who does and who does not play a role in crafting our national narrative. It is not about "us" versus "them." It is about letting young people make informed choices as they read and reflect on our history. In many ways the times we live in are far different from the 1920s, yet every day the news is filled with racially charged stories, whether it's about who is snubbed by the Academy of Motion Picture Arts and Sciences for the Oscars or about racial profiling by police. It is about making history relevant to young people. The story of eugenics is indeed a sad chapter in our history. But I'm not interested in portraying the Monacan and other Indian people of Virginia as victims. These people have long fought against the system, and it's for a very good reason that they want their story told. They are not looking for pity; they are looking for justice. The story of agency by any oppressed group is critical to making the narrative being taught much more authentic and robust.

As a teacher you can use examples from our present to illuminate the past. Let's take the previously mentioned Oscar snubs as an example. If I were back in the classroom, I would be cutting up and photocopying newspaper articles for students to read, including op-ed pieces. I'd get them to write reflective journals. I'd hold class discussions. In all of this I would ask my students to put their writing or their comments within a historical context.

I fully realize the time crunch teachers face and the constraints they are under with a curriculum that is a mile long and a quarter inch deep. But for every episode from our past there is a modern connection to be made. In many ways the book of Ecclesiastes has it right: "There is nothing new under the sun."

Putting It All Together

It is a little more than a week since our road trip, and Amy and I are hunkered down in a Northern Virginia bookstore. She has been really excited about pulling all this material together. With schools closed because of a blizzard, she has gone full bore on the documents. We have been in constant e-mail communication, with me sending her more primary source documents about the Virginia Racial Integrity Act that I have uncovered online. One of the more interesting documents we uncovered was a Virginia Department of Health Bulletin distributed to all Commonwealth employees, including teachers and nurses, advising them of the new regulation as dictated by the Virginia Racial Integrity Act of 1924. It is an amazing public document dripping with the odious nature of the age and tenor of the times (see Figure 1.1). We also discovered a post-1924 birth registration form in which the child has to be defined as black or white (Figure 1.2), which will be the hook of our planned lesson.

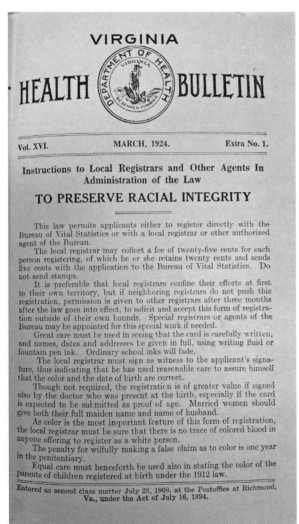

Because of the wealth of materials we have received from the National Archives and all the documents we photographed at the University of Virginia, it has taken some time to sift through everything and figure out what will work most effectively with the students. Early on we decided to frame the lesson around the idea of "identity" and why this most human of characteristics is important for people. It was also evident to us that the students would need some background about the topic and concept of eugenics. Still, we wanted to make sure the

FIGURE 1.1

Virginia Department of Health Bulletin

REGISTRATION OF BIRTH AND COLOR--VIRGINIA

FULL NAME...
[GIVEN NAME FIRST. GIVE FULL MAIDEN NAME IF MARRIED WOMAN OR WIDOW.]

PLACE OF BIRTH..DATE...................SEX..........

NAME OF HUSBAND ....
[IF MARRIED WOMAN OR WIDOW]

FATHER
    FULL NAME...

    BIRTH PLACE ....*COLOR...............
MOTHER
    FULL MAIDEN NAME ....

    BIRTH PLACE..*COLOR...............
REMARKS:

*A white person is one with no trace whatever of blood of another race, except that one with one-sixteenth of the blood of American Indian, unmixed with other race, may be classed as white. The date of birth may be omitted if desired.   Form 59—3-17-24—65M.
                                                                              (OVER)

FIGURE 1.2
Birth Registration Form

lesson was inquiry based while also ensuring it was student- and document-centric. It is important to both of us to let the documents do the teaching while we serve merely as facilitators. Again, because of the wealth of documents, we determined that the lesson would need to run for two consecutive days in a standard fifty-minute class period; we would ascertain if a third day was needed as we moved through the lesson. Amy thought the material we had found in our research was compelling enough to drop her planned instruction and devote time to having her students look at this material.

DAY 1

By the end of the first day of instruction students will be able to

- define the place of eugenics in American history;
- define Virginia's Racial Integrity Act of 1924 and its purpose;
- explain how the Racial Integrity Act of 1924 affected individuals, particularly American Indians; and
- examine and reflect on eight primary source documents to better understand history through the study of documents.

The Essential Questions to be explored are as follows:

- What is *identity* and how do you define it? How does our government define it?
- What is the Virginia Racial Integrity Act of 1924?
- How did the Virginia Racial Integrity Act of 1924 shape identity for Indians living in Virginia?

A short PowerPoint presentation will help fill in gaps where students need to have context as you work through the lesson.

For the warm-up, students are each given a copy of the 1920s-era birth registration card as they walk in the door. Students are asked to complete the card as part of the prompt.

At the top of each card are instructions for the students and questions for them to answer:

- What is this document?
- How does this card connect to *identity*?
- How might this card's information affect your life?

Once the bell has rung and students are settled, inform the students that on this day they will learn about the eugenics movement in the United States. On the screen will be the definition of *eugenics* on a slide provided by *Merriam-Webster's Collegiate Dictionary*, "a science that deals with the improvement (as by control of human mating) of hereditary qualities of a race or breed." The next slide depicts a time line of the eugenics movement in the United States.

For the first activity students will be broken into mixed ability groups, with each given several documents to study. They are also given a graphic organizer and ten minutes to complete it. Each group will need to select a spokesperson who can report what the group uncovered by studying the following documents and completing the graphic organizer.

- A letter to the editor from a Richmond, Virginia, newspaper endorsing the Virginia Racial Integrity Act

- A letter from Walter A. Plecker to Virginia registrars, clerks, and others about race mixing and the preservation of an all-white society; ask students to determine if there is any irony in the date of the letter being in 1943
- A document that explains Gregor Mendel's law of heredity and how that was applied to society
- The February 10, 1928, Virginia bill in which the term *blood* is defined
- An article about Virginia's vital statistics dated from 1923
- An article from a Virginia newspaper on the need to prevent mixed-race marriages
- A letter of inquiry from a resident in the District of Columbia about the possibility of the District of Columbia passing a law similar to the Racial Integrity Act

Next put up a slide of the Virginia Racial Integrity Act of 1924. This would be the first page of an eight-page Virginia 1924 Health Bulletin instructing state employees on how to employ the Racial Integrity Act. Briefly define it for students, as a pamphlet published for state employees to follow, particularly those who are responsible for keeping various records, and explain where it came from, who created it, and why.

As an exit ticket students will turn in the answers to the following questions:

- What implications do you think the Virginia Racial Integrity Act had for the United States? Explain.
- What implications do you think the Virginia Racial Integrity Act had for various cultures within the United States? Explain.

DAY 2

The second day of instruction will focus on the effect of the Virginia Racial Integrity Act and how it affected one particular group of Indians in Virginia, the Monacan. By the end of this class students will be able to

- identify the Monacan as well as where they are from;
- explain how the Virginia Racial Integrity Act affected Monacan history; and

- explain how the Monacan have been successful in (re)writing their own history.

The Essential Questions to be answered are as follows:

- Who were/are the Monacan?
- How did the Virginia Racial Integrity Act affect Monacan history?
- How are the Monacan and other Virginia Indian tribes fighting to be remembered today?

For the warm-up, provide students with a copy of the letter from Plecker dated January 1943.

Show a quick PowerPoint presentation that provides background on the Monacan, including their presence in Virginia for at least ten thousand years. Make sure to include a slide showing the number of tribes in Virginia that are recognized by the federal government. Once this is completed, move on to the following activities:

- Have students share some of the responses from the exit tickets from the previous day's lesson.
- Return to the idea of identity and how the effect of the Virginia Racial Integrity Act still has repercussions more than ninety years after it was passed.
- Explain to the students that the effect of the Virginia Racial Integrity Act on the Monacan will be seen from the source analysis today.

For the activity portion of the lesson, students will be paired to participate in a silent gallery walk where they examine multiple primary sources and respond to the question "How was Monacan identity affected by the Virginia Racial Integrity Act of 1924?" Have each pair record their responses on a sheet of paper and share what they learned.

As an exit ticket and/or for homework, have students read and then respond to another newspaper opinion piece called "Racial Integrity" from July 22, 1923. Using the modern Monacan perspective, explain how the tribe lives on despite the law, and how its members retain their rich identity.

Seven of the eight documents and quotes used for the gallery walk were taken from the book given to me by Karenne Wood, *Beyond Jamestown: Virginia Indians Past and Present* edited by Melanie R. Brimhall, Carole Nash, and Karenne Wood, and published by the Virginia Foundation for the Humanities. The last document is another letter from Walter Plecker that we found on our University of Virginia research trip.

Based on the gallery walk, students will write an obituary for Plecker from a Monacan viewpoint for homework.

Putting the Lesson into Play: Day 1

Alice Deal Middle School is neatly tucked away in the Tenleytown section of northwest Washington, DC. The school is named after the District of Columbia's first female principal, who also led the movement to create junior high schools for District of Columbia Public Schools. Deal celebrates its heritage in the main foyer of the building with a large tablet erected to its namesake by the Alice Deal Memorial Association. The school also embraces the local history of its place—it sits on ground that was once part of Fort Reno, which during the Civil War was part of the fortification network that encircled the nation's capital. Fort Reno was named after Union General Jesse Reno, who was killed in the battle of South Mountain in September 1862, during the Antietam Campaign. After the Civil War, a Freedman's Village sprouted up on the site of the fort, and after that a school for freedman was erected. Part of the building that dates to the late nineteenth and early twentieth centuries is not too far from Amy's classroom, Room 203G. It is in the portion of the building that connects the old structure to the more recent modern building, known as the Reno Wing. Just down the hall from Amy's room is a wall board that depicts the history of not just the school, but the sites itself. Teaching in such a space makes it easier to connect students to the past since they spend a good part of their day walking alongside the footsteps and spirits who have trod the ground before. In school settings like this, teachers, particularly those who teach history, should take advantage of the connections to the past that can be easily made. This gives the building itself a kind of life of its own.

I arrive at Amy's room about a half hour before her sixth-period US history class, where she will employ the first part of the lesson as described earlier. On her classroom door, facing the hall, is a poster of Chief Joseph of the Nez Perce tribe. I take it as an omen of good things to come as we move into the lesson we have developed. With winsome thoughts floating through my head, I look around the room decorated with historical posters and student-produced work.

Before her students arrive we go over everything again, just to make sure we are still on the same page. I will not take an active role in the instruction of the lesson, but Amy assures me that I can weigh in where I see fit. I beg Amy's indulgence and ask her if, after she introduces me, I can bring out my Tibetan bells and invoke the spirit of history. "Of course," she says with a big smile. We arrange the tables in the room for groups of three or four students to work together.

As the fifteen or so students filter into the room, Amy stands at the door and provides each of them with the warm-up activity: a copy of the birth registration card. There's also a digital image of the card on the screen in the front of the room. Amy asks the students to fill out the card as it relates to them, emphasizing that they should answer all the questions on the card. This hook works exceptionally well as students try to figure out what it all means. After the five-minute warm-up, Amy asks the students what they think the card was used for. The notion of it being some sort of registry is obvious, but the "For what?" question requires a bit of probing on her part. Some students liken the card to a driver's license, a form of government identification. That leads Amy to ask why people would need a government identification card. Some students answer that it provides a means for social order and legitimizes the person's ability to drive.

Once that part of the dialogue is complete, Amy moves on to the portion of the lesson that aims to set everything in context. For this she uses two quick PowerPoint slides: one that defines the term *eugenics* and another with a time line of the 1920s that addresses issues of race, immigration quotas, the passage of the Nineteenth Amendment, the 1925 March on Washington by the Ku Klux Klan, and the Harlem Renaissance. Then she puts up another slide with the question "What do you think would have been the tone of voices of those living in the 1920s who were not white males?" Students banter freely, providing various responses about it being an age of Jim Crow America. They have been able to bring prior knowledge to the table, which is good, and Amy makes sure to commend them for that. When she puts up the slide with the definition of *eugenics* on it, she first asks the students if they have ever seen the word before. None of them have. Then she asks students to read the definition and, when they are finished, determine what the definition might mean to them. Some students are quick to pick up the connection to science, with one student saying it reminds her of a film about genetics she saw the previous year in biology class.

Once a consensus is agreed upon about what the term means and students recognize that it has to do with genetic superiority, Amy asks them to provide examples of how genes are used. One student offers how dogs are bred to create purer breeds, which leads Amy to ask why it would be advantageous to breed animals or in this case, without directly saying it, "people." A variety of hands go up, and student replies range from crafting a particular kind of attractiveness to strength. She follows this up with the question "Do you know of any time in history where this has been done to human beings?"

One of the students she calls on says, "This was the sort of thing Hitler was trying to do in Germany to build a master race."

"Bingo!" Amy exclaims. "You got it."

Moving into the next sequence of the lesson, she provides the different groups copies of the documents we uncovered at the University of Virginia and the graphic organizer on which they need to record their responses to the documents. She gives the students about ten to fifteen minutes to do this. While they are working, there is a great deal of banter in the room as Amy walks from group to group, helping students with any problematic language and monitoring their progress.

Once they have completed the group activity, she asks each group to pick a spokesperson who can report on the document as an image of each document is displayed on the screen. The collection of documents consists of the first page of the March 1924 Virginia Health Bulletin (shown in Figure 1.1), some of the opinion pieces or letters to the editor of various newspapers in support of Virginia's Racial Integrity Act, and editorials and letters to the editor endorsing the formation of Anglo-Saxon Clubs. The students report on their respective documents, and with less than five minutes of class time remaining, Amy pulls everyone together to consider what, collectively, they might mean. By now the students have come to realize that all of this is not just about segregation as they might know it, but about a time period in which the procreation of the races was being monitored. Just before the bell rings, she asks, "What then was the purpose of the registration card [see Figure 1.2] that people had to complete in Virginia when a new child was born?" Now it's come full circle, and the students realize that the registration cards are a means by which the state can not only monitor and control interracial marriage, but keep tabs on people of particular races, particularly people who are black. Before the class is dismissed, she pushes one group with an opinion piece to determine who are trapped in the middle. The newspaper clipping addresses the issue of how Virginia Indians are trying to slip into the system as white people. She concludes the class by saying, "Tomorrow you will see how this law directly affected and continues to affect people today." As if on cue, the bell rings.

Putting the Lesson into Play: Day 2

Today's warm-up activity will be based on a projected slide with questions that refer to the prior day's lesson. Upon entering the room, students pick up the warm-up activity sheet from the shelf by the door, and before the bell rings, many of them are already working.

The slide shows this prompt:

> Read the facts about the Racial Integrity Act of 1924 on the slide. (The documents you were looking at yesterday were about this!) After reading it, answer the following questions:
>
> > What implications do you think the Racial Integrity Act of 1924 had for the United States?
> >
> > What implications do you think the Racial Integrity Act of 1924 had for various cultures within the US?

The following facts are listed on the right side of the slide:

- The Racial Integrity Act of 1924 was one of a series of laws designed to prevent interracial relationships.

- The Racial Integrity Act required that a racial description of every person be recorded at birth and divided society into only two classifications: white and colored (essentially eliminating all others, including American Indians).

- It defined race by the "one-drop rule," defining as "colored" those people with any African or Native American ancestry.

- It also expanded the scope of Virginia's ban on interracial marriage by criminalizing all marriages between white people and nonwhite people.

- In 1967 the law was overturned by the US Supreme Court in its ruling on *Loving v. Virginia*.

After the students complete the warm-up activity, Amy puts up a slide that provides the students with additional context that they will need to use for today's lesson: "In the 1920s, Virginia's registrar of statistics, Dr. Walter Plecker, was allied with the newly founded Anglo-Saxon Club of America in persuading the Virginia General Assembly to pass the Racial Integrity Act of 1924. The club was founded in Virginia by John Powell of Richmond in the fall of 1922; within a year the club for white males had more than four hundred members and thirty-one posts in the state."

The third slide illustrates the objectives of the lesson:

1. Identify who the Monacan are as well as where they are from.

2. Explain how the Racial Integrity Act of 1924 affected the Monacan tribes' history.

3. Explain how the Monacan have been successful in (re)writing their own history.

This is followed by a slide of the state of Virginia, noting the geographic location of Virginia's recognized and unrecognized Indian tribes, of which the Monacan remain one. Next is a slide that asks students to make inferences with the following prompts:

- How does being recognized as a tribe affect identity?
- How do you think the Racial Integrity Act affected the identity of Native Americans?

This is followed by a slide that contains the structure of today's lesson and the essential question that is being explored:

- Today, we're going to do a gallery walk. I'm going to put you in pairs or trios in front of one or two sources.

A gallery walk has public comments. In this case, students didn't have to identify which comment they made, but teachers could instruct them to write their name by their comment.

- Read the source and respond to this single prompt at each source:
  - How was the Monacans' identity affected by the Racial Integrity Act of 1924?
  - If someone has already written what you would write, you may respond to their statement, add more details, or write a related question to consider.

Around the room are seven stations on which various primary source materials that we pulled from our University of Virginia expedition are affixed to newsprint. The students break into their groups as Amy has assigned them and begin the gallery walk deeply immersed in reading the words of Plecker and other white supremacists. I like to think of it as a teaching moment when you let the protagonists hang themselves by their own words. There's no need in this instance to state the obvious, and from what the students are recording on the newsprint as they circulate from station to station, it is evident that they are picking up on the implications of what was said and written almost a century ago.

Before the students begin the gallery walk, Amy asks some leading questions about what they think might be some implications of the Virginia Racial Integrity Act. This generates a solid, well-thought-out conversation.

The prompt on the next slide directs the students as follows:

- Take the paper you started with back to your desks.
- Take three minutes to read the comments on the paper (since you last saw it) and summarize what was written as the answer to the prompt.
- How was the Monacans' identity affected by the Racial Integrity Act of 1924?
- Write a one-sentence summary at the bottom of the page and be prepared to share it with the group.

James, one of the students, explains that this law would be really problematic if someone fell in love with a person of a different race and that it might generate tension in their families' lives as well as between the individuals themselves and between them and the government. Rosalina is quick to point out that the law treats cultures other than whites as if they don't matter or exist. Alex adds that the law most likely tore families apart and provides little hope for children who have one black parent and one white parent.

Amy picks up on Alex's point and tells students that before 1967 if a black man and white woman fell in love in Virginia, they could, for instance, get married in the District of Columbia, or other states at the time that permitted interracial marriage; if they returned to the south bank of the Potomac River, they would be considered criminals. After sharing this tidbit, Amy pulls up a slide that explains who Walter Plecker and John Powell were in this story.

- In the 1920s, Virginia's registrar of statistics, Dr. Walter Plecker, was allied with the newly founded Anglo-Saxon Club of America in persuading the Virginia General Assembly to pass the Racial Integrity Law of 1924. The club was founded in Virginia by John Powell of Richmond in the fall of 1922; within a year the club for white males had more than four hundred members and thirty-one posts in the state.

Amy leads a quick discussion hearkening back to the previous day's documents that explored the belief among some people that it was important to preserve the purity of the race. She then puts up a slide that asks students to draw some inferences:

- How does being recognized as a tribe affect identity?
- How do you think the Racial Integrity Act affected the identity of Native Americans?

She does this through what she calls a "turn and talk" activity where students chat among themselves for two minutes, addressing the question on the prompts. A cacophony of voices fills the air as the students are fully engaged in the activity. When she calls time on the activity after three minutes, Amy asks students to report. Sage offers that this is a case in which people are clearly denied their culture and their culture is actually taken away from them. Amy nods approvingly, knowing that Sage has picked up on another thread of the lesson. She pushes them further with their ideas, particularly about why identity is so important to people. James replies, "In this case when you are part of a tribe, you have pride in something; you want to be connected to your ancestors."

Sage joins in, saying, "The law is all about being nonwhite."

This leads Amy to say, "If in this case I am an Indian in Virginia in the 1920s, what does that mean for me?"

Someone shouts out, "It means Jim Crow!"

Amy takes the point, and Nick says, "In this case not only is culture seized by the government, but rights are denied."

To which Amy asks, "Such as?"

Dakota chimes in, saying, "Their children would have, for example, no access to good schools, and it also impacts on the things that they have to share with each other."

At this point Amy is ready to launch the gallery walk. Before she starts students on their journey, she tells them, "Pay attention to the voices of the documents that you read at each station." They are given three minutes at each document to read it and record their responses on the newsprint next to it. She also directs students to "focus on how Monacan identity was affected by the Racial Integrity Act."

Below is the text for each of the gallery walk stations. All of the selections in quotations were taken from the book Wood gave me at our initial meeting, *Beyond Jamestown: Virginia Indians Past and Present.*

GALLERY WALK STATION 1

"Powhatan Red Cloud Owen, a member of the Chickahominy tribe and a Jamestown 2006 events planner, remembers being dressed in regalia as part of the opening ceremonies in 2004 for the National Museum of the American Indian Museum in Washington, DC. A Kiowa standing next to him turned and asked where he was from.

'Virginia,' Powhatan remembers answering.

'No, where are your people from?' the questioner persisted.

Powhatan said, 'Virginia. We're the Chickahominy.'

'Never heard of them,' responded the Kiowa.

'Well, we're here. We never left,' Powhatan replied."

GALLERY WALK STATION 2

"State Recognized Tribe Criteria (p. 1): According to the Code of Virginia (2.2.-2629), the Virginia Council on Indians shall establish criteria for tribal recognition and shall recommend to the General Assembly and the Governor in its biennial report those groups meeting the criteria that should be given official state recognition. The Council should receive the documents comprising a petition for recognition to carry out this function.

(*)The criteria that must be satisfied by a petitioning group in order to qualify for recommendation by the Virginia state recognition board can be summarized as follows:

1. Showing that the group's members have retained a specifically Indian identity through time.

2. Descent from an historical Indian tribe(s) that lived within Virginia's current boundaries at the time of that tribe's first contact with Europeans.

3. Ability to trace that tribe's continued existence within Virginia from first contact with Europeans.

4. Providing a complete genealogy of current group members, traced as far back as possible.

5. Showing that the community has been socially distinct at least for the 20th century, and farther back if possible from other cultural groups, preferably by organizing separate churches, schools, political organizations, etc.

6. Providing evidence of contemporary formal organization, with full membership restricted to people genealogically descended from the historical tribe(s)."

GALLERY WALK STATION 3

Virginia Indian History 10:

"Virginia first passed 'race laws' in 1705. These laws described Virginia Indians and other peoples of color and regulated their activities. Additional laws were passed in the 1800s. The Racial Integrity Act of 1924 declared that marriage between people of color and people determined to be white was illegal, and those who violated the law could be sent to prison."

Virginia Indian History 11:

"Walter Plecker, head of the division of vital statistics in Virginia for more than 30 years, was a staunch eugenicist and white supremacist. He changed many Indian people's birth certificates without any scientific evidence, from 'Indian' to 'colored.'"

GALLERY WALK STATION 4

Virginia Indian History 12:

"Virginia Indian students were not permitted to attend public schools until 1963. Mission schools, located near tribal populations, provided education up to seventh grade. For some tribes, high school education was not available at all. For others, the only option was to send their children to schools operated by the U.S. Bureau of Indian Affairs, located as far away as Oklahoma. Children who never left their home counties were given $200 and a train ticket. They were not able to return home until the school year ended."

GALLERY WALK STATION 5

Virginia Indian History 13:

"Eight Virginia tribes were recognized by the state of Virginia between 1983 and 1989. Although more than 560 tribes are recognized by the federal government today, the Virginia tribes are not. Six of the eight Virginia tribes have submitted a bill to the U.S. Congress requesting federal acknowledgment of their sovereign status. Their motto: 'First to welcome, last to be recognized.'"

Ashley Atkins, a Pamunkey, who is a PhD student in anthropology at the College of William & Mary:

"One hope and dream that I have is that the Federal Government will give the Virginia tribes the recognition they deserve."

GALLERY WALK STATION 6

Chief Anne Richardson of the Rappahannock:

"I think most people, when they think about the history of Virginia and the Indians in particular . . . think about these things like the dinosaurs that existed and died, and now we're writing about them and learning about them. But that's not the case with the tribes. They have vibrant communities that have been preserved for thousands of years."

GALLERY WALK 7

Chief Stephen Adkins of the Chickahominy:

"I remember once traveling with my father, and we pulled into a gas station because I had to go to the bathroom, and there was one bathroom marked 'white' and one bathroom marked 'colored.' I said, 'Dad, what do I do?' Dad would usually choose the closer one."

For the next ten to fifteen minutes banter fills the air as students plunge in and absorb the meaning and content of the different documents. As the activity winds down, Amy asks students to take down the newsprint where they are standing and describe their interpretations of the document by writing a one-sentence summary at the bottom of the newsprint.

The groups report the following:

> **Group 1:** Because of the Virginia Racial Integrity Act, tribes were not recognized as owning any land.
>
> **Group 2:** Monacan individuality was limited through strict criteria.
>
> **Group 3:** People of color were regulated by way of limits on their activities, as directed by Plecker.
>
> **Group 4:** There were limits placed on education, and children were socially restricted in whom they could encounter.
>
> **Group 5:** Only a few tribes were recognized, and those that were recognized got better benefits than unrecognized tribes.
>
> **Group 6:** Monacan people did not know where they belonged in public places—such as at water fountains or places to eat.

After the students report their findings, Amy asks, "Do the Monacan want to be seen as victims or would they want to do something to promote agency for themselves?"

Some of the students say, "Nobody wants to be a victim!" There's a palpable sense that the students know that being a victim diminishes one's humanity.

For the verbal exit ticket, Amy asks the students whether, based on what they have learned, the Monacan have been successful in (re)writing their own history.

Some of the students have picked up from the documents, particularly the one referring to the perception that the Monacan are like dinosaurs, that the Monacan want to be seen as active, thriving members of the community who make contributions to the well-being of all. Students are quick to point out that the Monacan can use their voices to speak out, that school history books should include their story, and that teachers should teach about them more often. Several students made comments similar to this one: "This is just like the story we learned in seventh grade about civil rights and Rosa

Parks, it just has a different face." Students also argue that the Monacan and others should not be remembered just for the negative things that have happened to them but for their contributions to society as well, citing the number who have become doctors, lawyers, and educators.

At one point I join in with Amy as I raise the question "How could somebody who has been dead since 1947 still affect people all these years later?" The class giggles when I share with them that Plecker was hit by a car as he stepped off a curb in Richmond in 1947. Powell succumbed to old age, I add. The question I raise, of course, is rhetorical but brings home the point about why it is crucial to know about history. It's like the line from the motion picture *Gladiator*: "What we do in life echoes in eternity."

As the bell rings, Amy pulls several students aside for me to speak with privately—James, Carlita, Nico, and Alex. With passes in their hands we head off to the multipurpose room, where we converse. First I ask them if they had ever heard of the Virginia Racial Integrity Act of 1924 and if they had ever heard of the Monacan. They all shake their heads. Next, I ask them collectively what they got out of the two-day lesson. James, whom I have learned is always willing to be heard and is never short on words, tells me, "This kind of lesson is good because it allows you to absorb a lot of information in a short time. The gallery walk keeps us engaged and allows us to learn and see things in a new and fun way."

Carlita follows up by adding, "The gallery walk gets us to see new views on new people and how other people interpret information. This allows me to create my own interpretation of history."

Nico asserts, "The lesson was very informative, as we were able to summarize what everyone said back in the 1920s and we learned from various opinions by looking at the documents themselves."

Alex tells us that the timing of this lesson was perfect for her because, "In English we are learning about civil rights, and this was a refreshing way to look at a new topic. I love Ms. Trenkle's use of the gallery walk. This lesson took the civil rights movement beyond blacks and whites. It was really new!"

As we continued chatting, the students said they found it hard to believe that this story was going on well into the twentieth and twenty-first centuries. All of them talked about how things really need to change for the Indian groups that remain unrecognized. I told them about my meeting with Karenne Wood and clued them in on her parting words to me: "We are still here!" I asked them what they thought she meant. "Look," said James, "these people lived in Virginia for generations because they lost their lands. Over time they were forgotten, and that is not okay! It's obvious," he continues, "that they thrive today."

The document with which they all resonated is the one by Chief Anne Richardson in which the Monacan are referred to by non-Monacan as "dinosaurs." Alex says, "Since people believed they were dinosaurs, they were treated like dinosaurs."

I turn the conversation to learning about identity. Nico says, "The fact that no one recognizes the tribe hurts people's pride. We should know about these people. By seeing this from the Monacan viewpoint, when I first read the question, I took it negatively, but as I continued to think, it is clear that they fought through it even though they were discriminated against."

The station in the gallery walk that upset all of them was Station 3, where a document written by Plecker ordered that people's identity be changed. Alex exclaimed, "Plecker changed people's identity, and he did it without their consent. This caused people to be lost." With frustration etched on her face she continued, "I still find it confusing as to why they could not have turned in their own classification."

I next mention that one of the documents that they looked at the previous day dates from 1943 and ask them what was going on in the world at that time. "World War Two," they all say in unison.

"So," I follow up, "what gives with that? Who are we fighting in 1943?"

"Nazi Germany" is the response, again in chorus.

"Does anything about this surprise you?"

James immediately offers, "People are hypocrites. It's in our nature. Plecker and Hitler decided what was right or wrong for people on a whim. In both instances it was an 'us versus them' story."

Carlita sees a direct connection to the Nazis and the Holocaust. "Hitler wanted a master race," she says. "He wanted to create a superperson. It all loops back to identity. Each one of us has a different identity and a different voice," she notes with emphasis.

"Plecker," says Alex, "did the same thing as Hitler. All of this stuff seems based on fear. White people were clearly afraid of [letting others be] on equal terms."

At this point I let the students take the lead in the conversation, which brings us to the current political climate in the United States. "Plecker built walls," says Nico, "and set race relations back. Anyone should have the right to marry whomever they wish. We want leaders today like Dr. King, who sought to tear down walls."

"We are seeing the same use of fear being employed by [political] candidates today. Why is that?" I ask.

"Because," James says, "emotions are powerful motivators that can either push people forward or hold people back. Humanity is a two-sided coin."

Carlita adds, "If Plecker had his way, in the end there is no possibility that President Obama would be remembered."

Alex explains that she is reading a book for her own enjoyment called *Uglies* by Scott Westerfeld, which is part of a young adult series. In this tale teenagers are surgically altered to be pretty once they reach the age of sixteen. She says that during the past two days, she's made connections to the book. Then she pauses and says, "We need people to be different. Differences make people unique and make the world different, because everyone contributes different things to the world."

We've been talking nonstop for a half hour. It's time for them to head off to their respective classes. Quite frankly the conversation has drained me, but in a good way. I don't want it to end because I want to know more about their thinking. What is blazingly clear, though, is that these young people are very clued in to the present moment, and I find real comfort in that. When I return to Amy's room to report to her, I tell her that her students are "amazing!" and that I miss working with kids.

Amy and I debrief about the lesson and what can be done to make it stronger. As veteran teachers we know that there is no such thing as the "perfect lesson." The longer I taught, the better I got at improvising as I taught. That comes with experience. You can't learn it in a Social Studies Methods class. We both agreed that had the documents from *Branham v. Burton* been less dense, we could have employed them. Amy and I teach by the philosophy "show, don't tell." To demonstrate the agency exercised by the Monacan in the 1943 court case, it might have been good to include a slide in the PowerPoint that addressed the case of the Monacan suing the government and winning. Unfortunately, none of the documents from the National Archives provided any sense of specific moments of agency. Because of their raw nature we also thought that documents from the University of Virginia were much more compelling in getting the story out. And it was those documents that guided us. As luck would have it, the day before we put the lesson into play, the *Washington Post* reported on the recognition of the Pamunkey tribe of Virginia. I brought the article in with me to show Amy, who had also seen it. We just didn't have the time to weave it into the lesson. These are the things you need to consider doing if the opportunity arises and you can get to your school's copier. Amy shared the story with her students, which gave a kind of immediacy to the lesson taught. Of particular interest is that the Virginia Racial Integrity Act really never applied to the Pamunkey, because they were descendants of Pocahontas, and a bunch of documents we looked at on our research trip clearly articulated that people descended from Pocahontas were exempt. No source specifically gave a reason, but there were some inferences that she was considered royalty once she married John Rolfe, one of the "founders" of Jamestown. Her baptism marking her conversion to Christianity, when her name was changed to Rebecca, is celebrated in a huge 18-by-12-foot canvas painted in 1839 by John Gadsby Chapman that hangs in the Rotunda of the United States Capitol.

Back on the Road

It's two days after the lesson has been taught and I am driving on Interstate 95 South to Richmond, Virginia. Amy and Priya are unable to be with me, and I miss them, because we gain such good, fun, informal professional development with our conversations. Yet I still have companions with me as I make the ninety-minute drive. I slip a CD called *In the Heat of the Summer* by my college friends Kim and Reggie Harris into my player. Track one is perfect as I hit the pavement. "Travellers" explores how we are all "travellers living in the passage of time." Kim and Reggie are African Americans who write, produce, and record their own brand of folk music. Last week Reggie and I got together for dinner. It had been at least a decade since we had seen each other, and we both agreed that our meeting was long overdue. Reggie has been deeply immersed in genealogy of his own, recently learning that his great-great-great-great–great-grandfather was the Confederate general and slave owner Williams Carter Wickham. There is a heroic statue of Wickham in full Confederate garb in Richmond's Monroe Park. Reggie traced his ancestry to one of Wickham's enslaved women, Bibhana Hartlett, who lived on his plantation, Hickory Hill, near Ashland, Virginia, twenty miles north of Richmond. Reggie has taken it one step further and reached out to his white cousins who live in Richmond, even writing a song about their meeting, "Hickory Hill." Given the common ground between my work and theirs, our conversation turned to Plecker, Powell, the Monacan, and race in general. I know I am in good company today, with Kim and Reggie's music.

In some ways I have been dreading this road trip. I have tromped through dozens of cemeteries over the years, and whether it's walking along Author's Ridge in the Sleepy Hollow Cemetery in Concord, Massachusetts, communing with Emerson and Thoreau, or channeling Civil War photographer Mathew Brady and the twenty-one women killed in the DC Arsenal Fire at Congressional Cemetery in Washington, DC, it's always done with a sense of homage to the people whose graves I am visiting. I also find that visiting famous people's graves humanizes them and, in turn, me. Today, however, I am headed to the Mecca of the Confederacy and the "Lost Cause," Hollywood Cemetery in Richmond, where both Plecker and Powell were laid to rest. So much ambiguity filled me before this road trip that I brought it up with the students I met with at Deal Middle School after Amy's class. My ambiguity stems from the fact that I am visiting the graves of people who are anathema to my own sense of personal values. There's nothing heroic or worth admiring about Plecker and Powell. To a student they thought it was actually a cool idea and helped calm my anxiety by reminding me that we can't forget the past and that visiting their graves is not necessarily paying homage, but remembering them for what they did to people.

I must confess I have a feisty side, and it is in full force today. I can feel it. It is a gray, drab, chilly day. I spend a half hour looking for a sweatshirt I purchased many years ago from the Crow Indian Nation Reservation in Montana on the outskirts of Little Big Horn National Battlefield, site of Custer's Last Stand, in 1876. On it was a map of the United States that included the names of all American Indian tribes and where they were located. I want to make some kind of statement by wearing something appropriate. I could not find the sweatshirt, so instead, I pulled on the polo shirt I bought in Cincinnati at the National Underground Railroad Freedom Center when I took students there in 2009. I am cool with the status of my attire.

As I cruise I-95, music playing, just north of Fredericksburg, site of a lopsided Confederate victory in December 1862, I spot a huge Confederate battle flag flapping in the breeze just off the interstate. I address the contentious nature of the Confederate battle flag later in the book, but for now its presence seems to fit with my destination. Ninety minutes after leaving home I arrive at the cemetery entrance. I pull out the large map sent to me when I first made inquiries about Plecker and Powell's graves. The staff person who sent me the map highlighted their grave sites on the map. It's been at least twenty years since I have been to Hollywood Cemetery, where you will find the tombs of Presidents James Monroe and John Tyler, who also served in the Confederate Congress. Additionally, visitors will find the graves of Confederate luminaries President Jefferson Davis and Generals Henry Heth, John D. Imboden, John Pegram, George Pickett, and James Ewell Brown Stuart—better known as Jeb—among a host of other Confederate knowns and unknowns. Plecker and Powell share with them the 135 acres of rolling hills on a bluff over the James River, which is swollen and raging this particular day. I make a connection between the river's course and velocity and my particular emotions as I have worked with this story. Plecker's grave is alongside one of the cemetery's interior roads. It's a nondescript grave that he shares with his wife, Kate Houston Plecker. He was born on April 2, 1861, just twelve days before the South launched what Plecker called the War Between the States. I don't get out of the car. I don't even roll down the window. But then a moment of genius seizes me, making this trip much more worth it.

Kim and Reggie's CD has a song called "All My Relations," which is based on the Lakota Indian prayer of the same name and expresses sentiments about balanced relationships between people, the earth, and all of creation, and living a life filled with goodwill. Indian tribes of Virginia express the same sentiments. According to Oliver L. Perry—chief emeritus of the Nansemond tribe, along Virginia's southeast Atlantic Coast, and board member of the National Governor's Interstate Indian Council—Virginia Indians, like many other America Indians, have adopted the following philosophy: "Live in harmony with Mother Earth and Father Sky. Honor your ancestors. Respect your elders. Love, protect, and educate your children. They are the future—ours and yours." I crank up the volume and let the music blast, laughing to myself, saying, "Here you go, Dr. Plecker! Listen up! How do you like these 'Negros in feathers'?"

The song ends, and with a smug smile I drive to Powell's grave. His marker is equally nondescript, but he has a better viewshed and vista of the James River. I am, however, struck—and struck hard at that—by the inscription on his headstone: "His Work, A Singing With His Hands." I know it's a reference to his work as a composer, but Powell believed only Anglo-Saxon Americans had the skills to create beautiful and meaningful music, and he wrote vociferously about it. His work on the famed White Top Mountain Folk Festival I referred to earlier, a Virginia celebration of the state's Appalachian music, banned African American musicians from performing and prohibited blacks from attending. On the Virginia state historical marker that identifies the site of the festival, there is no reference to this attitude. I crank up Kim and Reggie's CD even louder at Powell's grave with these words from one of Powell's letters in my head: "I commend 'White America' to all Virginians. If Virginia leads in making America as a white nation such service will be infinitely greater than any that the state has performed throughout its glorious history" and "History, ethnology, and biology all bear out the Anglo-Saxon conviction that one drop of Negro blood makes the Negro." The ambiguity of my visit dissipates as I pull out of the cemetery and head home.

Your Next Steps

Where do you go with this? There are numerous avenues you can pursue even if you teach in Peoria, Illinois. One way would be to employ the idea of identity with how sports teams use mascots, specifically addressing the name of Washington, DC's, NFL franchise. You can find on the Internet all matter of opinion pieces on this. If you want additional resources to support your efforts, visit www.changethemascot.org. Challenge your students to consider why American Indians might want the name to be changed and again, what that says about identity. Or, consider showing the scene in the Disney cartoon motion picture *Pocahontas* where the entire ensemble, British settlers and Virginia Indians alike, sing a song called "Savages." Explore with your students how that term cuts both ways, with regard to race, within the context of the song.

Since the United States was originally inhabited by American Indians, you can have your students conduct research about the native peoples from your region and create state historical markers that reflect what they have learned about them. There is a template for state historical markers in Appendix 1.2. Another place in your curriculum where this lesson, or a similar one, might fit is in a unit on the 1920s. The 1920s are jam-packed with all kinds of episodes tied to race in America, and the eugenics movement was in full force as part of what white supremacists saw as an amalgamation of the races. You could also make a STEM connection here, by demonstrating how scientific data is often misused to defend a particular position.

You could also choose to replicate this lesson when you teach about the civil rights movement, but bring in the story of the parallel American Indian movement, which was also under way in the 1960s and 1970s and is often overlooked in classrooms across the country. Students could research the American Indian takeover of Alcatraz Island in San Francisco Bay, which lasted from November 20, 1969, to June 11, 1971, and was put down by federal officials. They could do a faux news report of the event, putting everything into context about the takeover and the American Indian movement. Or you could have them research the 1972 events of Wounded Knee, South Dakota, where leaders of the American Indian movement again confronted federal officials. Have your students consider how the civil rights movement of African Americans influenced the American Indian movement. Unlike the civil rights movement, the American Indian movement had a flag. After students study the American Indian movement, have them design a flag for it and then compare and contrast the flags that they create with the original design.

Something else you can have students study is Virginia Governor Mark Warner's denunciation of Virginia's role in the eugenics movement in the form of an official apology on the web at https://www.washingtonpost.com/archive/local/2002/05/03/warner-apologizes-to-victims-of-eugenics/87a14c82-da36-4551-9c28-98d001131bfc/.

Many years ago I used to teach Dee Brown's classic, *Bury My Heart at Wounded Knee,* about the Plains Indian Wars of the 1870s–1890s. One student challenged me on reading the book because his father thought, and told him as much, that the bottom line was that the United States "needed the land." I remembering explaining to the student that this was really about looking at our history through a different lens and that he did not have to accept Brown's premise. I was more interested in the perception of interpretations. He gave me a strange look and shuffled out the door. Three weeks later when the reading was due, he stayed after class and said, with a smile, "Mr. Percoco, I am glad I read this book."

As I pass through the cemetery gates, once more Karenne Wood's words, "We are still here!" resound in my head. Yes, the Monacan and other Indian people *are* still here and *are* making a difference, whereas Plecker and Powell are six feet under.

CHAPTER 2

The M and Ms of the Journey—Montpelier and Monticello, Madison and Jefferson

n his six-volume biography of James Madison, Irving Brandt argues that the long-standing relationship between Madison and Thomas Jefferson was a "perfectly balanced friendship." Scions of the landed gentry from the Virginia Piedmont, the men shared an equal amount of ambition, temperament, intellect, and vision, and could, when together, look like the oddest of couples. Jefferson at six foot two towered over his diminutive friend and confidant, who stood a mere five foot four. Yet it is Jefferson whose face adorns Mount Rushmore and who has an impressive memorial on the National Mall in Washington, DC. Madison seems like a forgotten founder. We know he is there in the shadows but are not quite sure where he fits in among other founders such as George Washington and Benjamin Franklin. It appears as if Madison has been lost in the dustbin of history, yet Madison is one of a number of founders whose influence is felt in daily American life.

"The influence of these two mighty minds upon each other is a phenomenon, like the invisible and mysterious movements of the magnet in the physical world," wrote John

Quincy Adams (1839, 111). It is imperative that teachers and their students recognize Jefferson and Madison's place in our ever-unfolding national narrative, because both men believed in a strong, civic-minded society and played a significant role in establishing the foundational principles upon which the United States rests. This is particularly true given that continuing results of the National Assessment of Educational Progress, often referred to as the "nation's report card," indicate that not only are our students failing history and civics, but they don't have a fundamental understanding of our democratic system of government. Because we are a nation established on a set of ideals and principles based on the foundation of an active and informed citizenry, students need to understand that in many ways they hold the future in their hands. Their participation in elections helps determine which people set policy for the nation. As Sandra Day O'Connor and John Glenn so ably pointed out in a 2015 *USA Wall Street Journal* op-ed, "We want to give students an immersive civic-education experience that inspires them to learn how to use the legal system, the legislature and the electoral process to solve problems in their communities and effectively communicate with their government."

"A popular government without popular information or the means of acquiring it," wrote James Madison, "is but a prologue to Farce or Tragedy or perhaps both. Knowledge will forever govern ignorance, and a people who mean to be their own Governors must arm themselves with the power knowledge gives." Thus the material presented in this chapter will be of benefit to not only history teachers, but teachers of government and civics as well.

The homes of Madison and Jefferson, Montpelier and Monticello, are both within the Journey Through Hallowed Ground National Heritage Area, twenty-five miles apart from each other. The National Trust for Historic Preservation, which manages Madison's home, Montpelier, and the Thomas Jefferson Memorial Foundation, which operates his home, Monticello, are crucial partners who help shape the Journey's identity as the "birthplace of the American ideal." Both sites have developed extensive educational materials related to the lives, ideas, and homes of these men.

Jefferson was the ultimate idealist, whose ideas Madison deeply respected. Madison at heart was more of a realist and measured human beings based on what they were, not on their aspirations. Teachers often find that Jefferson's words and ideas are easier to unpack than Madison's, which may be why Madison is somewhat overshadowed by Jefferson in today's curriculum. Yet it is important that students encounter both men in their course of studying and analyzing US history. Unless they understand their political alliance, friendship, and ideals, students will fail to recognize the passage of the nation at its inception from loose confederation to federal republic and with it the tangential rise of the two-party system. This was a time filled with crisis and intrigue, and although we hold Jefferson and Madison dear in our national memory, at times they acted against political opponents, some of whom they had called friends, out of self-interest and in the name of politics.

The other important issue when studying these founders is that they both were practitioners of the institution of slavery. Here rests a central dilemma of not only their lives and legacy but of the United States as well. This is something that is not easy for many contemporary Americans to grasp. Americans tend to like to celebrate rather than remember the sordid side of our past. Yet if we are to become a more perfect union, we as a nation must wrestle and struggle with America's "original sin," even if that means making our heroes more human and getting them placed on lower pedestals; to not do so is a disservice to history and to ourselves. It is true that neither Jefferson nor Madison were "great" on slavery, but that does not discount the fact that they were great in other aspects of their lives. Students have a hard time grasping that.

Suffice it to say, much has been written on the lives of these two signature founding figures. The books listed in the selected bibliography reflect the most recent scholarship and offer a depth of reading for you to probe the lives and minds of these giants of American history and political thought. But while we are talking background, I think it would be good to give a nod to one of our own, the 1988 National Teacher of the Year, Phil Bigler. Phil is also a Madison scholar. I highly recommend you consult his *Liberty and Learning: The Essential James Madison,* which can be downloaded for free at www. scandalous-son.com.

Where to Begin

Where do teachers begin when teaching about two of the nation's foremost founders? The best place is to look at critical primary material and have students analyze their words, both in significant documents and personal correspondence. I suggest you begin with a Venn-diagram-type activity that uses the outline of their homes to fill in. Write on the board or project onto your screen the word *idealist.* Provide students with a 3-by-5-inch note card and ask them to define this word and list some of its attributes. Then do the same with the word *realist.* Discuss with students their respective definitions and attributes.

Next provide students with the following excerpts of Jefferson's documents to read. These four can be found on the panels of the Jefferson Memorial in Washington, DC, and you can locate them on Monticello's website, www.monticello.org. They are the preamble to the Declaration of Independence, a Bill for Establishing Religious Freedom, *Notes on the State of Virginia*, and a letter from Jefferson to H. Tompkinson. On the same website you will find not only the excerpts, but the full text of all these documents. For classroom use, the excerpts should be sufficient. After the students read Jefferson's words, ask them to determine if these are the words of an "idealist" or those of a "realist." I would also use Jefferson's "The Earth Belongs to the Living" found at http://lachlan. bluehaze.com.au/lit/jeff03.htm and then Madison's incredible response found at http:// founders.archives.gov/documents/Jefferson/01-16-02-0101.

Once these activities have been completed and discussed, follow the same procedure for Madison's words, using the text from these documents: "Vices of the Political System of the United States" (1787), "Federalist 10 and 51" (1788), and the US Bill of Rights (1791). Conclude this portion of the activity the same way you did with the Jeffersonian documents, asking students to determine if Madison was an "idealist" or a "realist." By this point in the activity, it should become evident that Jefferson was the "idealist" and Madison was the "realist."

I found great success many years ago crafting what I called Historical Heads (see Figure 2.1), which were empty templates of the human head that students had to fill in with images related to the person we were studying. Here I've flipped it a bit, calling this Historical Houses. Why not? The Journey is loaded with them! Provide students with schematic outline images of Monticello and Montpelier (see Appendix 2.1) and have them fill in the homes with significant terms from the documents that relate to Jefferson as the "idealist" and Madison as the "realist." Students can pull images off the web that represent these ideas or cut images out of magazines and paste them inside the template; if they are afraid of their artistic merits, they can simply use words. It's a great way to generate intellectual creativity and make the assignment very hands-on.

After you complete this portion of the activity, you are going to want to see where their ideas come together. Next provide a schematic map of the United States (the Lower Forty-Eight will work fine) with the Journey clearly delineated inside the map. Have the students pull together their thoughts and ideas, identifying concepts or ideas about Madison and Jefferson that apply universally to the United States. For example, students

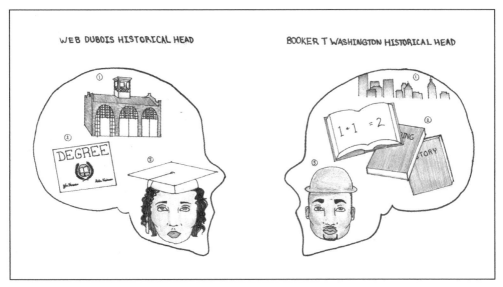

FIGURE 2.1
Historical Heads

could locate sites on the map related to events of the civil rights movement and write, "All men are created equal" next to those locations. You could take this to a whole other level by posting the map of the Journey included with this book on your classroom wall and then having your students post their respective schematics around it.

THE EYE OF THOMAS JEFFERSON

A film I really enjoyed using in my classes to help students understand Jefferson's wide range of interests was *The Eye of Thomas Jefferson,* produced by the National Gallery of Art for a special exhibition they created honoring the third president. If you show this film after the map activity previously discussed, Jefferson's broad interest in many things will be made even more apparent. This film in particular looks at Jefferson's work as an architect and the ways in which he decorated his home to reflect his values and beliefs about the United States. For Jefferson, the dome was the greatest single contribution to architecture, as well as the greatest embodiment of Republican virtues, thus the designs at Monticello and the Rotunda at the University of Virginia, both of which he designed. A few years ago, PBS aired an exceptional miniseries titled *American Visions* about American art and architecture. The episode on the founders is spectacular, and the corresponding print book that accompanied the series is still in print, making a great resource.

The Eye of Thomas Jefferson is available in DVD format on WorldCat. One of the many ways you can incorporate the film into your classroom is to have students examine how mathematical principles influenced Enlightenment thinkers and are reflected in Jeffersonian architecture. Similar to the formerly mentioned Historical Houses activity, use a template of a building with a dome and have students fill it in with Jefferson's ideas as articulated in the film. For closure, share with them Jefferson's quote, "You see, I am an enthusiast of the arts" and ask students to consider why he devoted as much time to architecture and the arts as he did politics. What value do the arts play in shaping one's vision of government? You can also have students consider the idea that Jefferson believed he represented "the common man" of America. How does that square with the Jefferson who built an elaborate home, decorated it with fine works of art, and maintained a large wine collection? What does this say about Jefferson's persona, and about his role as a leader?

A great way to follow up this film is to employ the Teaching with Historic Places Lesson Plan "Thomas Jefferson's Plan for the University of Virginia: Lessons from the Lawn" that can be found at https://www.nps.gov/nr/twhp/wwwlps/lessons/92uva/92uva.htm. In this lesson students explore Jefferson's thoughts on education and how that education played a role in shaping our democratic republic. The lesson also explores Jefferson the architect, so if you are looking for a STEM connection, you can find it here.

JEFFERSON AND MADISON ON CIVIC ENGAGEMENT AND NATIONAL IDENTITY

Since the Journey focuses extensively on civic engagement, one approach to your students' work on Madison and Jefferson could be the examination of how the two men shaped both the idea of civic engagement and the foundation of our national identity. Both men emphasized the need for an informed citizenry. The approach I outline here will also engage students in different readings from American literature, bolstering literacy skills in the process. By defining *national identity* and *civic engagement* within the context of Jefferson and Madison, students will explore not only what the term *national identity* meant when these Founding Fathers were alive, but also what it means today and how civic engagement in modern America is rooted in their principles and values. Your starting point for this will be materials prepared by the creators of the What So Proudly

We Hail curriculum, found in their anthology of the same name, *What So Proudly We Hail: The American Soul in Story, Speech, and Song.*

You can access the curriculum at www.whatsoproudlywehail.org. The purpose of What So Proudly We Hail is to help build a robust American citizenry by reading significant, yet digestible, elements of American literature in an effort to not just understand American ideals but more fully appreciate their citizenship. For discussion purposes here, your students will be reading seminal pieces of American literature found in the anthology. Specifically for this lesson approach, students will be reading the short stories "The Man Without a Country" by Edward Everett Hale, "The Promised Land" by Mary Antin, and "In a Strange Country" by Ralph Ellison.

Students should be directed to read Jefferson's writings on education, also found in the anthology, as well as these primary documents: the Declaration of Independence (1776), the Virginia Statute of Religious Freedom (1786), the Virginia Resolution (1798), his Letter to the Danbury Baptists (1802), Jefferson's directive to Meriwether Lewis (after the Louisiana Purchase, 1803), and the Embargo Act (1807). They can be found at https://www.monticello.org/site/families-and-teachers/jefferson-documents-and-quotes. You will need to put each of these documents in historical context for your students by giving a minilecture on each that should last no more than five minutes. To ground yourself in these particular Jefferson readings you should consult the following: Peter Onuf's *Jefferson's Empire: The Language of American Nationhood,* Chapter 1, "We Shall All Be Americans," and John Ragosta's *Religious Freedom: Jefferson's Legacy, America's Creed.* You might also wish to consult Robert Linder's article "Civil Religion in Historical Perspective: The Reality That Underlies the Concept," *Journal of Church and State* (1975). I would also recommend participating in Onuf's Massive Online Open Course, or MOOC, titled The Age of Jefferson and developed by the University of Virginia with assistance from the Thomas Jefferson Foundation. It is available on iTunes U and via Coursera. The link to the free course on the Coursera website is https://www.coursera.org/learn/ageofjefferson.

Once again you will write or project the terms *national identity* and *civic engagement* on the board. Provide each student with a note card and ask them to define these two terms in their own words, and then come to some consensus as a class on the working definitions that you can use for the rest of the activity. Post these working definitions somewhere in the classroom for reference.

After students have read, most likely for homework, the short stories by Hale, Antin, and Ellison, brainstorm with the class as a whole what these stories have to say about "national identity" and "civic engagement." As you discuss the readings, record student responses on the board.

- Break the class into seven groups with three to four students per group.
- Provide each group with a piece of newsprint and a copy of one of the Jefferson documents.
- Ask each group to read their document.
- Have the students note on their newsprint points from their document that address ideas of national identity and civic engagement.
- When students are finished, debrief as a class.
- Provide each student with a note card and have them use one side to complete the following sentence: "Thomas Jefferson believed that national identity was . . ."
- Have students flip the card and complete the following sentence: "Thomas Jefferson believed that civic engagement was . . ."
- Discuss the students' responses and come up with a class consensus on Jefferson's definition of both *national identity* and *civic engagement*.
- Write the class's consensus on a piece of newsprint and post it next to the newsprint that was posted earlier in the lesson.
- Finally, ask students to compare and contrast what they view as Jefferson's definition with the definitions they arrived at earlier.

You can expect this activity to take two forty-five-minute classes or one ninety-minute block period.

For the next part of the lesson you will essentially repeat the activity, but with a focus on James Madison and his writings. This will get your students actively engaged in the same kind of process historians use when dealing with lofty ideas.

In line with teaching about Jefferson and national identity I suggest you also have your students work with his role in the Louisiana Purchase. You can find his instructions to Meriwether Lewis at https://www.ourdocuments.gov/doc.php?doc=17, which include his secret message to Congress for his justification of purchasing the Louisiana Territory.

After you look at the web link provided and share with students the document found there, have them take the virtual tour of Monticello, looking particularly carefully at how Jefferson decorated his front parlor entrance with many of the artifacts Lewis and William Clark sent back to him. Ask students to consider what this says about Jefferson and his ideas about national identity. Why would he use his front parlor to showcase such artifacts? What does this say about him?

TEACHING "FEDERALIST 10" AND "FEDERALIST 51"

To best understand the years 1787–1789, one should recognize the role that *The Federalist Papers* played in securing ratification of the Constitution. It is important for young Americans to understand how our government works and what role the founders, particularly Madison, played in defining the direction the new government would take. *The Federalist Papers* are like notes left behind by the founders that help explain the need for, and the process of, the new American government. They need to be taught in a way that makes them palatable to students so that students don't view them as just some moldy documents written by a bunch of dead guys a long time ago that they are being forced to read.

Write on the board the term *ordered liberty*. Ask students what they think it means. Then ask them why drivers are required to stop at stop signs or red lights, even when there are no other cars in sight, or better yet, no police officers in sight. Have students consider the reasons we behave in such ways. Then ask them, "If we are a free nation, why can't we just do as we please when we want to?" The founders, who had just fought a tyrannical Great Britain, wanted a society of "ordered liberty." Ordered liberty is the notion that a free society is possible, provided people recognize that everyone has certain rights that must be respected, which ultimately allows for the structure of government to organize that society by creating laws and norms. They wanted a nation that mostly protected them against government oppression. That is the fundamental purpose of the Bill of Rights: to protect the individual from an abusive state. At the same time, the founders sought to create a government that was both stable and energetic, a delicate balancing act between liberty and government action.

Careful attention should be given to *The Federalist Papers*, particularly numbers 10 and 51. "Federalist 10" is about factions. *Merriam-Webster's Collegiate Dictionary* defines *factions* as "a party or group that that is often contentious and self-seeking." The founders were very afraid of self-interest, and some saw the state governments within the federal structure as being particularly self-interested. In "Federalist 10" Madison creates a paradox by arguing that more factions—not fewer—were needed because the more you have, the more they will keep each other in balance.

A way you can impress upon your students the idea of factions is to talk about school life. In your discussion interchange the word *faction* and the word *clique*. Ask your students about the nature of the cliques in your school. Follow this by raising the issue of self-interest and asking how these school groups are self-interested. Chances are, students will respond that they often think these groups are exclusionary and don't let anyone in unless a person has some kind of connection to what the group holds dear. The same is true in politics, but whereas school factions can't influence policy, political factions can.

In the founding of the nation, a fragile question had to do with the idea of majorities, particularly what was perceived as the "tyranny of the majority." The nation that was established was not a direct democracy, but rather a representative democracy. Madison brilliantly concluded that the more factions operating in society the better, for they will counterbalance each other. It was an argument for a large republic rather than a small republic. According to Kass, Kass, and Schaub (2011), editors of *What So Proudly We Hail*, "Political struggle will be moderated not by moral and religious instruction aimed at making citizens more moderate and virtuous, but instead by the moderating effects of multiplicity."

Because *The Federalist Papers* can be a difficult read for students, I suggest you have them read the essays in class rather than as a homework assignment. This will allow you to be there as students struggle with terminology and the nuances within the documents. You can help clarify points as they read. Because these are lengthy readings, you can break them into sections and have students read the sections aloud. When students complete each section, review with them what they have read, checking for understanding. In doing so you will allow students to digest the material much more easily than if you wait until finishing all of Madison's writings.

It's important to remember that Madison always wrote his ideas within the context of his perception of human nature. The What So Proudly We Hail curriculum asks teachers to raise the following questions with students after reading "Federalist 10":

- **What assumptions about human nature inform this ingenious solution?**

- Why is heterogeneity preferable to homogeneity, and what, if any, might be its defects or costs?

- What sort of human character—with what sort of passions, virtues, and vices—is produced by a large commercial republic?

- What might be the advantages and disadvantages of bigness over smallness in public life?

It took me about fifteen years to mature into the teacher I became. One of the things I struggled with in the first half of my teaching was developing hooks to launch my lessons. I owe the changing of that to abolitionist Frederick Douglass. I had seen the PBS film *Frederick Douglass: When the Lion Wrote History*, which is an incredible resource for teachers. In looking around for curricular materials on how best to use this film in the 1990s, I contacted the staff at the Frederick Douglass National Historic Site, in Washington, DC. This National Park Service unit honors Douglass by interpreting Cedar Hill, the house in which he lived after the Civil War. I was invited to come and talk with the staff and took them up on their offer.

During our meeting I was given an extensive packet of materials to use for the classroom, including a generic video guide. But within the video guide was a terrific nugget! It was a different kind of hook, and it launched my teaching in a new formidable direction that paid off in dividends. Frederick Douglass struggled all his life to determine the year of his birth. This was no small matter to him, and it weighed on him daily—he spent years trying to determine it. By the time he died, he figured he had been born in 1819, but records uncovered since his death in 1895 indicate he was off by a year and was most likely born in 1818. The video guide suggested engaging students before showing the film by asking them, "How would you feel if you never knew when your birthday was?" The strategy was ingenious because students perceived the question as being random and their curiosity was piqued, as in, "What is Mr. Percoco up to with asking this question?" I looked forward to this every year, because as I walked around my classroom and asked the question of particular students, I could watch their faces and see their reactions: puzzlement, wide-eyed wonder, and a scrunching of foreheads. Most students replied with responses such as "I'd feel lost" or "I would question my identity." After I had asked a good number of students, I would tell them that the question was meant to get them to think about it in the light of the life of Frederick Douglass, who wrestled with this lack of identity all his life. All of a sudden Douglass would become a human being to them, his life having been brought down to a level of humanity with which students could relate.

I quickly realized how powerful this hook approach could be, and from that point on frequently used the same technique with other moments or historic personalities. Thus, I recommend that when you introduce the study of Madison and his important "Federalist 51," you use the same approach, by asking this question: "What would life be like if we had a different system of government, like that of China or Russia?" Once you run through this exercise, write on the board or project on the screen the seminal line from Madison's "Federalist 51," "If men were angels, there would be no need of government." Break the class into mixed-ability groups of four or five students, and provide each group with a piece of newsprint and markers. Ask the groups to brainstorm and list the ways in which government affects their lives on a daily basis. When the students are finished, ask them to share their responses with their classmates. I have a hidden agenda at work here: I want students to consider how our lives are influenced every day by the role and function of government, something upon which Madison was particularly keen.

You have probably noted by now that I am a fan of having students record their group findings on newsprint. I do that so that they can see their handiwork on the walls of the classroom while allowing other groups to see what they have discovered.

Like many Americans today, young people tend to be cynical about government and politics. We often hear how our government has become dysfunctional and that our system is gridlocked. Since this is the public perception, you could start out the lesson with an anecdote like this: "One day I went to the supermarket to buy milk, but the milk was at the back of the store. I asked the clerk why the milk was at the back of the store, and he said, 'I don't know, I just work here.' So I went to the store manager and asked the same question and he said, 'I don't know, it's just always been like that.' Next I asked the store owner the same question, and he told me, 'Because that is the way the architect designed the store.' My curiosity got the better of me, and I headed to the local library to look at the architectural renderings of the store. In the library archives I found a note from the architect that explained that by putting the milk in the back of the store, people would have to walk by the processed food and might purchase something else while they were in the store to buy milk. This would provide profit and stability for the store." In some ways, as architect of the Constitution, this is exactly what Madison wanted, particularly in a nation that had ideas of expanding geographically. Given his long, careful review of history, particularly the rise and fall of nation-states, Madison was shrewd in recognizing human behavior. In some ways he wanted a cumbersome form of government because he knew that a cumbersome system was a bulwark against government abuse. For modern Americans this might seem like anathema—we like immediate results, but government takes its time.

Americans should be familiar with "Federalist 51," because it is all about divisions of power. In fact, if you read "Federalist 51" and not the others, that would be fine, because "51" is arguably the most important essay in *The Federalist Papers*. Students will have to be guided in their reading to understand the division of power within and between governments in the proposed federalist system as offered by Madison. History has demonstrated time and again that governments can become abusive. So the question for Madison and the other founders was how to construct a government that prevented tyranny. To do this Madison devised a scheme that we take for granted today; we call it federalism. Madison explains in "Federalist 51" that the best way to avoid tyranny is to divide government within itself, as in the three branches of government. He takes it a step further, however, by dividing the government into two spheres—the federal or national government and the state governments, which become other centers of power. Thus power is divided geographically in a compound republic.

Madison and others at the time wanted to diffuse power in a way that would produce political stability while protecting liberties. He offers us other clues to this in "Federalist 51." It takes a supermajority to change laws in the United States; to secure the passage of a constitutional amendment, two-thirds of both houses of Congress must agree to pass it, and it still requires three-quarters of the states to ratify it. Madison keenly knew that it was about geography and time, particularly because passions cool and change over time and the geography of the age in which Madison and his compatriots were living did not lend itself to rapid communication.

You can take the exercise a step further by having students consider human nature. Pair students up and ask them to interview their partner about human nature. Have them record how their partner describes human nature and then share those descriptions with classmates. You can tally on the board the number of individuals who see human nature in a positive light, then those who see it in a negative light, and then get them to consider how Madison settled on the belief in a need for government and how that belief is enshrined in "Federalist 51."

These are complicated readings and topics with which you are asking your students to wrestle. One approach to helping them, particularly those who have learning disabilities or are English speakers of other languages, is to front-load all of this by showing the video *The Birth of the Constitution, Charlie Brown*. The issues that the new nation faced, and the questions that were raised at the time, are addressed in cartoon format in this thirty-minute video, making the topic easier for students to digest. Because it's the Peanuts Gang doing the narration, it also alleviates fears that this material is beyond them.

I suggest that you conclude your investigation of Madison with a reader's theater of the preamble of the US Constitution, the text and process of which can be found in Appendix 2.2. There is a lot of power in having students participate in reader's theater; it makes learning fun and pulls all students into the activity. When you are finished with the reader's theater, take the points addressed in the preamble and write them on the board. These would include, for instance, "Insure Domestic Tranquility," "Promote the General Welfare," "Provide for the Common Defense," and so on. Then discuss with students how government fulfills these functions today. List those functions that you brainstorm under the correct heading. In doing this activity you will have divided the various functions and role of government as envisioned by the founders and made students more keenly aware of how the work of individuals more than two hundred years ago plays out today in the United States. If you want to build on what you taught about Jefferson and places connected with him, you can easily do the same with Madison. I encourage you to use the lesson from Teaching with Historic Places, "Memories of Montpelier: Home of James and Dolley Madison." In this lesson students look at daily life at Montpelier, including that of enslaved people. Once more you can engage students with the idea that our founders' behavior often conflicted with their ideals. Given the tenor of our times, ask students to consider or complete a journal entry discussing whether anything has changed in America since the founders wrote such stirring words. As a teacher, I really struggled with the paradox of the lives and actions of the founders who were slave owners. It's easy to give them a pass and for simplicity's sake not deal with the historical reality. But deal with it we must, for if we don't, we are being untruthful not only to the narrative of American history, but also to the enslaved people who had no voice.

THE DECLARATION OF INDEPENDENCE AND BEYOND

When I taught Thomas Jefferson to my students, I always placed my instruction within the context of the great Enlightenment thinkers, particularly John Locke. I referred to Locke's philosophy as he outlined it in his *Two Treaties of Government*. Locke was one of

Jefferson's favorite philosophers, and he gleaned a great deal from Locke when writing the Declaration of Independence.

What students need to recognize is that the decision to separate from Great Britain in 1776 was truly revolutionary. Rarely in history had a colonial people broken away from their mother country. The men who gathered in Philadelphia in 1776 knew they were making history, but they couched their decision to part from Great Britain in language that had been written a century before. I framed my introduction to the Declaration of Independence by breaking the document down into its essential parts and looking at different clauses. I could do this much more easily after I had employed a reader's theater on the Declaration of Independence (Appendix 2.3). I also augmented my instruction with useful clips from the PBS film *Liberty*. The nice thing about *Liberty* is that it is divided into short, easily digestible segments. The one on the Declaration of Independence in Episode 2 is particularly good at breaking down the meaning of the document at the time it was written and then laying out where, as a document principally dealing with social justice, the Declaration has led people in their thinking.

I have mentioned that "the hook" at the beginning of class is critical. These first five to ten minutes of instructional time are crucial for setting the tone of the class and subsequent lesson. Two great hooks for students dealing with the independence movement between the colonies and Great Britain can be found on YouTube. The first is a satirical rendition of the song "Apologize," by the band New Republic, called "Too Late to Apologize," in which the founders are turned into rock stars singing about their reasons for declaring independence. Students will love it and be pulled into the popular culture connection. The other YouTube source features Eric Langhorst's eighth-grade class, in Liberty, Missouri, writing a breakup letter to a boyfriend or girlfriend. The clip is nine minutes long and perfect for inspiring your instruction, because you can see Langhorst and his students in action as they work through the lesson.

With my students I often equated the American Revolution with teenage rebellion, something to which most grades 7–12 students can relate. In my early years of teaching I had a student respond to an essay question I asked about the causes of the American Revolution with a long screed about how she was just like the colonies and her parents were just like Great Britain. She listed, as did Jefferson in his document, the various grievances against her parents and how they were tyrants controlling her life. Teaching the American Revolution does give teachers an opportunity to make history personal.

One approach is having students write their own Declaration of Independence from their family. Have them look at the various clauses in the Declaration that address specific grievances, and then, with some proper guidance on your part, ask them to determine why they might want to separate from their family. You just have to make sure students feel safe enough to engage in such an activity, knowing they will not be judged and you won't rat them out. I often was able to do this later in the school year, getting students to express how they compromised with their parents when we studied the Great Compromise of the Constitutional Convention or the various compromises that forestalled the Civil War. I generally did it through journal-writing exercises. The key to teaching history to young people is having them make their own connections between people and events in the past. This goes a long way in keeping them focused and engaged in your instruction.

For younger students, special needs students, or students who are English speakers of other languages, a terrific resource available through Monticello's online bookstore is Bentley Boyd's short graphic novel from his Comix with Content series, *Constitution Construction*. This twenty-four-page comic book addresses a variety of themes for teachers to use with their students, including John Locke's ideas, the notion of religious freedom, and the creation of the United States Constitution. Bentley riffs on Jefferson, Madison, and the other founders in a creative use of comic-strip-type illustrations connected with popular culture.

Another exceptional resource, also secured through the Monticello bookstore, is *Thomas Jefferson for Kids: His Life and Times with 21 Activities* by Brandon Marie Miller. This is a great go-to source for getting students to look at a variety of Jefferson themes, including his work as a statesman as well as an architect. There is also an American Adventure Game Discovery Book called *Thomas Jefferson and Monticello* by Steve Benson and Ron Toelke that you can use with your students to have fun. There are ten different games from which to choose. Playing games in history classes changes up the pace. The various games in this book are not difficult to employ in the classroom, the directions are simple, and once more, it is a look at the myriad sides of Jefferson, from planter to architect to statesman. It's another cool way of connecting disciplines across the humanities.

When teaching the Declaration of Independence I also sometimes used a film clip from the Hollywood musical *1776*, particularly the scene where the Continental Congress debates Jefferson's clause over slavery in the Declaration of Independence.

This scene illuminates the problem of slavery in American history on many levels. The song performed by delegate Edward Rutledge from South Carolina, powerfully portrayed by actor John Cullum, exposes the hypocrisy of Northern delegates who claim that the institution of slavery is immoral, offensive to God, and opposes the idea that "all men are created equal." Rutledge points out in the song "Molasses to Rum," that it is New England seafarers who are complicit in the slave trade and that essentially everyone's hands are dirty. Northern states did not begin to abolish slavery until after the American Revolution when people recognized the contribution African American men were making to the Continental Army. Even George Washington, a slave owner, came to recognize that black soldiers could fight as well as white soldiers. And during the American Revolution approximately five thousand African American men served in the Continental Army alongside their white counterparts. Many of them endured the bitter winter encampment at Valley Forge, Pennsylvania, and in 1995 a memorial was raised at Valley Forge National Historical Park to honor the sacrifices of these black patriots. Washington was the only founder who emancipated his slaves, but not until his death.

It should be noted that in the scene I recommend you share with your students, there is a glaring historical inaccuracy. Before Rutledge launches into his soaring anthem, Thomas Jefferson claims that he has already resolved to free his slaves. Nothing could be further from the truth. A few of Jefferson's slaves were emancipated upon his death in 1826, mostly members of the Hemings family. But by the time he died, he was so far in debt that he was unable to free his slaves. And herein lies the conundrum of the founders and slavery. For planters such as Jefferson and Madison, freeing their slaves would have been financial suicide. Even Rutledge in his fictional conversation with Jefferson before he sings says, "Then, sir, you have brought about your own financial ruin."

Another place to look for good dramatic film clips on the Declaration of Independence is the HBO miniseries *John Adams*. Since it is based on David McCullough's Pulitzer Prize–winning book of the same name, it is not a costume pageant, as *1776* might appear. You can compare and contrast the scene in *John Adams* with the last fifteen minutes of *1776* or John Trumbull's iconic painting, *The Presentation of the Declaration of Independence*, which hangs in the Rotunda of the US Capitol.

To be honest, the record seems to indicate that Madison felt the disconnect between maintaining the institution of slavery and the founding principles of the United States more than Jefferson did. Several times during the course of his life he lamented this fact, calling it at one point, "a sad blot on our free country." During his lifetime Madison owned more than three hundred slaves, and as was the case at Jefferson's Monticello, black people outnumbered white people at Montpelier. David O. Stewart's book *Madison's Gift* delves at length into this problem, and I highly recommend it as a resource, because it is a well-written biography and a fair assessment of Madison. Also consider introducing students to the efforts of the America Colonization Society, a national effort to address the institution of slavery. No one was blamed for the system since no one alive in the nineteenth century had anything to do with its creation. The world changed in 1831 with William Lloyd Garrison's publication of *The Liberator* and Nat Turner's slave rebellion.

In some ways our collective memory has resulted in the South getting a bum rap regarding slavery. Yet, as I explained, it was not solely a Southern phenomenon. Many Northern bankers and insurance companies supported the "peculiar institution." Northerners also carried race prejudice; even abolitionists did not necessarily think that blacks and whites were social equals. For example, in the early years of the American republic as the political party system developed, African Americans were disenfranchised in 1828 not so much because of race but because of party affiliation. If you want to bring this into a contemporary context, you can have students study the current issue of congressional redistricting, otherwise known as "gerrymandering," to keep certain parties in control of congressional representation in the US House of Representatives.

In the Ken Burns film *The Civil War* Burns quotes American author John Jay Chapman, who said slavery was the "serpent beneath" the carpet at the Constitutional Convention. The framers of the Constitution knew that slavery was a problem, yet for political expediency they permitted Southern states to count each slave as three-fifths a person when calculating the population for congressional representation purposes, ultimately setting in place the framework that allowed the slave trade to continue until 1808. They left future generations the task of figuring out what to do about slavery, and the future decided the matter during a horrific war that cost more than six hundred thousand American lives.

It is our obligation as teachers of history to ensure that our students know this fact. You can either tell them or show them by having them analyze primary documents that address the issue. There's an equally powerful scene in the film *Founding Brothers* in which historian William Fowler discusses Thomas Jefferson's farm book and how it lists, in addition to how many pigs, chickens, and cattle Jefferson has, the number of slaves he owns, some of whom were probably his own offspring. The scene is instructive because it addresses just how inhuman the whole sordid affair was while reminding us that a guy who practiced this behavior is enshrined on Mount Rushmore and on the National Mall.

That said, I don't believe in tearing down monuments. The German word for monument is *Denkmal*, which translated means "thought object." If we are clever, we can use these monuments, including those to heroes of the Confederacy, to be instructive by interpreting them within their context. Students love to debate topics like this. And a well-led and thoughtful conversation can pay dividends for you as a teacher. I address some of these issues more fully in the chapter on the Civil War.

One of the ways you can have students study the institution of slavery through the prism of the American Revolution is to have them study Virginia Colonial Governor Lord Dunmore's 1775 proclamation that offered freedom to enslaved people who left their plantations to serve in the King's Army. These former enslaved people were mustered into what became known as Dunmore's Ethiopian Regiment and wore uniforms with a badge reading "Liberty to Slaves." Provide your students with copies of the document to read (it's not dense at all) and then project onto a screen an image of men serving in the Ethiopian Brigade. Ask the students to determine the irony that took place in America at the time. They should easily see that Dunmore was turning the tables on Virginia by issuing his proclamation. As Virginians and other colonists argued they were being made slaves to Great Britain, here was something that exposed the flaw in their argument. In some ways Dunmore's proclamation was genius as both policy and propaganda. Nothing put the fear of God into slave owners more than the idea of enslaved people with weapons. It sent shivers up the spines of white Southerners who feared insurrection and is one of the reasons George Washington balked at permitting black soldiers into the Continental Army.

One of the hardest things about teaching sensitive topics in American history is the tendency to make judgments with a sense of presentism—that is, placing our standards on people who lived long before us. No doubt it is tempting to hold folks like Madison and Jefferson accountable for their flaws. It is a very human response. But presentism is ahistorical. The founders and others need to be viewed through the prism of their times, not ours. Madison and Jefferson were raised in a society that embraced slavery. That was their world, and it was what they knew. For them it was normal, despite the fact that they knew deep down that slavery in a nation espousing equality was problematic. In 1820, during the congressional debates that led to the Missouri Compromise, the first slave-related political crisis of the nineteenth century, Jefferson famously said that slavery was like holding "the wolf by the ear, and we can neither hold him, nor safely let him go." He also said in 1820 with regard to slavery and the Missouri Compromise that the issue was "a fire bell in the night." Run those quotes by your students and see what they think they mean.

When it comes to teaching about Locke's philosophy and Jefferson's use of it in writing the Declaration of Independence, students have to really wrap their minds around certain abstractions. Take, for instance, the idea of the "state of nature," into which, according to Locke and other Enlightenment thinkers, people are born. I had a colleague who brilliantly got students to understand this concept. He would open his class by talking "about" the state of nature by having his students actually reenact the social contract. In his classroom closet he kept a faux loincloth and a garden hoe. He would gleefully go into his closet, slip the faux loincloth over his clothes, and emerge with the hoe in his hand. Then he would pretend to be tilling the soil as a simple agrarian person who lives in a semi-paradise kind of condition, explaining that it was from this state of nature that governments were to be organized so that some structure could be crafted for society. By now all of his students were rapt with attention, focused on what was to come next. Having done his bit of showmanship, he secured his students' attention and they could then better learn about how, according to Enlightenment philosophers, a social contract was formed between those being governed and those governing. The stage was set by reviewing what students had learned previously in world history, focusing on how the Gutenberg Bible, Martin Luther, and René Descartes opened up the idea of reason and deduction and weakened divine truth, thereby weakening the thinking of divine right as the basis for the rule of monarchs. Philosopher Thomas Hobbes, who had studied Euclidian geometry, was impressed with the idea of using similar deductive reasoning to determine a moral basis for the existence of the state. If one can build a system on the assumption that two parallel lines never meet, might one be able to do that with politics? Hobbes imagined the state of nature when life was "nasty, brutish and short."

My colleague would break his students into small groups, telling each that they were farmers who planted beans or raised cattle. Next students reenacted the first social contract, in which two people would shake hands and agree to not murder or steal each other's crops or cattle. What students rarely realized is that there was no one to enforce the contract. Hobbes stipulates that in making such a contract, we cede power to another—an enforcer, if you wish. He called his enforcer The Leviathan, which at the time would have been represented by an omnipotent monarchial figure. Now along comes Locke, who says that in his reconstruction of the social contract (remember, this is not anthropology but a game of deduction) the enforcer is given only as much power as needed to enforce the rules. Should he exceed them and rob us of liberty, we retain the right—under the contract—to rise up and replace the enforcer. Students accomplished the lesson by role playing and reading sections of Hobbes and Locke. They had fun and learned an important concept in a compelling fashion.

The social contract is best understood as a relationship. When I covered it in class as a preamble to understanding Jefferson and the Declaration of Independence, I would write three terms on the board: *offer*, *acceptance*, and *consideration*. Then I would break each word down contextually, explaining that in the social contract the people/society voluntarily "offer" governing power to some authority. Before moving on I would ask students, "How do we do this today?" Most students would get it and respond, "We vote." The next step takes place when the authority "accepts" the responsibility and the power that has been vested to them. Finally—and this is important—the authority has to take into "consideration" what the people want. That is the critical point. Power rendered voluntarily now becomes a contractual arrangement between those governed and those governing. For Locke and Jefferson, the idea is that communities have the right and responsibility to replace or remove government power if government becomes abusive and violates the social contract. Again I would ask students, "How do we do this?" and again the refrain would come back, "We vote them out of office."

Since the colonies were breaking off from a king, they could not vote him out, so they had to have a revolution. The bottom line is that the Declaration of Independence is all about the violation of the social contract. Colonial leaders believed that Great Britain had become too abusive in its relationship to its colonial populations and needed to be replaced. They chose to declare independence, which also happened to be an act of treason and war. You can easily weave clips from Episode 2 of *Liberty* into this exercise, because the film provides exceptional actors portraying Jefferson and others who give voice to the words and articulate the arguments for separation.

WAS THOMAS JEFFERSON A BLACK PANTHER?

During the heyday of the Teaching American History grants program offered by the US Department of Education, I had the privilege and honor to work alongside Dr. Yohuru Williams, dean of academic affairs and professor of black studies at Fairfield University in Connecticut. Williams, also one of the National Humanities Council advisers to the

Journey, and I share a very similar philosophy when it comes to teaching history, and we often discussed pedagogy, content, and how best to deliver historical information to students. Williams also understands the struggles of teachers today and remains an advocate for high-quality teaching. His background in history and pedagogy makes him the perfect ally to have alongside you, particularly when it comes to teaching issues of social justice.

In 2008, for the *Magazine of History*, published by the Organization of American Historians, Williams wrote a provocative lesson plan called "Was Thomas Jefferson a Black Panther?" Williams and I believe that making connections for young people is crucial for student understanding and success. We always discussed and presented in a way that explored how teachers can use crossovers of time regarding historical content. This is but the first step in helping students develop historical thinking skills while also helping them see that history doesn't happen or unfold in a vacuum. Williams and I always talked between ourselves and with teachers about the changing nature of American history across time and how democratic principles have shaped—and continue to shape—the United States.

Williams is very creative with his use of acronyms in teaching. He even developed lesson plans about Supreme Court cases by crafting a character based on the well-known acronym of the Supreme Court called SCOTUS (Supreme Court of the United States) that leads students to understand the complexities of a variety of Supreme Court decisions. In this particular lesson he encourages the students to compare the nation's founding documents with other expressions of freedom and liberty across time. The goal of the lesson is not only to appreciate the importance of our founding documents, but also to help students appreciate how they continue to shape contemporary understanding of democracy as well.

In this particular lesson, Williams uses the acronym EQUAL, with each letter standing for one of five points of comparison:

- The document should contain an *Enumeration* of basic rights and principles.
- The document should address *Quality* of life issues.
- The document should promote the cause of community *Unity*. Here, the concept of community can be broadly construed as that which is in the interest of the nation, or narrowly interpreted as the causes and concerns

of a particular interest or group. These can include any number of factors such as race, class, gender, and spirituality, among others. In this sense, certain reform movements have projected unity even if they are limited to the issue that they hope to affect.

- The document should be related to an *Antecedent* document, just as the Declaration of Independence was a forerunner to the United States Constitution.

- The document should express an appreciation of freedom and/or *Liberty.*

Like many social and political movements before them, the Black Panthers used the principles established in the most sacred of American documents, the Declaration of Independence, to point out the hypocrisy of the American practice of not living up to its principles. In doing so, they followed a time-honored tradition of engaging the founders in a dialogue eloquently expressed in the Declaration of Independence. In each instance, from David Walker's *Appeal* in 1829 to the Seneca Falls Declaration of Sentiments in 1848 to Jacob Coxey and his ragtag army in 1894, protesters and reformers have interpreted these documents to support their cause. This raises a provocative question: what if your students could have a conversation with Thomas Jefferson? If Jefferson and the Black Panthers could dialogue, what might they agree on, what might they disagree about, and what turns would the conversation take? Would Jefferson find the Black Panther Party—Ten Point Program (see Appendix 2.4) "equal" to the Declaration of Independence?

Because Jefferson was a prolific writer, there are certainly enough of his writings to engage with questions ranging from religion to justice to education. His declaration embodied the sentiments of a revolution, which makes the question all the more provocative when compared with the writings of other reformers and revolutionaries. Because the 1960s have a kind of mystique all their own, students naturally gravitate to learning more openly about this conflicted era in American history. In part that is what makes this lesson so powerful and intriguing.

You could spend a lifetime digging through Jefferson's writings in libraries, archives, and on the Internet in search of relevant passages you can use for this lesson, which should take one ninety-minute block period, or two fifty-five-minute class periods. One of the best Internet sites on Jefferson, Thomas Jefferson on Politics and Government, is maintained by the Electronic Text Center at the University of Virginia. This site is tailor made for an EQUAL activity, as passages and quotes from Jefferson are searchable by topic and keyword. To jump-start your search you will find here four quotes from Jefferson that correspond with points 2, 5, and 10 of the Black Panther Party program, excerpts of which should make for lively discussion in your class (http://etext.lib.virginia. edu/jefferson/quotations/index.html).

First discuss the concept of EQUAL in class with your students. Choose a document such as the Seneca Falls Declaration of Sentiments, discuss how it illustrates Enumeration, Quality, Unity, Antecedent document, and Liberty. For homework, provide your students with copies of the Black Panther Party—Ten Point Program (Appendix 2.4) and a selection of quotations from Thomas Jefferson (Appendix 2.5). To help students analyze these documents, distribute copies of the National Archives and Records Administration's Document Analysis Sheet (http://archives.gov/education/lessons/ worksheets/written_document_analysis_worksheet.pdf).

Have students answer the following questions based on the National Archives and Records Administration's Document Analysis Sheet:

1. What type of document is it?

2. When was the document written?

3. Who is the author (or creator) of the document?

4. For what audience was the document written?

5. What does the document tell you about the author's background?

6. List three things the author said that you think are important.

7. List three things the document tells you about life in the United States at the time it was written.

8. Were the Panthers and Jefferson "EQUAL"—that is, on the same page—about certain issues? On what things might they agree? On what things might they disagree?

Next, divide students into groups of two or three and have them list on newsprint three questions they may have about Jefferson or the Black Panthers. Finally, ask the students to develop and list three questions they would like to ask Jefferson or the Black Panthers if they could have a conversation with them. Post the newsprint around the room and have the students share their questions with the class. Then lead a discussion that tries to answer the main questions students asked.

As a homework assignment assessment, have students assume the identity of Thomas Jefferson and write a letter to Huey P. Newton and Bobby Seale, leaders of the Black Panther Party, responding to their ideas in the Black Panther Party—Ten Point Program. Have the students read their letters in class and discuss their findings.

The Black Lives Matter movement has taken a central place in American life. Here might be a good place to discuss with students how they see the Black Lives Matter movement. I know it is an emotionally charged issue, but if we are to resolve the social ills that afflict the United States, we need to have the long-needed conversation about race. A good place for starting that conversation is the classroom.

If you want to follow this up with a video, I suggest you use the last few minutes of the last episode of the film series *Liberty*, "Are We to Be a Nation?" in which an actor portraying an enslaved person named Luke discusses his thoughts on the newly established nation that maintains the institution of slavery. You could also use the thirty-minute film *Dreams of Equality,* produced for the visitor center at Women's Rights National Historic Park in Seneca Falls, New York. This is an exceptional film that directly addresses the points in this lesson with regard to women's rights in the United States. I think it resonates with students because many of the issues or topics raised about women's rights are addressed by teenagers in the film.

Another way to approach this is to frame this within the context of the Black Lives Matter movement. Given what students have thus far learned about Jefferson and the founding documents, how is the Black Lives Matter movement connected to his ideas and the principles articulated in the Declaration of Independence? How does the Black Lives Matter movement demonstrate the changes in democracy over time?

Taylor Branch, eminent civil rights historian and Pulitzer Prize winner, argues, "It is vital to have white people involved in the issue of police justice because it makes it not purely a racial issue of black versus white. This is about right versus wrong" (Schwartzman 2016).

TEACHING FREEDOM OF RELIGION AND CONSCIENCE

One of the great gifts that Madison and Jefferson gave to the United States was the idea of freedom of religion. This tenet of our national faith is secured in the First Amendment to the Constitution. To really understand Madison and Jefferson's belief in freedom of religion, which they also argued included the freedom not to believe in any religion, you have to understand the world of Virginia in which they lived. The

Church of England, or Anglican Church, was the established church of colonial and early American Virginia. When people tithed, they were giving money not only to the church, but also to the state or colony. What Madison and Jefferson found most reprehensible was that the Anglican Church discriminated against other faith groups in Virginia, most notably Baptists, Quakers, and Presbyterians. They thought it was unjust for people of these other faith groups to, by virtue of their paying taxes, help defray the expenses of the Anglican Church. Like many other founders they looked at European history as a litany of wars caused by the mischief of religion. In the new nation, for which they saw plurality as tantamount to success, they believed people should be free to exercise or not exercise any faith without fear of being penalized. Jefferson wrote the Virginia Statute for Religious Freedom in 1777, but it was not adopted by the Virginia General Assembly until 1786. Jefferson wrote, "We the General Assembly of Virginia do enact [Be it enacted by the General Assembly] that no man shall be compelled to frequent or support any religious worship, place, or ministry whatsoever, nor shall be enforced, restrained, molested, or burthened in his body or goods, nor shall otherwise suffer, on account of his religious opinions or belief; but that all men shall be free to profess, and by argument to maintain, their opinions in matters of religion, and that the same shall in no wise diminish, enlarge, or affect their civil capacities."

Madison's "Remonstrance" is a powerful statement on religious liberty and was the driving force behind the adoption of Virginia's Statute for Religious Freedom in 1785 (at the time, Jefferson was still in France). You can find it at www.revolutionary-war-and-beyond.com/memorial-and-remonstrance-against-religious-assessments.html. Another great resource for this topic is the First Freedom Center; related materials can be found at http://thevalentine.org/firstfreedomcenter#.

As a history teacher I tried more often than not to "show" students something rather than "tell" them something. I never wanted to be perceived as the teacher in the Charlie Brown cartoons who is a squawking, unintelligible voice. Often, as I have indicated, I tried to show how periods of time in our history are related to one another. When teaching about freedom of religion and conscience, you can start your class by projecting onto a screen an image of one of Norman Rockwell's war-bond drive prints related to President Franklin D. Roosevelt's Four Freedoms speech, which he delivered before the United States entered World War II. In his State of the Union address delivered on January 6,

1941, Roosevelt outlined not just for Americans, but for the entire world, what he saw as the four essential freedoms that should be afforded to every human being.

> In the future days, which we seek to make secure, we look forward to a world founded upon four essential human freedoms. The first is freedom of speech and expression—everywhere in the world. The second is freedom of every person to worship God in his own way—everywhere in the world. The third is freedom from want—which, translated into world terms, means economic understandings which will secure to every nation a healthy peacetime life for its inhabitants—everywhere in the world. The fourth is freedom from fear—which, translated into world terms, means a world-wide reduction of armaments to such a point and in such a thorough fashion that no nation will be in a position to commit an act of physical aggression against any neighbor—anywhere in the world. That is no vision of a distant millennium. It is a definite basis for a kind of world attainable in our own time and generation. That kind of world is the very antithesis of the so-called new order of tyranny which the dictators seek to create with the crash of a bomb.

The Four Freedoms were enshrined in the United Nations Charter and Universal Declaration of Human Rights. In 1943, American artist and illustrator Norman Rockwell, painted his images of what the Four Freedoms looked like. These were later used as propaganda images on war-bond drive posters.

To kick off this particular lesson, project onto the screen the image of Rockwell's *Freedom of Worship* and ask students to study it. After a few minutes, ask them to describe it to you. They should pick up the words at the top of the image, "Each according to the dictates of his own conscience." Ask your students how effective they think Rockwell was in portraying this particular freedom and why they think that is so. Students should be able to point out that the image includes a variety of worshipers from different faiths, including Islam and Hinduism.

Next provide each student the excerpt of Jefferson's Virginia Statute of Religious Freedom that is found on one of the panels inside the Jefferson Memorial. You could also note to your students at this point that the Jefferson Memorial was built and dedicated during Franklin Roosevelt's presidential administration and that Roosevelt often saw himself as an heir to Jeffersonian ideas. To demonstrate this, project onto the screen an image of Roosevelt at the dedication of the memorial on April 13, 1943, and ask students to explain to you what it might say about him.

When we studied the idea of religious freedom, I sometimes projected onto the screen images of churches, temples, and mosques in the Springfield, Virginia, community where I taught. This drove home the point even further for students, because they all knew these places and passed them every day; in this Jeffersonian context, the buildings took on new meaning. That is something you can easily replicate in your community.

At this point in the lesson, you might want to hold a class discussion about the differences and similarities between the terms *religion* and *conscience*. Take a random poll of your students and ask them to define each of the words. Have one student serve as a secretary, writing down the differences and similarities noted. Then ask them to reread Jefferson's statute and see if their definitions of *religion* and *conscience* have changed. Raise the hypothetical question with your class of whether it is reasonable for people to think what they want to think. Ask students to consider if there are times when what some people think conflicts with what other people think. Obviously the answer to that is "Certainly," but how then do you resolve differences of opinion? Do you have to resolve them at all? Ask students to explain whether Jefferson opened a Pandora's box by writing his Statute on Religious Freedom.

We hear a great deal about words such as *tolerance* and *acceptance* in the news. Write both words on the board and ask students to consider if they mean the same thing. There are two noteworthy documents from the early federal period that you can follow up with as teaching exercises to have students study when looking at the issues of freedom of religion. The first is the 1790 letter from President George Washington to the Jewish community in Newport, Rhode Island, where he assures congregants that the government of the United States "happily gives to bigotry no sanction" and reaffirms the American idea of toleration. An excellent lesson plan on this letter can be found at http://teachingamericanhistory.org/library/document/letter-to-the-hebrew-congregation-at-newport.

The other document is Thomas Jefferson's 1802 Letter to the Danbury, Connecticut Baptists. In this letter he discusses his beliefs about freedom of religion, particularly the establishment clause of the First Amendment to the Constitution. It is in this letter that we find the words *separation between church and state*. A lesson that gets students to consider how high the wall is, or should be, between the two can be found at www.firstamendmentschools.org/resources/lesson.aspx?id=13064.

MR. MADISON'S WAR: TWO LESSONS

One of the often overlooked conflicts of American history is the War of 1812. I think it gets overlooked because it is wedged between the American Revolution and the Civil War. In fact I wager that students in Canada understand the War of 1812 better than our own students do, because it is taught as a central component of Canadian history. Yet it was a formative conflict that led to the creation of the longest undefended border in the world. It's also the first time the United States declared war on a foreign government. The first of two lessons presented here deals with the causes of the War of 1812, and the second lesson explores the results of that war.

The first lesson is designed to provide teachers and students with a means for understanding the political dynamics that brought the United States into war with Great Britain in 1812. Students will consider a variety of significant events and people who shaped them and how those events eventually led to the newly formed United States going to war with Great Britain. The lesson will take one ninety-minute block class or two fifty-five-minute classes.

Using primary and secondary sources, students will be able to analyze events, motivations, conditions, and actions leading up to the outbreak of hostilities between the United States and England in 1812. Students will also use this material to identify and give examples of the economics of the politics of the time that brought about conflict. When finished, students will be able to explain the different political viewpoints of the Federalists and the War Hawks, identify key figures of both groups, and trace the chronology of events that led to the rupture between the United States and England.

To prepare for the lesson you will need to divide the classroom into two sets of desks; one will serve as the seats for the Federalists, and the other desks will be for War Hawks. Cut thirty strips of paper and label half of them "Federalists" and the other half "War Hawks," and provide enough online access for both groups of students to do basic research on historical events and figures using laptops, tablets, or other digital devices. You will need a copy of the History Time Line Template (Appendix 2.6), two sheets of newsprint or several sheets of loose-leaf paper, and 3-by-5-inch note cards. You will also need copies of the following primary documents, which can be accessed online:

- James Madison: Special Message to Congress on the Foreign Policy Crisis—War Message, June 1, 1812, http://millercenter.org/president/madison/speeches/speech-3614

- James Madison: Proclamation of a State of War with Great Britain, June 19, 1812, http://millercenter.org/president/madison/speeches/speech-3615

- Treaty of Ghent, 1814, http://avalon.law.yale.edu/19th_century/ghent.asp

- A Kentucky Soldier's Account of the Battle of New Orleans, http://kynghistory.ky.gov/Our-History/History-of-the-Guard/1812%20Additional%20Resources/ThebattleofNewOrleans_s.pdf

- Harry Smith: The Aftermath of the Battle of New Orleans. *The Autobiography of Lieutenant-General Sir Harry Smith,* 240–244 (from "Late in the afternoon" to "our military fame"), https://books.google.com/books?id=xnNnAAAAMAAJ&pg=PA240#v=onepage&q&f=false

- Letter from Andrew Jackson to James Monroe, January 13, 1815. *Memoirs of Andrew Jackson* by Samuel Putman Waldo, 224–226, https://books.google.com/books?id=NHAEAAAAYAAJ&pg=PA224#v=onepage&q&f=false

- James Madison: Special Message to Congress, February 18, 1815, http://millercenter.org/president/madison/speeches/speech-3627

- James Madison: Seventh Annual Message to Congress, December 5, 1815, http://www.presidency.ucsb.edu/ws/?pid=29457

For the "hook," discuss with students how one event can be perceived from multiple viewpoints. Brainstorm with students some recent episodes in the United States that have polarized the American people. Have students consider why people join particular "camps" or "sides" on such issues. What drives them to believe what they believe and to perceive that their position is the right one? Explain in no more than ten minutes that by 1812 the new United States was often caught between the politics and policies of the world's two superpowers—Great Britain and France—which were often at war with each other. The Federalist Party, the party of Alexander Hamilton and George Washington, tended to lean toward maintaining good relations with England based on economic, commercial, and industrial ties, whereas the Democratic-Republicans, the party of Thomas Jefferson and James Madison, tended to be pro-French, based on the alliance between the United States and France during the American Revolution and on Republican values, which found monarchy to be anathema. As hostilities between the United States and England increased, the Democratic-Republicans aligned themselves with those who sought further expansion of the territory of the United States, including the acquisition of Canada and the elimination of the Indian threat on the frontier, which they believed England was antagonizing. These Americans took up the moniker "War Hawks."

Have students pull slips of paper from a hat that designates them as either a "Federalist" or a "War Hawk." Once all slips have been drawn, ask students to move to the side of the class designated either "Federalists" or "War Hawks." Have both sets of students use the list of primary source documents as well as online or in-class sources to research the background causes of the War of 1812. Give them about thirty minutes to complete their research. Have them develop a series of arguments, based on their party affiliation, about why the United States should or should not go to war with Great Britain. Then have them list on two separate sheets of newsprint the names of the major players in their party and their reasons. Have each group select a spokesperson to present their side's argument to the class. The spokesperson needs to articulate his or her party's position as it actually was.

Bring the class together as a group, providing each student with a 3-by-5-inch note card, and ask them to complete the following sentence: "The United States went to war with Great Britain in 1812 because . . ." Tally responses on the board. Next, provide each student with a copy of "The Road to War" History Time Line Template and ask them to fill in the causes of the War of 1812 chronologically. Students may decide to start in 1807, when President Thomas Jefferson signed the Embargo Act, which had the unintended consequence of putting into motion the steps that eventually led the United States into war.

You can then spend the next two periods exploring the War of 1812 by using the board game Invasion. It might be interesting to have students consider the particular name of this game before they play it, because in our collective national memory, we Americans don't generally see ourselves as invaders. Though we feel more comfortable in the role of being noble liberators, the historical record is clear that our foreign policy has often led us into wars of aggression. The War of 1812 is one of those wars.

After students have played Invasion, teach the following lesson about the conclusion of the War of 1812. This lesson is designed to provide teachers and students with a means of understanding the outcomes of the war, both at home and abroad. Andrew Jackson's stunning January 1815 victory over the British at New Orleans was fought after the Treaty of Ghent had been signed, when word had not yet reached America that the war was over. Yet Jackson's victory over some of England's finest troops who had engaged Napoleon's Grand Army in Europe electrified Americans and launched the nation into what has been called the Era of Good Feeling. American nationalism was boosted as a result of the war. Under Madison's leadership, America stood up to the greatest political, military, and economic force in the world, defending her honor admirably. The war also put Andrew Jackson on the road to the presidency. Students will consider a variety of primary source documents in relationship to the end of the war. For fun, teachers might wish to play the 1959 number one hit, "The Battle of New Orleans," written by Jimmy Driftwood and performed by Johnny Horton, as part of the lesson. The lyrics can be found online.

The aforementioned lesson will take one ninety-minute block class or two fifty-minute class periods, with the goal that students will be able to assess and explain the results of the War of 1812.

Once this next lesson is completed, students will be able to analyze events and American and British attitudes about the conclusion of the War of 1812, be able to define the term *status quo antebellum*, explain the definitions of *national identity* and *nationalism*, and articulate why the largest battle of the war—and one of the most important in American history—was fought after the Treaty of Ghent had been signed. Before starting the lesson, review the previous lessons on the background causes of the War of 1812 and the course of fighting that war.

You can augment this lesson by showing the last thirty minutes of the Hollywood motion picture *The Buccaneer*, which is the story of pirate Jean Lafitte's role in the story. It is a compelling clip and demonstrates really well Andrew Jackson's improvised fortifications. The film is available on YouTube. You will once more need to provide students with 3-by-5-inch note cards.

For the "hook," discuss with students how they often bring closure to conflicts with parents or siblings. Does the resolution of these conflicts include compromising? When the conflict is resolved, what changes internally within individuals and between the conflicting parties?

Next write the term *status quo* on the board, ask students if they know what it means, and settle, as a class, on its definition.

Finally, share with students a copy of the Treaty of Ghent and be sure they note the date it was signed. Then share with them one of the accounts of the battle of New Orleans, being sure that they note the date of the battle. Since the battle was fought after the treaty was signed, ask students to speculate how that might have happened. Next have students reread from the "Causes of the War of 1812" lesson President James Madison's "War Message to Congress" and his "Proclamation of War." Ask students to make a list of Madison's causes for fighting the British, tallying these reasons on one half of the board. Then have students review the terms of the Treaty of Ghent, and on the other side of the board list the negotiated agreements for peace.

Now with both the grievances and how they were addressed written on the board, ask students what changed between 1812 and 1815. Students should see that nothing really changed and that the statuses of both nations were returned to where they were when the war began.

Next have students read James Madison's "Special Message to Congress" from February 1815 and his "Seventh Annual Message to Congress," December 1815. Students should be able to define the tone of these speeches and write those terms on the board. Next have them read "National Aegis: 'The Peace'" from February 1815 (found in *The War of 1812: Writings from America's Second War of Independence*, edited by Donald R. Hickey). Ask students to define the tone of this reading and compare it with Madison's words. Then ask students to describe, based on the reading of Madison's "Seventh Annual Message to Congress" and the "National Aegis," the mood of the nation after the War of 1812.

Follow this by writing the terms *national identity* and *nationalism* on the board, and brainstorm with the class the meanings of those terms. Come to a class consensus and write it on the board. Next provide each student with a 3-by-5-inch card and ask them to write a complete sentence about how the results of the War of 1812 helped to create a kind of national identity for the United States and boosted nationalism in America. Have the students share with the class.

Next give each student a handout with the lyrics to the song "The Battle of New Orleans." Play the song; the 1959 Johnny Horton version can easily be found on the web. Then have students read the three accounts of the Battle of New Orleans. Have students compare and contrast the lyrics in the song to the accounts in the primary documents. Hold a discussion with students about why a lighthearted, almost comedic song would be written about an American battle from the War of 1812. Have students consider what that says in general about American national identity.

After this class discussion provide each student with another 3-by-5-inch note card and ask them to list their top three results of the War of 1812, explaining why they chose them. Next provide students with another 3-by-5-inch card and ask them to complete this sentence: "The War of 1812 is often called America's Second War for Independence because . . ." Discuss student responses with the class.

You can follow this with a brief discussion about *The Buccaneer*. Explain to students that this film was made in 1958. Ask them to consider what was going on in the United States at the time. You may need to give a five-minute lecture or show a quick PowerPoint presentation if they are unable to pull from prior knowledge that the Cold War was in full swing. There's a critical scene in the movie in Andrew Jackson's office before the battle, when the character Mr. Peavey asks Jackson, as he points to an American flag, "Andy, should we bring this?" Jackson replies, "I guess so, since we are going to have to fight for it." What I want you to be able to do is get your students to see this film as a subtext about Cold War America. Many of the historical pageant films produced in the 1950s and early 1960s were really about our conflict with the Soviet Union. If students can see this connection, they will also be able to understand how Hollywood has often played a role in shaping how Americans view themselves: as heroic, self-righteous, and always defending liberty. This is deeply ingrained in American national identity. Once more, you will have made connections and crossovers through historical content.

One of the War of 1812 sites inside the Journey is the grave of Francis Scott Key, author of "The Star Spangled Banner," who is buried in Frederick, Maryland. On the top of a column rising above his grave is a portrait statue of Key holding the national anthem in his hand. An interesting way to approach this with your students is to compare an image of this portrait sculpture of Key with the monument erected in his honor on the grounds of Fort McHenry National Monument and Historic Shrine in Baltimore, Maryland. The monument is a heroic-sized bronze sculpture of the Greek muse Orpheus, representing music. After playing board games about the War of 1812, where students will have to address the British attack on Fort McHenry in 1814, put the images of both monuments on the screen and ask students to consider which is more appropriate to Key. Of course there is no right answer and the point is debatable, so you can have some fun with them as you discuss it. This is another way to get students to consider ideas of public memory and national identity.

THOMAS JEFFERSON'S GRAVE ACTIVITY

One of the more intriguing facts about American history is that both Thomas Jefferson and John Adams died on the same day—July 4, 1826, the fiftieth anniversary of the congressional adoption of the Declaration of Independence. At the time, many Americans viewed the fact that two of the key leaders of the Revolution passed away on this particular day only hours apart as an act of divine providence. Jefferson's last words reportedly were "Is it the Fourth?" Adams's last words were "Jefferson survives." Jefferson actually died earlier in the day than Adams did.

Thomas Jefferson also designed his own tombstone. There were three things he had done during his life that he most wanted to be remembered for, and he had them etched into his tombstone at Monticello. It was always fun to have students determine, after spending a few classes learning about Jefferson, which contributions from his remarkable life he most wanted to be remembered for. The secret to this activity is to do it in class so that students can't look up the correct answer beforehand. Have them make a list of the three things they think Jefferson chose. When the students are finished, go over their responses. Then project onto the screen an image of Jefferson's tombstone, which reads "Author of the Declaration of Independence," "Author of the Virginia Statute of Religious Freedom," and "Father of the University of Virginia." Have students compare their responses with Jefferson's choices.

REFLECTIONS ON WHAT OTHERS HAVE SAID ABOUT JEFFERSON AND MADISON

It's always fun to have students play around with what people have said about famous people. I like having students rewrite quotes in their own words, because it gives them a look into the life of the person they are studying while at the same time providing them with their own individual agency in making historical interpretations. I also like having students consider what significant people have said about other significant people, because it lends a shred of credibility to the former. After completing the Historical House activity, students will be well enough versed in the lives of Madison and Jefferson to be able to manage the following quote activity. The first quote about Jefferson is from the pen of American author Henry Adams. Henry Adams was the grandson of President John Quincy Adams and great-grandson of President John Adams. The second quote is a famous quote about Jefferson uttered by President John F. Kennedy.

Adams wrote in his *History of the United States of America During the First Administration of Thomas Jefferson,* "A few broad strokes of the brush would paint the portraits of all the early Presidents with this exception . . . Jefferson could be painted only touch by touch, with a fine pencil, and the perfection of the likeness depended upon the shifting and uncertain flicker of its semi-transparent shadows" (1909, 277).

At a 1962 White House dinner in honor of all living recipients of the Nobel Prize, Kennedy said, "I think this is the most extraordinary collection of talent, of human knowledge, that has ever been gathered together at the White House, with the possible exception of when Thomas Jefferson dined alone."

Ask your students what they think these quotes mean, and record their responses on the board. Then ask them which quote seems to fit their impression of Jefferson and why. Take the Adams quote and have the students rewrite it in their own words, sharing with each other what they wrote. Ask the students to consider why Kennedy's quote has become part of the way Americans remember Kennedy's presidency.

Joseph J. Ellis, contemporary and popular historian and Pulitzer Prize winner, offers the following on James Madison: "If God was in the details [of a law], so the saying went, Madison was usually there to greet Him upon arrival" (2001, 54). Author Garry Wills, another Pulitzer Prize recipient, claims, "As a framer and defender of the Constitution [Madison] had no peer" (2015, 164). Do the same activities with these two quotes about Madison that you did with the Jefferson quotes.

My favorite quote about Madison is from the American poet Robert Frost, who said, "I've decided that the best dreamer was Madison . . . I think I know . . . what Madison's dream was. It was just a dream of a new land to fulfill with people in self-control." Now have your students look at Madison in the context of Frost's quote. How do they, based on what they have learned thus far, see Madison as a dreamer? Ask them if in their opinion the United States is a land filled "with people in self-control." You might wish to make this a writing assignment in the form of a journal reflection. Ask students to discuss in their reflection specifically where we as a nation have succeeded in being a "people in self-control" and where we have missed the mark. Follow this with a classroom discussion.

Each July 4, in front of Jefferson's beloved Monticello, a naturalization ceremony is held. Here, people who long to be American citizens can find the beginning of their dreams as they aspire to fulfill what Jefferson and Madison envisioned. These new Americans find the beginning of their journey as full-fledged citizens of the United States at the southern terminus of the Journey Through Hallowed Ground National Heritage Area in an effort to make the United States live up to its ideals and promises, and thus their journey continues, as does that of the nation. Be sure to bring your students along for the ride.

CHAPTER 3

Harpers Ferry: A Confluence of History

Ask most history teachers about Harpers Ferry, West Virginia, and you're likely to get a response that invokes the name of John Brown and his October 1859 raid on the federal armory and arsenal. Brown's goal was to secure arms and munitions and start a slave uprising along the Appalachian Mountains, and his raid is considered one of the major triggers of the Civil War. Even though Brown's raid was a failure, there remains a thread between Brown, his motivations, and the dilemma Americans continue to confront with regard to race. Like all matters of history, there are no easy answers to be found as you walk along the cobblestones in Harpers Ferry or step inside John Brown's Fort, the U.S. Armory and Arsenal's firehouse where Brown and his raiders made their last-ditch stand. The good study of history requires that we wrestle with events, personalities, and outcomes if it is to be rigorous. In reality there can never be one definitive tale, for history is full of nuance and shades; that is why the reflective aspect of studying history is so important.

I first visited Harpers Ferry in the spring of 1981. Naturally I made the obligatory first stop the National Park Service Visitor Center and watched the introductory film *To Do Battle in the Land*. Acclaimed African American actor Ossie Davis narrates the film, which focuses on a contemporary conversation about property rights and asks people to decide whether they think Brown's 1859 actions were justifiable. It's a terrific vehicle for looking at the complicated implications of American slavery. Several years later on a return trip to Harpers Ferry, I was delighted to see that the film was available for purchase in VHS format. I bought a copy to use in my classroom. When it came out on DVD, I bought it again. I can honestly say that of all the different materials I used to teach history over the years, this film—in spite of it being made in the late 1970s—held up in my classroom. It took on an even more powerful relevance after the 9/11 terrorist attacks on the United States, because early in the film, Davis, looking directly at the audience, says, "But when does freedom fighting become terrorism?" The historical story remained the same, but the context had changed. The film is now available on YouTube.

Tackling the Homework Dilemma: A Strategy

Like many teachers I struggled with the issue of homework. I believed in its use as a pedagogical practice, but as my high school demographics dramatically changed, I encountered more and more students who simply would not do homework. The reality really hit me one day as I was collecting homework assignments. When I asked one student, who frequently slept during my class, "Why don't you have your homework again?" he looked at me with pleading eyes and told me he had to work late at his job on weeknights to help supplement his family's income. I was flummoxed. I remember standing there as he put his head back down on his desk, closed his eyes, and went back to his dreams. For me it was a bit of a moral crisis. How could I best assess students' learning while remaining humane and compassionate about the ever-growing strains placed on them? I gave deep thought to it and decided I had to figure out an alternative means for assessing students. Thus was born the 3-2-1 note card activity, which proved to be a game changer for me, my approach to teaching, and subsequent student learning.

Employing the 3-2-1 note card activity is quite simple, really. You just need to be willing to secure a plethora of note cards for your classroom. You can use this technique for films, readings, and other class assignments. Simply provide each of your students with a note card and have them write their name at the top of one side. Then ask them to record on one side of the note card three important things they learned from the film, reading, and so on, two things about which they would like to know more, and finally, one thing from the film, reading, or activity that will stick with them. On the back side of the card they are to write in one complete sentence the main idea conveyed by the film or reading. Once students completed the card, I would randomly call on individuals to report on each of the points.

It's a good, quick way to check on student learning and retention. Once they were completed, I would collect the cards, review them, log their completion into my grade book, and then return them to the students. I discovered that students really liked this activity, because it permitted authentic assessment to take place within the confines of the class period, did not tax them with homework, and forced them to focus on the topic at hand. It also liberated me as a teacher from contending with the homework dilemma. Every time I would try to collect homework from students, I felt like I was their adversary. That feeling really grated on me and made me feel sad, because I always viewed myself as a teacher who was doing my work on the behalf of others. The 3-2-1 note card in a way saved me as well as my students.

For the film *To Do Battle in the Land* I modified the activity a bit. I gave each student a note card and asked them to write down the word *terrorist* and then define it in their own words. Once they did that, I randomly called on students to share their definitions. There was a range of responses, such as "A terrorist is someone who uses violence to secure a particular objective" and "A terrorist is someone who commits murder or creates a chaotic atmosphere."

Once we discussed some of their responses, I showed the film. When the film was over (it is thirty minutes long), I asked them to answer the following question on the back side of the note card: "Was John Brown, in your opinion, a terrorist or not? Please explain." This generated a lot of conversation and discussion once we began sharing responses. Clearly in our contemporary worldview the word *terrorist* has come to mean something quite specific, particularly since the 9/11 terrorist attacks on the United States. All of the students I was teaching near the end of my career had been raised in the shadow of 9/11. Thus there was undoubtedly some confusion on the part of some students about this request to respond on the card. For many students, terrorism is a modern concept, and they found it difficult to apply it to an event from the middle of the nineteenth century. Nevertheless the prompt for this card activity got students thinking about Brown and his motivations for instigating a slave rebellion. Responses were all over the place when it came time to discuss. Some students said that Brown was a terrorist because he used violence and fear to make a point, whereas others said he was not a terrorist because his motivation to liberate slaves was based on a sense of concern for them. I am not advocating for a particular response or saying there is one correct answer. There really isn't, and that in some ways is what can make history fun, because it can be an argument without any end.

In employing this technique, students get to wrestle with the past in a very direct way, and that, in part, is what the National Park Service does so well at Harpers Ferry—they are in the business of raising questions, not necessarily providing answers. To be sure, a specific historical event took place here in 1859, but so what? Many people who visit Harpers Ferry National Historical Park do so with the intent of seeing a place where history happened, which is a fair reason to visit. But the Park Service will have done its job if visitors or students leave with more questions than answers.

HARPERS FERRY AND AMERICAN MEMORY

The longer I taught, the more I began to realize that young people can, in fact, deal maturely and rationally with difficult historical questions. Increasingly I was drawn to bringing the idea of studying American memory into my classroom. This helped students see that there was a purpose behind studying the past and that history is more than just the names of people and dates. It's a rich mine that produces a great deal of grist for the intellectual mill. The last fifteen years I was in the classroom saw an explosion of the historiography of American memory. Scores of books were written to address various events in American history and how the nation has chosen to either remember or forget some things. Academic conferences sponsored by the Organization of American Historians and the American Historical Association often addressed themes of American memory. The Lincoln Bicentennial in 2009 and the Civil War Sesquicentennial provided a wealth of scholarship addressing memory as it relates to Lincoln and then the Civil War. I was captivated by all of it. Reading about American memory recharged my intellect and opened a door for me to get my students to consider why history is presented the way it is. There is that old saying that "History is written by the campfire of the victors."

There are essentially two voices competing with each other when studying past events. There is the "historic voice," which is the analytical voice that looks at history through a lens of cause and effect. Then there is the "commemorative voice," which is generally reflected in the words of the participants. The "commemorative voice" is generally laden with emotion. It is very hard to reconcile the two voices. In some ways the parallel study of American history infused with a dose of American memory is also a heck of a lot of fun. Memory is more closely linked with the "commemorative voice."

It has a feel-good component to it. Historian Richard White of Stanford University has often said, "Americans like to celebrate, not necessarily remember." I loved watching students engage with material that forced them to think, and saw that they enjoyed being challenged as well. And one of my biggest tools in my arsenal was from the television series *The Simpsons*. In Season 7 there was an episode called "Lisa the Iconoclast" that is great for classroom instruction. And when you tell your students they are going to be watching an episode of *The Simpsons* in school, well, watch the delight on their faces; it's priceless.

This particular episode is tailor-made for the classroom because it involves Lisa Simpson working on a history project for school and having to encounter the difference between myth and actual history. During her research project on Jebediah Springfield, the founder of the Simpsons' hometown of Springfield, Lisa uncovers some unseemly things about his past, just as the town is getting ready to celebrate a holiday in his memory. Lisa is put in the position of having to decide whether it's better to let the myth live on or reveal the sordid truth.

I loved showing this thirty-minute episode in class because students can connect on many levels; there is certainly the popular culture element to watching this during school, but there is the equally thoughtful element at play, too. I often showed it before taking students to visit Harpers Ferry. Even though I was able to take them there easily, there is a way you can employ this activity in your classroom, too.

Before our trip to Harpers Ferry I always introduced the topic by showing *To Do Battle in the Land*. Before watching it I would simply ask students to write down or focus on the name Heyward Shepherd, who is mentioned in the film. When the film was over, I asked students to recall the tale of Heyward Shepherd from the 1859 raid. He was the free black baggage master of the train station at Harpers Ferry and the raid's first fatal victim. His death is a huge irony in American history, given that Brown wanted to start a slave rebellion and had African Americans as part of his band of raiders. In the 1930s the United Daughters of the Confederacy and the Sons of Confederate Veterans erected a memorial to Shepherd that reads as follows:

> On the night of October 16, 1859,
> Heyward Shepherd, an industrious
> and respected colored freeman,
> was mortally wounded by John

Brown's raiders. In pursuance
of his duties as an employee of
the Baltimore and Ohio Railroad
Company, he became the first
victim of this attempted
insurrection.

This boulder is erected by
the United Daughters of the
Confederacy and the Sons of
Confederate Veterans as a
memorial to Heyward Shepherd,
exemplifying the character and
faithfulness of thousands of
Negros who, under many
temptations throughout
subsequent years of war, so
conducted themselves that
no stain was left upon a record
which is the peculiar heritage
of the American people, and an
everlasting tribute to the best
in both races.

Generally when I took my students to Harpers Ferry, a visit to the Heyward Shepherd Memorial (Figure 3.1) was our last stop. That was intentional. By the time we had reached this point on our field trip, the students had been steeped in the story of John Brown and his raid. When we reached the memorial, I would ask the students to gather around and then pick a student with a strong voice to read the inscription on the memorial aloud. With this information in hand they had the context for responding in their journals and writing their reflections there, on site, at the memorial. For the next twenty minutes or so, students feverishly wrote their thoughtful reflections. Becky, who was on our

ON THE NIGHT OF OCTOBER 16,1859, HEYWARD SHEPHERD, AN INDUSTRIOUS AND RESPECTED COLORED FREEMAN, WAS MORTALLY WOUNDED BY JOHN BROWN'S RAIDERS. IN PURSUANCE OF HIS DUTIES AS AN EMPLOYEE OF THE BALTIMORE AND OHIO RAILROAD COMPANY, HE BECAME THE FIRST VICTIM OF THIS ATTEMPTED INSURRECTION.

THIS BOULDER IS ERECTED BY THE UNITED DAUGHTERS OF THE CONFEDERACY AND THE SONS OF CONFEDERATE VETERANS AS A MEMORIAL TO HEYWARD SHEPHERD, EXEMPLIFYING THE CHARACTER AND FAITHFULNESS OF THOUSANDS OF NEGROES WHO, UNDER MANY TEMPTATIONS THROUGHOUT SUBSEQUENT YEARS OF WAR, SO CONDUCTED THEMSELVES THAT NO STAIN WAS LEFT UPON A RECORD WHICH IS THE PECULIAR HERITAGE OF THE AMERICAN PEOPLE, AND AN EVERLASTING TRIBUTE TO THE BEST IN BOTH RACES

FIGURE 3.1

Heyward Shepherd Memorial

October 2007 trip—and who went on to be a writer after graduating from William & Mary—wrote this:

At the Heyward Shepherd Monument Oct. 5, 2007

This monument is full of terrible irony. Confederate support groups erected a monument to a free black man, claiming that his death represented the ideals of the Confederacy. It is propaganda at its worst: using the noble, tragic death of an individual to support a cause that he himself would never have supported.

The engraving says that Heyward "exemplified the character and faithfulness of thousands of negroes." Those "negroes" were not faithful because they chose to be, they were faithful because they were forced to be by cruel masters who used their labor for profit. Shepherd was merely doing his job, and definitely was not supporting the Confederacy. The monument speaks of blacks as if they were children, who withstood "temptation" as if freedom and liberty were sinful desires to which they had no right.

The fact that this was erected 70 years after the end of slavery shows how pervasive prejudice is.

Most students over the years have reflected Becky's sentiments. Today our young people are sensitive to race and to people in the United States who are marginalized and maligned simply because of who they are. At the Heyward Shepherd Memorial, students encounter history in a deep and provocative way. This activity within its historical context strikes a chord in them, and I have found students willing to stand up and express the deepest longings of their heart in such circumstances. A visit to the Shepherd Memorial gives them great insight into the various shades of the human condition and allows you as a teacher to engage in rich, meaningful conversation with them.

To replicate this activity in your classroom you can use the film *To Do Battle in the Land* and the episode from *The Simpsons* I discussed, and then project an image of the Heyward Shepherd Memorial on the screen in front of your classroom and either have students do a journal activity or hold a conversation with them. Be sure to have a student read aloud the inscription on the memorial.

I have laid out for you the manner in which I raised the topic of Harpers Ferry and American memory with my students, but there's one more element I included: showing the last bit of the 1940 film *Santa Fe Trail*, starring Ronald Reagan and Errol Flynn. For the last three decades historically based Hollywood films have made a comeback as an American genre. Consider, for instance, *The Patriot, Saving Private Ryan,* and the HBO productions of *Band of Brothers* and *John Adams.* Many people take film as fact, particularly when it is on the big screen. Creating visually literate, as well as historically literate, students is important to me, and any time I could use a film to demonstrate that Hollywood is Hollywood and not history, I did so. But truth be told, there is a place for historically based films in our culture, particularly if they generate a curiosity among people to go out and learn the facts. I remember bumping into one of my students at the public library the summer *Saving Private Ryan* came out. He was carrying a stack of books on D-Day. As we saw each other, he said to me proudly, "Look, Mr. Percoco. I saw *Saving Private Ryan* the other night and just checked out a bunch of books to read about D-Day." So we as a community of educators cannot be completely dismissive of Hollywood films, provided students are guided and then willing to take the next steps to continue their learning.

Santa Fe Trail is about the years just before the Civil War breaks out, chronicling the story of Jeb Stuart, portrayed by Errol Flynn, and George Custer, played by Ronald Reagan, and their time at Fort Leavenworth, Kansas, just as the violence of Bleeding Kansas breaks out. John Brown and his sons played a large role in the violence perpetrated against pro-slavery Kansans. Brown is portrayed in the film by Raymond Massey, who would go on to play Abraham Lincoln the following year in *Abe Lincoln in Illinois.* I do not show the whole film, but just the last twenty minutes, which depicts the events of Brown's raid on Harpers Ferry. In particular the climax of the film is the battle waged in Harpers Ferry between the raiders and the US Marine detachment led by Colonel Robert E. Lee. The scene is set inside Brown's Fort, which was the arsenal's firehouse.

When I visited Harpers Ferry with students, Brown's Fort was an obligatory stop. If you have ever been to Harpers Ferry and stopped in to visit the fort, then you know just how small it is. In *Santa Fe Trail* the fort is transformed into this impregnable structure that is huge. It is so bogus and over the top that students who have been with me to Harpers Ferry break out in convulsive laughter because they have experienced the reality and know the history. The students quickly get the point, too. After leaving my class they all know that they must bring a skeptical eye to history films produced by Hollywood.

You can replicate this activity in your classroom by showing students images from the interior of John Brown's Fort on the screen. They will clearly get the sense of how small and cramped the space actually is, so that when you show them the clip from *Santa Fe Trail*, they too will get it.

RAN AWAY READER'S THEATER

One year when I brought my students to Harpers Ferry, the ranger assigned to my group was Catherine Bragaw. Bragaw developed a reader's theater for school groups based on the slave advertisements that appeared at the end of Charles Dickens's (1842) book *American Notes for General Circulation*. Called *Ran Away*, it is a very powerful strategy to employ. I had just begun using other reader's theaters in my regular US history classes with great effect. On days when the class was performing a reader's theater, I'd create what I called the Spirit of American History Players, which I would announce with great fanfare, making a trumpeting sound with my voice and hands.

The Spirit of American History Players was a staple in my classroom, but the players always changed, and I made sure that all students participated in one way or another, since we did seven or eight of these per school year. Reader's theaters are very engaging ways to bring history alive with and for students, and they get the students out of their chairs and sometimes out of their comfort zones. Rarely did students not want to participate.

Here is what you do for the play *Ran Away*. Take the script (Appendix 3.1), cut out each of the separate newspaper advertisements, and fasten them to a larger piece of construction paper. You will then have eleven advertisements that your students will read. When you get the students who are to perform assembled at the front of your classroom, direct them to begin reading their advertisement when the student before them gets to the name of the runaway slave being sought. Every student will start the same way, with the words *ran away,* just as the newspaper advertisements begin. In this way it becomes a bit of a round robin approach, but it has a measured beat when read.

The effect of all these newspaper advertisements for runaway slaves is very powerful; what is doubly powerful is that they are primary sources. Dickens, who traveled to the United States in the 1840s, was most struck by the place of the institution of slavery in American life. So disturbed was he by its presence that he concluded his travel narrative by listing a bunch of these advertisements. You can make it even more powerful for your students by having images of enslaved people who were photographed in the 1850s or some of the antislavery images drawn by abolitionists projected on the screen as the students read.

I would also recommend using this reader's theater with students as young as upper elementary school. The language is easy enough, and the point will be made. Teachers at this level may not feel comfortable with showing the associated graphic images of those enslaved.

It is very important to remember to approach the topic of American slavery and the life experiences of the enslaved with sensitivity. Because we still confront racial division in the United States, it is incumbent upon you as a teacher to help your students develop a sense of historical empathy. You want your students to understand, in the case of this activity, why slaves would opt to run away to freedom. Reader's theater is also a good method for addressing the topics of abolition, the fugitive slave crisis in America during the 1850s, and the coming of the Civil War.

BIRTH OF THE VODCAST

The "Of the Student, By the Student, For the Student" vodcast project is an award-winning program and the centerpiece of the Journey's curricular programs. It received the Award of Merit from the American Association of State and Local History, and the Advisory Council on Historic Preservation presented its Award for Federal Preserve America Accomplishment to the National Park Service for its integral role in the service learning project. It is addressed in much greater detail in Chapter 5. In essence this is a student-researched and student-produced mini-movie in which National Park staff works with local schools and Journey staffs to have students create movies for various parks. With the help of adults, students research a park-related topic using only primary material, write a script, film, and then edit their vodcast, which becomes part of the official interpretive material of the park.

There are five vodcasts for Harpers Ferry National Historical Park. The first is *Troubling Water: John Brown as a Child*, which examines what made Brown a leader, a radical, and a martyr. Here students from Harpers Ferry Middle School interpret what occurred in Brown's life that propelled him to take action against slavery. *John Brown: Children of the Raid* answers the question of what was it like to be a kid on October 16, 1859, when Brown and his raiders came to town. This vodcast interprets the pivotal event as seen through the eyes of Harpers Ferry children (www.stenhouse.com/harpersferry). *JB: Getting Down with Our History* examines John Brown from a historical perspective and his relevance today. *Harriet and Dangerfield Newby: A Story of Love, Family and Courage* tells the story of Dangerfield Newby, who struggles to buy the freedom of his wife and children and joins John Brown. In this vodcast the students uncover his remarkable and haunting tale, which is filled with pathos. One of his letters is key to the story and subsequent vodcast. Finally, *Jump to Freedom: Slavery and Harpers Ferry* examines the role and institution of slavery as it played out in this community.

After five months of hard work, the students premiered their work. On June 25, 2009, Robert G. Stanton, deputy assistant secretary of the Department of the Interior and the director of the Office of Youth joined the JTHG Partnership in Harpers Ferry National Historical Park for the official unveiling.

> On behalf of the Secretary of the Interior, Ken Salazar, and President Obama, I want to commend the students of Harpers Ferry. Students, you exemplify the spirit of service, you exemplify what Dr. King would remind us is the most urgent question that we face collectively and individually: What are you, what am I, what are we doing for others? That is the most urgent question of all. What you are giving of yourselves for this noble cause of preservation stands as a hallmark which I will share beyond the state of West Virginia, beyond the state of Virginia, beyond Maryland and Washington, D.C. If they want to see an example, if they want to see a model of citizen engagement, a connection to our youth, they only have to come to Harpers Ferry. (JTHG 2009)

The big payoff of the vodcast is that all the students assume the ownership of their learning. There's nothing better than student success when you work with young people either as a teacher or as a mentor. The first Harpers Ferry vodcasts were produced in 2009, and by the summer of 2015, three of the students who participated in the first series of vodcasts had returned to work at Harpers Ferry National Historical Park as seasonal park rangers. "It's inspiring," Dennis Frye, chief of Interpretation and Educational Partnerships at the park, related to me during a conversation, "to see people who were in the park as sixth and seventh graders in the uniform." For Ashley Pugh, Adele Fischman, and Blayne Ott, participation in the vodcast project put them on a path to their current status and bright-looking futures. All of them want to stay connected to the National Park Service when they graduate from college. I was able to spend some time over the summer with them discussing their work.

For Pugh the experience was in part to get more involved in a different approach to learning. "We always knew our town had a lot of history," she said, "but we didn't know the extent of it and how that history still impacts the town today. The best thing about being involved with the vodcasts was the working side by side with park rangers and learning how to work with [peers] with whom you would not ordinarily work. As a ranger I now get to live out the idea you always hear that if you find a job you love, you will never work a day in your life. Everybody here at Harpers Ferry loves their job."

"I always liked history in the classroom," said Fischman, "but working on the vodcasts and with the National Park Service gave me a hands-on approach to learn history a different way." Her plan is to attend the Savannah College of Art and Design to study industrial design. She hopes to bring the skills learned in college back into play at some point for the National Park Service. Fischman said she appreciates the opportunity to come back and work in the same park that helped her define what she likes doing in an adult capacity.

Taking the lead on getting these vodcasts created was Joe Spurgas, principal of Harpers Ferry Middle School. "None of the vodcast success at Harpers Ferry Middle School would have been possible without his willingness to experiment, take risk, challenge convention, and grasp our shared vision," Frye said.

In a world driven by testing mania, Spurgas believes in thinking and doing outside of the box. "There is no question that I took a substantial risk in working with . . . the Journey and Dennis at the National Park," Spurgas told me in a chance conversation. "But their pitch meeting was so filled with enthusiasm that I couldn't say no."

Spurgas is a devotee of the value of authentic service-learning projects. As a school administrator, he believes community involvement is very important; so, too is building trust with students and staff. Some of his faculty demonstrated some pushback when he pledged to engage the students in his school in such a manner. "They questioned the time commitment," he said, "wanting to know how this was more important than seat time. But I'm a firm believer that service learning engages students in real-world application, because it involves hooking students with successful careers. It connects people with experience, and the best kind of learning is rooted in experience."

Spurgas can back that up from his own wellspring of informal service learning, having worked for the United States Forestry Service. An academic background in science led him to work for the federal government early on. A lover of the great outdoors, he also became a National Park Service buff in his early adulthood, hiking trails and drinking in the natural beauty at places such as Zion National Monument, Yellowstone, Yosemite, the Grand Tetons, and a host of others. His experience working in California and sojourning through the National Parks persuaded him to become a science teacher, and in 1981 he joined the faculty at Harpers Ferry Middle School in just such a capacity. He remained at the school for thirty-three years, serving as principal for twenty-two of them.

Developing the whole child is important to Spurgas. "No matter how smart you are," he says, "if you are not a good person and are not healthy in mind and body, then you don't succeed." In part, that is what made him so energized and enthused about the Journey's Of the Student, By The Student, For the Student vodcast project. He points directly to the success of Pugh, Fischman, and Ott as examples of why and how the vodcast projects work. "Those three young ladies just blossomed," he said. "I can remember when they started out as sixth graders and how shy and timid they were. Now look at them!"

Every student at Harpers Ferry Middle School was invited to participate in the vodcast program, and most students wanted in on the action. "Participation in the vodcasts helps students grow," Spurgas said. He is particularly proud of the special education students who participated. "It was amazing to see students with learning disabilities become successful in front of a camera." At the end of the first year of the project, parents were repeatedly telling Spurgas, "This has been an incredible experience. My child has really grown by participating."

Equally compelling for Spurgas and Frye was that the students were able to bring their own perspective to the interpretation of history, whether it was about the short-term implications on the town after Brown's raid, the numerous times it changed hands during the Civil War, or the struggle for rights, equality, and dignity by African Americans. At its core, working on a vodcast gets students to look at the range of emotions and experiences of a local community through the eyes of the people who lived that particular history.

As much as Spurgas is an idealist, he recognizes the realities teachers face today in an already crowded curriculum and an environment of high-stakes testing. Spurgas wants students to leave Harpers Ferry Middle School with four traits: reading excellence, quality of character, a greater awareness of personal health and well-being, and success on state-mandated testing. "You need all four to succeed in today's world," he believes. He also wants his students to "care for each other, themselves, and the National Parks."

Each year before the round of West Virginia state-mandated testing commenced, Spurgas would hold a schoolwide testing pep rally and tell his students he had gone to bat for them to keep the vodcast project alive for subsequent generations of students. "I did this for you," he told them. "Now you need to be successful on these tests for me." The students had no trouble responding, and based on their solid across-the-board test scores, Spurgas was able to persuade district officials to maintain the vodcast program.

What is equally terrific is that the educational staff at the Journey have developed lesson plans to accompany many different vodcasts, reinforcing the basis of the project: that students teach each other. Watching the vodcasts, you can see the joy and enthusiasm on the faces of the students participating, and that can pay dividends in your classroom on several levels. It is peer-to-peer instruction, which for young people carries great credibility. It can encourage your students to take risks, too. Nothing of value or merit just happens—it requires risks, and although there may be bumps in the road, much of the American success story has depended on people willing to take physical, intellectual, and emotional risks. Just ask Joe Spurgas and his students—they are the kind of adult and student leaders we need to emulate in all of our schools from coast to coast.

THE SEARCH FOR FREEDOM IS A CONSTANT STRUGGLE

For Frye, Harpers Ferry National Historical Park is about a unique continuum of the struggle in America for freedom and dignity. "Harpers Ferry is the epicenter of that story," he says. It may have started with John Brown in 1859, but it resonates today. It was no accident that Frederick Douglass delivered the commencement speech at the predominantly black Storer College in 1881. Years after John Brown's raid, Douglass famously said, "I could live for the slave, but John Brown could die for him." It was no accident, either, that W. E. B. Du Bois held the second meeting of the Niagara Movement at Harpers Ferry in 1906. Both Du Bois and other black intellectuals, such as Ida B. Wells, were locked in a fierce debate with Booker T. Washington on how best to achieve equality for African Americans. Washington, the founder of Tuskegee Institute, had laid out his philosophy of accommodation with whites in his 1895 Atlanta Compromise. To Du Bois and others in his camp this was anathema. When Du Bois came to Harpers Ferry in 1906, he delivered what he called an "Address to the Country." He deliberately delivered his remarks in the long shadow of Brown's 1859 efforts. Once again, American history is defined and set against a particular historical point of reference, not unlike Martin Luther King Jr.'s "I Have a Dream" speech delivered on the steps of the Lincoln Memorial in 1963.

I always introduced the debate between Du Bois and Washington to my students by reading aloud to them Dudley Randall's poem "Booker T. and W. E. B." The meter is perfect, and it sets their argument in stark contrast. But you need to take this a step further and delve into the inner world of each man.

First have your students read Douglass's 1881 address http://www.archive.org/stream/johnbrownaddress00doug/johnbrownaddress00doug_djvu.txt. Rather than give them a worksheet based on it, I recommend employing the 3-2-1 technique outlined earlier in this chapter. If you do this as a class assignment, project onto the screen a picture of Douglass, which adds to the reality of the activity and puts a face to a name. Next have students read Washington's Atlanta Compromise. Again, use the 3-2-1 technique and project Washington's image onto the screen. Finally, wrap up by having students read Du Bois's "Address to the Country." Now provide the students with a blank Venn diagram, asking them to complete it based on what they have read. Don't be surprised if you don't see much overlap—there really wasn't much.

When you have completed these steps, ask the students to consider race relations in the United States today. Ask students to use a journal to respond to where they see the country. Have we changed at all? If so, what has changed? If not, what needs to change? Again, remember you are treading on sensitive ground here, so make sure to create a safe classroom environment where students are encouraged to speak their minds, knowing that you as well as their peers will respect their positions even if differences emerge.

Another way you can approach this is to have three students role-play Douglass, Du Bois, and Washington. Because Douglass's remarks are lengthy, you will need to edit them down. Have the rest of the class serve as newspaper reporters, with some being assigned the role of op-ed writers. Ask the regular reporters to write a general news story highlighting each man's remarks, and have the op-ed writers respond appropriately based on their opinions.

Another creative approach is to divide the students into three groups, with each group representing Douglass, Du Bois, or Washington. Have them create a faux Facebook page for their character, complete with a list of friends, posts, and so on. I did this about twice a school year for different historical personalities and found it to be a great success.

You could also create a cereal box project based on the concept of American freedom fighters. In this activity you provide each student with the name of someone who worked for social justice in the country. In addition to Douglass, Du Bois, and Washington, you could add names such as Harriet Tubman, Sojourner Truth, William Lloyd Garrison, and other Americans who took a stand for social progress, freedom, and equality. You then have students design a cereal box based on their character. For example, one year when I did this for the Gilded Age, I had a student who had drawn the name Jacob Riis from a hat create Jacob Riis Krispies. Students put important information about the life of the person in the place on the box where the ingredients are normally listed, and design a game that people could play on the back of the box, such as a word search or crossword puzzle. I usually gave the students one class period to research their person and a second class period to work on their box. On the day the assignment was due, I had the students post the boxes around the room and then provided them with paper so they could walk around, examine each box, and jot down important information.

These next two suggested activities give you a way to disseminate a great deal of information that covers a broad scope of time. Although chronologically you may be in late-nineteenth- or early-twentieth-century American history, the school year calendar allows you to cover events into the late twentieth century by bringing into play people such as Dr. King, Cesar Chavez, Dorothy Day, and other figures from more recent history.

For the Civil War Sesquicentennial the National Park Service cultivated a theme, "From Civil War to Civil Rights." This was an effort to demonstrate the connection between the Civil War, what it wrought, and how the struggle continued well after the guns went silent at Appomattox. The Park Service also launched a program for their 2016 centennial called "Find Your Park." One way to approach racial history in the United States is to have students go online and pick a National Park site that is somehow connected to the broad struggle for equality and freedom. Ask your students to "Find Their Park" about social equality and civil rights and in a journal entry explain why they picked that park. To take it a step further, you can follow up by asking students to explain what they think they might see when visiting such a site.

Then take the map of the Journey Through Hallowed Ground National Heritage Area that came with your book, and post it on the wall adjacent to a map of the United States. Have all your students use a length of yarn or ribbon to start at Harpers Ferry on the JTHG map and connect it to the other civil rights sites on the adjacent map of the United States. You're not just going to find the yarn leading to places of significance for African Americans, such as Selma, Alabama, and Little Rock, Arkansas. The yarn may go to places important to the struggle for Native American rights, such as Wounded Knee, South Dakota, or Sand Creek, Colorado; and to places commemorating Latino American history, such as Cesar Chavez National Historic Park in California, or Asian American history, such as Manzanar National Historic Site, the location of one of the Japanese internment camps during World War II. You also might find yarn going to New York City to either the African Burial Ground National Monument or the site of the Stonewall Inn, which is part of the heritage of lesbian, gay, bisexual, and transgender people's struggle for equality.

If you have opted to frame your entire curriculum around the Journey's mantra, "Where America Happened," you can next ask your students to reflect in a journal entry or on a 3-by-5-inch note card how the concept of the Journey as "Where America Happened" has played out over the course of our history. Ask the students to consider why we always come back to the Journey as our starting point. What does that say about what took place in the Journey? Why does it make preserving the Journey important?

THE FURIOUS 1850s

You can also approach teaching about the events of Harpers Ferry within the context of the other triggers of the Civil War by asking students to weigh which events of the 1850s played a role in leading the nation to the Civil War.

Write the following historical events on the board or screen:

- The California Compromise
- The Fugitive Slave Law
- Personal Liberty Laws
- The Underground Railroad
- The Kansas-Nebraska Act
- The Dred Scott Decision

- The Caning of Senator Charles Sumner
- The Lincoln-Douglas Debates
- John Brown's Raid on Harpers Ferry

Divide your class into groups of three to four students, and provide each group with some markers and a piece of newsprint. Ask students to research these events either through a class set of textbooks or by using the web, ranking them in order of significance in bringing the nation to civil war. Have them record them on the newsprint from one to nine. When the groups are finished, have them post the newsprint on the wall and select a spokesperson to explain why they ranked the events the way they did. I would be very surprised if John Brown's raid is not at the top of the list. For argument's sake let's say that is the case. Then write on the board or project onto the screen author Herman Melville's quote: "John Brown was the meteor of the Civil War." Ask the students to explain what they think Melville meant.

A fun way to follow this up is to set up a series of dominos and label each one with an event from the 1850s, including the date. John Brown will come last, in 1859. Set them up and then knock them down, demonstrating how one event can lead to another and so on. The students will automatically get the point. My only caveat with this is that you need to tell your students that history isn't always like a set of dominos. We can view the past this way only because we know how it turned out. People living in the middle of the nineteenth century didn't have the hindsight we have.

John Brown was tried by the Commonwealth of Virginia and found guilty of treason and sentenced to hang. Brown's last words before the hangman's noose snapped his neck were prophetic. "I John Brown am now quite certain that the crimes of this guilty land: will never be purged away; but with Blood. I had as I now think: vainly flattered myself that without very much bloodshed; it might be done." When you have completed your unit on the Civil War, post this quote and ask your students to respond in a journal entry or on a note card. What do they think Brown meant, and why do his words seem to have a resonance of truth given the awful carnage of the Civil War? It's ironic, too, that Harpers Ferry is only seventeen miles north of Antietam National Battlefield, site of the war's highest number of casualties in a single day.

Not surprisingly, John Brown is extolled in American art. John Steuart Curry painted a mural featuring Brown for the Kansas State Capitol, calling it *The Tragic Prelude*

(1938–1940). Project an image of that painting onto the screen and hold a conversation with your students. Have them list the things they see in the painting, particularly noting how Brown is portrayed with his arms outstretched like a cross. Ask your students whether it is appropriate to have such a depiction of Brown in such a public place, particularly a seat of government.

Another sympathetic artistic portrayal of Brown is Thomas Hovenden's *Last Moments of John Brown* (1884). You can do the same thing with Hovendon's interpretation, in which Brown is depicted kissing a young black child held up to him by a mother as he is being led to the gallows. Further, ask students to determine Hovenden's interpretation of history based on what they see. Don't tell them the title of the painting, but have them craft their own title for the image and share it with the class.

After Brown was executed, many of his Northern supporters, including intellectuals such as Ralph Waldo Emerson, likened Brown to Jesus Christ. Since Christ was a man of peace, you may want to challenge your students and ask them to determine if Brown, too, was a martyr. Conversely, Southerners saw Brown as the incarnation of Satan. You can demonstrate the deep divisions within the country in 1859 by using Brown as a kind of litmus test, providing students with quotes from both the Northern/abolitionist perspective and from people in the slaveholding states. For many of these individuals the thought of a gun in the hands of a black person raised deep-seated fear. Many still recalled the horrors of Nat Turner's Rebellion in southern Virginia in 1836. You can discuss with your students whether in 1859 those fears were justified.

Here are some quotes you can use to help your students see the different perspectives held with regard to John Brown. You can write them on the board, project them onto the screen, or make a handout and distribute them to your students.

Northern Supporters of Brown

While I cannot approve of all your acts, I stand in awe of your position since your capture, and dare not oppose you lest I be found fighting against God; for you speak as one having authority, and seem to be strengthened from on high.

—Letter from "Christian Conservative" in West Newton, Massachusetts, quoted in the Annual Report of the American Anti-Slavery Society (1861)

That new saint, than whom nothing purer or more brave was ever led into conflict and death—the new saint awaiting his martyrdom, and who, if he shall suffer, will make the gallows glorious like the cross.

—Ralph Waldo Emerson in "Courage," lecture at the
Boston Music Hall (November 8, 1859)

He done more in dying, than 100 men would in living.

—Harriet Tubman, as quoted in *Bound for the Promised Land: Harriet Tubman, Portrait of an American Hero* (2004) by Kate Clifford Larson

Southern Antagonists of Brown

I looked at the traitor and terrorizer with unlimited, undeniable contempt.

—Diary of John Wilkes Booth, quoted in *The Secret Six* (1997) by Edward Renehan

I say, let him hang.

—*Charleston Mercury* (1859) newspaper

What More Recent Americans Have Said About Brown

If John Brown were still alive, we might accept him.

—Malcolm X, when asked if white people could join the
Organization of African Unity, from "Mystery of Malcolm X" by
Hans Massaquoi in *Ebony* magazine (September 1964)

Ideas made the opposite impact in the Confederacy. Ideological contradictions afflicted the slave system even before the war began. John Brown knew the masters secretly feared their slaves might revolt, even as they assured abolitionists that slaves really liked slavery. One reason his Harpers Ferry raid prompted such an outcry in the South was that slave owners feared their slaves might join him. Yet their condemnations of Brown and the "Black Republicans" who financed him did not persuade Northern moderates but only pushed them toward the abolitionist camp. After all, if Brown was truly dangerous, as slave owners claimed, then slavery was truly unjust. Happy slaves would never revolt.

—James W. Loewen, as quoted in *Lies My Teacher Told Me: Everything Your American History Textbook Got Wrong* (2008, 193)

Ask your students to consider these quotes and then indicate on a 3-by-5-inch note card which one feels most accurate them and why. Before collecting the note cards hold a class discussion, making sure to ask students why people from contemporary America would even want to weigh in on John Brown and his actions so many years after the event.

A PUPPET SHOW

In speaking with teachers across the country over the years, I have come to appreciate the frustration that many elementary school teachers feel when it comes to teaching history. In high school, teachers are pretty much specialists, but in elementary schools they have to be generalists, because they teach everything.

One of the best history activities my daughter participated in as a fourth grader was a puppet show about Virginia history. It was a very clever way to prepare elementary students for the Virginia Standards of Learning test. Each student was given the name of a famous Virginian, and one of my daughters, Stephanie, had James Madison. She had to do some basic research on Madison, including his life and accomplishments, and then make a puppet to take to class and use to tell Madison's story.

Elementary teachers could approach teaching the events of John Brown's raid on Harpers Ferry the same way. There were twenty-two raiders, including Brown, three of his sons, and five African Americans. There were also the Secret Six, the New England abolitionists who funded Brown's raid: Thomas Wentworth Higginson, Samuel Gridley Howe, Theodore Parker, Franklin Benjamin Sanborn, Gerrit Smith, and George Luther Stearns. This gives you twenty-nine characters with which to work. You can also adjust by deleting a few or adding to the mix Lieutenant Colonel Robert E. Lee, who led the detachment of United States Marines to Harpers Ferry to put down the raid, and his adjutant, Lieutenant J. E. B. Stuart, or Brown's daughter, who accompanied him to Maryland, from where the raid was sprung. At Stephanie's back-to-school night that year, some of the students performed for the parents. It was fun to watch the students engaged in such a way with their learning. Although some of the more existential issues might be a bit deep for elementary students, the story of Brown's raid will resonate with them. It will also serve as a good way to introduce the variety of characters involved in the story and provide a kind of context for their future learning about the raid when they get to middle and high school.

BOARD GAMING THE ABOLITIONIST MOVEMENT

One creative way to teach about the abolitionist movement is through board games. Academy Games has taken the lead in developing historical board games for school use that focus on learning and collaboration between players rather than on winning. The Civil War Trust, which I discuss in the next chapter, has purchased seven copies of the game Freedom: The Underground Railroad, which it circulates at no cost among teachers who sign up to use them. For classes of twenty-five students or more you will need seven copies of the game to complete the instruction. Phil Caskey, of University High School in Morgantown, West Virginia, uses the games successfully and reported in an e-mail exchange,

> Educating our youth about the institution of slavery is one of the most challenging topics to teach because of the heavy complexities regarding the human capacity for introducing, cultivating, and maintaining evil through forced servitude and bondage. One of the bright spots during this terribly tragic time period in American History, however, are the success stories of the Underground Railroad and the abolitionists determined to end slavery in this country by rescuing as many as possible. One way to express and convey this is through simulation, as it gives students legitimate chances to re-create and role-play through higher depths of understanding and knowledge through analysis and synthesis. Through simulation learning, and utilizing Academy Games' Freedom: The Underground Railroad, students in both my American Civil War Studies classes took on the roles of abolitionists during Antebellum America. They were tasked with working in a collaborative group of three to four against the game, rather than against each other, to free and save as many slaves as possible. Quickly, moral dilemmas arose in

the simulation because it became apparent that not every soul could be saved as a race against time (the game). It became very challenging for students to run slaves to Canada, avoid slave catchers, yet move them out of the South's plantations prior to the slave market repopulating new slaves. "Who do we save? We saved three here but lost one there, so is that considered a success? Maybe. But, we still lost slaves while others were set free." It was very powerful for my students to see and experience firsthand.

The two weeks of simulating Freedom: The Underground Railroad and the abolitionist struggle proved to be one of the highlights of our year-long, comprehensive study of the American Civil War, as it set the tone for the rest of the year. The foundation of slavery had been laid and my students then had simulated the firsthand struggle to abolish that institution. It was very powerful and rewarding.

You can find the game video tutorial at https://www.bing.com/videos/search?q=free-dom+board+game+&&view=detail&mid=4B23178933ECEA89D6054B23178933EC-EA89D605&FOR. You and your students will have loads of fun using it to teach and learn.

HISTORICAL FICTION FROM HARPERS FERRY

I always found using high-quality historical fiction to teach about the past to be of real value when I taught. When a gifted novelist has done his or her own research, historical fiction makes history personal for me and adds insight into a certain time period. Generally, historical fiction raises the moral components found in history in compelling ways that a narrative historian might not be able to pull off as effectively. Two historical novels I read as a youth and then taught in my classroom were Howard Fast's *April Morning* and *The Hessian*. Both books are about teenagers caught up in war, which makes them relatable for middle or high school students. When teaching about Harpers Ferry you can use James McBride's *The Good Lord Bird;* its protagonist is Henry Shackleford, an enslaved teenager from the Kansas Territory, who by a twist of fate ends up as one of John Brown's raiders. You can find exceptional lesson materials for *The Good Lord Bird* on the Teaching Books.net website at https://www.teachingbooks.net/qlu74kt. If you prefer, you can again play historian and have your students evaluate the book and its tale against the study of real history. After the students do some independent research on Harpers Ferry, ask them to measure McBride against the yardstick of actual history. Where did he get it right? What seems off base?

I once heard filmmaker Ken Burns speak at a teachers' conference, where he discussed narrative structure and the telling of history. According to Burns, everything relating to our past and human condition is summed up in the Old Testament's book of Ecclesiastes, particularly the verse that says, "there is nothing new under the sun." Teachers, myself included, often frame their instruction around the famous George Santayana quote, "Those who forget the past are doomed to repeat it." In all fairness to the philosopher Santayana, that quote is so overused that not only has it been trivialized, but it is also cliché. If you can get your students to recognize and understand that all of history is a story of humanity—our foibles as well as our triumphs—they may be better served. Certainly as we look at the world around us today, both at home and abroad, we see that in some ways nothing has really changed, given human behavior. People continue to struggle. I don't have any answers to solve this conundrum, but maybe in using the story of what took place at Harpers Ferry in 1859, our students can see our shared humanity—the good and the bad.

Life itself can be thought of as a journey, and you can use the Journey Through Hallowed Ground as a metaphor for the American story and its journey. That is what makes it such a compelling parcel of land. Using the material in this chapter will help you provide terrific "food for thought." Your students will have to make decisions and interpret history for themselves, and will encounter the notion that history is always a confluence of sorts, no matter where and when it happens.

CHAPTER 4

Battle Cries of Freedom—Where Brothers Fought Brothers

n his 1873 satirical novel, *The Gilded Age,* Mark Twain says the Civil War "uprooted institutions that were centuries old, changed the politics of a people . . . and wrought so profoundly upon the national character that the influence cannot be measured short of two or three generations" (168). Six generations removed from that fratricidal conflict, it sometimes seems that we are still fighting the Civil War and living in its long shadow. We debate the place of the Confederate flag in American life and still struggle to determine the war's root cause. Another American man of letters, Robert Penn Warren, called the Civil War the American Oracle. Given the tenor of our times it would be remiss of history educators to dismiss the Civil War as an arcane event, relegating it to the dustbin of history. In fact one nationally recognized school system has gone so far as to encourage its teachers not to dwell on military history at all. That's too bad, because whether we like it or not, much of our history has been shaped by military actions, and many young people, like myself when I was their age, are drawn to the study of history by virtue of military exploits.

We can learn a great deal about our national character by studying the American Civil War, the people who emerged at the forefront of its history, and its difficult legacy. The Journey Through Hallowed Ground National Heritage Area is home to the most concentrated swath of soil touched by those who wore the blue and gray. Two of the war's most significant battles took place inside the Journey—Antietam and Gettysburg—altering the landscape of the war and shaping the America we know today. In 2015, the General Assembly of Virginia recognized the Journey with a special commendation for "their commitment, dedication, and partnership with the Virginia Sesquicentennial of the American Civil War Commission." Many of the educational endeavors of the Journey were part of this commitment.

Before launching your students into studying the Civil War, it would be helpful for you to view two videos of John Hennessy, chief historian for Fredericksburg & Spotsylvania National Military Park, discussing why the Civil War matters today. Hennessy, whom historian Brooks Simpson says is a "true gem of the National Park Service," speaks at the Spotsylvania Unit of the park, the site of heavy combat during Ulysses S. Grant's 1864 Overland Campaign. This battle site is inside the Journey. You can see the videos at https://www.youtube.com/channel/UCOkeeHJWWOPq18E3sounJAQ, and they are worth sharing with your students for reflection and discussion. By showing these videos you can also have your students play around with William Faulkner's famous quote "The past isn't dead. It's not even the past." Place Faulkner's remarks in a contemporary context, particularly when discussing hot button topics such as the Confederate battle flag and Confederate iconography in public monuments across much of the South and on many of our national battlefield parks. In this chapter I lay out some terrific resources that can help you and your students understand the many complicated sides of a war that continues to define us 150 years after the guns went silent.

The Civil War Trust

Like the National Park Service the Civil War Trust is one of the Journey's strongest partners. I view the educational work of the Civil War Trust as your one-stop shopping place for all things Civil War related. The staff of the education program of the Civil War Trust works hard to develop teacher-friendly materials to assist them in teaching about the Civil War. They have developed Battle Apps for several Civil War battle sites including Gettysburg. Meant to assist visitors who like and rely on technology when visiting historical sites, the Battle Apps can be used just as effectively in the classroom without having to take students to the site. As schools increasingly rely on technology to augment teaching and determine how students can use their personal digital devices to learn, these apps are great tools for use in the classroom because they put the teaching devices in the palm of your hand. The Battle Apps can really enhance a visitor's experience to a site. Users can download pictures, videos, and animated maps, and employ the GPS components to help them better understand the flow of battle and troop movements. You can actually walk in the footsteps of the nineteenth century with a twenty-first-century learning tool at your disposal. More and more learning is being viewed as an integrated part of life in which formal and informal learning coexists, and the National Park Service is leading the way in this movement. As such, it should come as no surprise that Gettysburg National Military Park would be participating in this cutting-edge learning technology.

I used these apps in conjunction with a class field trip to Gettysburg, where students could pull up videos and look at primary source documents and animated maps that showed troop movements where they actually occurred. (See Figures 4.1–4.3.) With the pulsating GPS blue dot steadily moving along the digital map as a guide, students quickly grasped how empowering the apps could be. They were in control, visiting sites, accessing information, and consuming supporting media at their own pace. With the Battle App as their guide, the students were able to find some of the area's "hidden gems," such as the Strong Vincent marker or Bullet Hole Rock. Using information gleaned from virtual signs and historians' videos, students engaged in spirited and thoughtful discussions of complex topics ranging from military topography to the effect of battles on the home front.

Each student at the beginning of the year purchased a marble composition book in which to record his or her responses to class field trips. On our trip to Gettysburg, I asked them to not only weigh in on the intellectual components of the visit, but to comment on the effectiveness of the Battle Apps. Some students found the uses of the apps greatly beneficial, whereas for others they were less so. John wrote in his journal, "The trip to Gettysburg was a very engaging experience using the Civil War Trust Battle Apps. I got more out of being on the battlefield using the app, walking around to the various sites and learning from the information provided. Some sites' pages on the app also provided a small clip with further information. In this respect, the app also allowed me to connect more with the battlefield, especially when learning about what happened about Gettysburg. The battlefield was not an isolated place but became an extension

FIGURE 4.1–4.3
Students use the Battle Apps on
our class trip to Gettysburg.

of the classroom when coupled with the app. I learned from what I saw but could also draw from the information provided on the app and this personalized the experience on the battlefield."

Courtney said in her journal, "I absolutely loved using the app because it really brought history to today. We're obviously the generation of technology so to be able to learn about history in something that we're so comfortable with really helped me visualize the battles."

I appreciate that many readers can't just up and take their students to Gettysburg, or any other Civil War battle sites, but the really terrific thing about these Battle Apps is that they can be employed in the classroom, too. Anyone with access to digital devices can use the Battle Apps, regardless of their location. When unable to bring my United

States History classes to Civil War sites, I divided the students into groups of three or four and assigned each group one of the Civil War battles covered by the Battle Apps. The Battle Apps cover First and Second Manassas, Antietam, Chancellorsville, Brandy Station, Cedar Creek, Fredericksburg, Malvern Hill, Petersburg, Vicksburg, the Atlanta Campaign, the Overland Campaign, and Appomattox, all important battles fought in both the eastern and western theatres of the war. Each group also received a large piece of newsprint and several markers. At the top of the newsprint students wrote the name of the battle and its date. Using the Battle Apps they determined the winners of the battles and the important generals who led the armies in the field, and established the significance of the battle in the course of the Civil War.

Once this was done, the pieces of newsprint were posted in chronological sequence on the back wall of the classroom. Each student group made their presentation in the correct sequence of battles while the other students took notes. In this way I was able to cover much of the war in one ninety-minute-block class. I would follow up by providing each student with a 3-by-5-inch note card and asking them to list three important things they learned collectively, two things about which they wanted to know more, and one important thing from the lesson that would stick with them. I then collected the note cards for assessment purposes. Students enjoyed this approach to learning because it tapped into their particular comfort zone by allowing them to use their personal electronic devices to complete an activity. It also permitted movement around the room, so the kinesthetic elements worked well, too: students had room to move physically and weren't confined to a chair and desk.

In addition to their Battle Apps, the web resources of the Civil War Trust are of very high caliber, state-of-the-art, and cutting-edge. For example, they have a series of videos called The Civil War In4, a wide range of exceptional four-minute videos about a host of topics. Included are biographies of Frederick Douglass, Robert E. Lee, and Ulysses S. Grant, among others; videos about the social history of the war such as one on religion, one on the role of African American soldiers, and one on the role of women; and others focusing on specific moments such as Lincoln's issuance of the Emancipation Proclamation and his delivery of the Gettysburg Address. They work perfectly in the classroom because they are short and concise, and address the war's major themes. One way teachers could employ them is to assign each student a different video to watch for homework and have them report on it during the next class period while their peers take notes. In this way you avoid using vital classroom instruction time to show a raft of videos. The learning also becomes student-centric, because you are letting the students assume ownership of their learning and not lecturing or telling them about history; rather, you are showing it to them. It's also a very different kind of homework assignment, and that usually delights students.

Another engaging web resource provided by the Civil War Trust is the collection of 360 Battle Panoramas. These panoramas allow the user virtual access to many battle sites and show in clear, crisp detail the actual topography of various Civil War battlefields, giving the user the sensation of actually standing there. *Civil War 360* is a great way to digitally tour battlefields in 360 degrees—from your classroom.

Additionally, the trust's *Civil War Curriculum Guide* is another exceptional resource. Matched to both the National US History Standards and the Common Core, the lessons in the curriculum guide can be used to teach the entire Civil War. The lessons use the additional resources developed by the trust so that it all seamlessly fits together when teachers use the web-based resources in their classrooms. One great thing about the trust is that staff members take teacher feedback seriously and work with teachers from across the country to develop materials. For instance, when teachers noted that the curriculum guide didn't include lessons on Reconstruction, a particularly difficult topic to teach, the staff made sure the updated version ended with a lesson on that era. What is so cool about this lesson is that it incorporates features from the National Park Service's Corinth Civil War Interpretive Center's showcase memorial in Mississippi called the Stream of American History, which connects the Civil War to the twentieth-century struggle for civil rights.

The Civil War Trust also hosts an Annual Teacher Institute at a significant Civil War site. There is no cost to attend, and the trust provides travel scholarships for teachers who need help with their travel expenses. The Annual Teacher Institute brings together hundreds of teachers who are passionate about the Civil War for several days, giving them the opportunity to hear from major Civil War historians, participate in field trips, and select from a host of concurrent workshops.

Additionally the Civil War Trust has a field trip fund to which you can apply to help defray the cost of student travel to a Civil War site up to $1,500.00. The trust is committed to and has the funds for promoting all kinds of learning opportunities. Many teachers look to the trust for financial assistance to take their students to Civil War–related sites, including museums and historic houses, not just battlefields. Many states far removed from the battlefields have sites connected to the legacy of the Civil War, such as

Saint-Gaudens National Historic Site in Cornish, New Hampshire, the home and studio of the great American public sculptor Augustus Saint-Gaudens, who sculpted for the nation various important public statues, such as the *Standing Lincoln* in Chicago, the *Shaw Memorial* in Boston, and the *Sherman Monument* in New York City.

An estimated 70 percent of all Civil War documentary photographs were shot as "stereoviews," the nineteenth-century equivalent of 3-D. The trust's photography special, in conjunction with the Center for Civil War Photography, will let you see Civil War photos as the photographers intended—in three dimensions. The trust will provide each school with one free pair of 3-D glasses for students to use. For twenty dollars you can order a set of thirty 3-D glasses for your classroom. Teachers can find related lesson plans on the trust's website. Many of these famous images were taken at Civil War sites inside the Journey.

The trust, like the Journey, loves to work with teachers, building positive relationships and creating a community of like-minded educators. The Civil War Trust has taken this to a whole new level by creating what is known as the Teachers Regiment, the brainchild of board member William Hupp, a major supporter of the trust's educational initiatives. Hupp explained to me via e-mail what motivated him to establish this resource:

> The Teachers Regiment was born from wanting to reach more history teachers and give these teachers more resources than we could through just the [Civil War Trust's] national and regional Teacher Institutes. I was thinking about how lonely and unsupported my wife felt as a new teacher having the responsibility for teaching English to all sophomores at her school. It struck me that for many US history teachers, they are also the only ones teaching this subject in their school. If some of the great mentoring and idea sharing that teachers experienced in our Teacher Institutes could be freed from geography and time using on-line tools, then we could have that bigger impact on more students by getting timely help to more teachers from their fellow teachers. A national community of US history teachers, administered by senior, "master" teachers, supported by the CWT, might also find new ways and methods to advance the teaching of US History. And of course, the future of preservation lies in the historical knowledge and love of history created by a favorite teacher.

The Teachers Regiment has a Facebook page where posts are made weekly to keep members informed of various activities and learning opportunities. Postings on Facebook also coincide with major landmark moments of the Civil War, such as Lincoln's issuance of the Emancipation Proclamation and delivery of the Gettysburg Address. IN4 videos related to these themes and others are often posted so that teachers are made aware of materials they can employ in the classroom. Teachers also are able to share their lesson plans with each other. The trust has discovered that members really appreciate this kind of community building and awareness.

Under the umbrella structure of the Teachers Regiment are various companies formed by members of the regiment who serve as those company commanders. For example, there are companies formed around Civil War and Instructional Technology, Civil War Ancestry, Civil War Journalism, and Civil War Memory, among others. Though they enter as privates, teachers who make contributions to the trust by posting on Facebook, participating in battlefield fund-raising efforts, engaging students in service-learning projects, and other activities can earn promotion points and perks.

David Kendrick, history teacher at Duluth High School in Duluth, Georgia, a longtime stalwart of the educational efforts of the trust and the 2015 Civil War Trust Teacher of the Year, is the company commander of the Civil War Ancestry Company. "The Civil War Trust Teachers Regiment is an incredible set of resources for differentiated and collaborative instruction of our Civil War," he told me via e-mail. "It has expanded and enhanced the way I teach because the resources are constantly being added by teachers and educators! I now have access to more primary sources and materials that I previously could not have accessed. We are able to suggest and revise, as our opinion is valued and requested. In other words, the Teachers Regiment is a living, breathing unit that allows for keeping the Civil War alive and relevant in the twenty-first century."

For teachers who want to make the Civil War come alive in their classroom but can't take students to Civil War sites, the trust can help by sending them their Traveling Trunk, which provides reproduction Civil War artifacts, books, music, and various other materials for teachers to use during their Civil War instruction. The trunk fosters a greater interest in the American Civil War and in battlefield preservation by allowing students to have an immersive tactile, hands-on experience. And, like all the trust's resources, it is free to teachers.

Another opportunity for you and your students is the Civil War Trust's postcard and essay contests. The trust sets a theme each year, and students submit postcards and essays based on the theme. For example in 2015 the theme for both was "1864–1865: Bringing the War to a Close." The final days of the Civil War were filled with human drama. Old ways were dying, and new horizons were imminent. The essays or postcards incorporate the importance of preservation and the study of history into the theme. (See Figures 4.4–4.7.) Cash prizes are awarded, and winners receive a free membership to the Civil War Trust. There are two divisions of the contests; the senior division is for students in eighth to twelfth grades, and the junior division is for students in the fourth to seventh grades. Criteria and rules for the contests can be found on the education tab of the trust's website at www.civilwar.org.

If you are looking for classroom resources to help you unpack the complexity of the Civil War in all its facets, it would serve you and your students well to check out what the

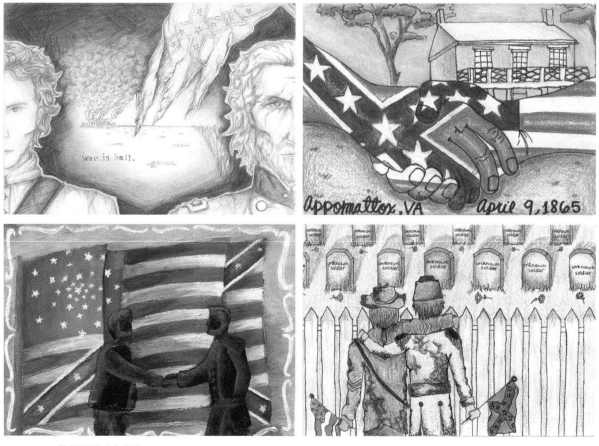

FIGURES 4.4–4.7
Student entries in the Civil War Trust's postcard contest

Civil War Trust has to offer. Chances are, you and your students will be so drawn in by the plethora of resources available for no cost on the web that you will spend hours just searching and looking for personal pleasure as well. The resources previously discussed are only a small sample of what is available on the education page of the website www. civilwar.org.

THE LIVING LEGACY PROJECT

During this country's most defining moment, approximately 620,000 soldiers died. In 1860s America that amounted to 2 percent of the American population; translated into today's population that would equal roughly six to seven million people. Every American living at the time of the Civil War was affected in some way. Many of these fallen soldiers fought on the battlefields within the Journey Through Hallowed Ground National Heritage Area. As a living commemoration for their individual and combined sacrifices, the Living Legacy Project is planting one tree for each American who sacrificed his or her life in that conflict, creating a unified color palette that reminds visitors that they are, indeed, on hallowed ground. The trees planted are redbud, red oak, red cedar, and red maple, all of which invoke the color associated with honor and valor. Upon completion, this initiative will create the first 180-mile landscaped allée in the world and the only allée dedicated to honoring the most defining moment in American history.

The Journey Through Hallowed Ground Partnership is engaged in raising the necessary funds to complete this initiative. Schools from across the country can contribute to the project in a number of ways, including $100.00 contributions to support and plant each tree. Donors may select a soldier to honor, and the trees will be geo-tagged to allow visitors to learn the story of each soldier, providing a strong educational component to engage interest in the region's historical heritage and literally bringing the tree to life. Those who opt to participate in this project by conducting research on a particular soldier do not have to pay the $100.00. Students can help bring to life the stories of the 620,000 soldiers who made the ultimate sacrifice during the American Civil War. By rediscovering the stories of these individuals, they will help bring healing to those who need it while establishing a connection with local history and people from their community who served in the Union and Confederate armies and participating in the creation of the first national Civil War memorial.

The education staff at the Journey will help you in a number of ways should you wish to participate:

- identifying the soldier(s) you will research
- providing you with a variety of resources and subscriptions to use throughout the research process, including connecting you with ancestryK12.com
- training students in historical research skills, as needed
- assisting with any research troubleshooting
- communicating details pertaining to the planting site(s) for your soldier(s) so that you may attend a dedication ceremony

When applicable, students are often invited to attend the dedication ceremony for the planting site of the soldier(s) they have researched, where they can read a brief biography of these men they have come to know so well. The Civil War Trust allows their Field Trip Fund to cover the costs of bringing students to plant the trees and then attend the dedication ceremonies.

Once you have connected with the Journey to identify your soldier(s), they will provide you with numerous online resources to visit while researching. Our partner, fold3.com, has begun the immense task of creating an honor wall for every American veteran. As students locate information, documents, or photos, we ask that they upload them directly on to their soldier's honor wall page—it is this site that our interactive map (www. hallowedgroundtrees.org) links to when displaying a soldier's biography. In so doing, you and your students will be working to create the most comprehensive collection of fallen Civil War soldier biographical information known. For each tree-planting site, the Journey Through Hallowed Ground Partnership hosts a dedication ceremony, in which we pay tribute to the sacrifices made over 150 years ago.

Many teachers across the country are already eagerly participating in this project, including Joe Foster, teacher at Waynesfield-Goshen High School in Goshen, Ohio, and Joe Fulton, middle school teacher at Linus Pauling Middle School in Corvallis, Oregon. As Fulton explained via e-mail,

> The . . . Living Legacy Project has been an enlightening experience for our students. They became "pen-pals" with young men who lived over 150 years ago. All I provided was a name, a regiment, and a company. They discovered their soldier's hometown, family, occupation, battles,

camps, and in many cases their height, weight, and eye color. But then their pen-pal died and they somberly found death registries, headstone receipts, and, of course, the location and picture of their graves. This opportunity proved to be a powerful learning experience. History became very personal for our students, fulfilling, at least for that moment and hopefully a lifetime, a primary goal of every history teacher.

Some of Fulton's students reported the following based on their participation in the project. Anika said, "Researching my soldier made me feel connected with the past. That feeling makes you feel *alive*!"

Kari said, "Researching about my soldiers made me really aware that they were actual people that sacrificed their lives for our country. Real people, with families, with friends . . . People I can picture in my head, with brown hair and gray eyes."

And Olivia reported, "I think the most profound idea I took away from this experience was realizing each soldier that died was an individual. We learned about their family, their job, and their lives. You hear about the . . . soldiers who died in the Civil War, but until now, I failed to understand that these people were, in fact, people."

Joe Foster believes, "Undertakings like the Living Legacy Project enable students to make personal connections to the soldiers we honor. Rather than a mere name on a page, we were able to research Lieutenant Sumner Paine and discover his grandfather, who signed the Declaration of Independence. Kids laughed when they found a record of his discipline from Harvard University. And we felt sorrow and pride as we read his letters home. And for the rest of their lives these students will be able to point to a spot on a map or a tree along the highway and know that was the living tribute to a man whose life was given for them" (personal correspondence).

Foster's student Connor, a junior, reported, "The Living Legacy Project is a creative way for us to remember and understand where the soldiers stood, fought, and died."

Another junior, Jonnell, said, "Remembering our national heroes from the past is just as important as acknowledging our fallen heroes today. Planting these trees will help us do just that."

"Planting these trees will bring new life to those who have fallen defending our country and will let their legacy be remembered by each future generation," opined Bobby, a senior.

And Stephen said, "The Journey Through Hallowed Ground has allowed students to remember and honor the fallen heroes of the past."

Just imagine that students who engage in this project will be able to bring their grandchildren to the Journey Through Hallowed Ground National Heritage Area for the Civil War Bicentennial and not only share with them the story of the life of the soldier they researched, but show them the tree they helped to plant, providing a dramatic connection that evolved over a two-hundred-year span.

FREDERICKSBURG & SPOTSYLVANIA NATIONAL MILITARY PARK'S COMMUNITY AT WAR VIRTUAL CLASSROOM

National Park Service staff at Fredericksburg & Spotsylvania National Military Park under the leadership of Chief Historian John Hennessy, Ranger Peter Maugle, and Teacher-Ranger-Teacher Rebecca Capobianco have crafted a unique virtual classroom that provides students with a glimpse of a variety of topics in Civil War history. Though specific to their park, affectionately called "Spotsy," the Community at War virtual classroom uses topics germane to the entire Civil War.

This web-based curricular site is designed to be an interactive educational resource for teachers and students alike. Here you will find that the curriculum does not tell the same old story of the Civil War, but incorporates new and unique perspectives into a dynamic, multidimensional, and comprehensive lesson about the experience of a war we're still trying to understand today. Ultimately, this is about more than just a war that changed America; it is also about the role of individual people in determining the course of their nation's future. Consequently, it can be used to facilitate discussion about historical inquiry, civic engagement, and the democratic process while answering questions such as "How can disenfranchised people find a voice in our nation's future?" and "How do individual people make a difference in a national cause?"

Maugle told me that when they began the process of creating Community at War, they wanted something that was atypical of what can be found on the web. The park wanted to make sure that they told the larger story of the Civil War through the microcosm of individuals who lived in the boundaries of the park. "We wanted," he said, "a new way of looking at web-based curriculum, taking it to another level and making it interactive and more than just a place where teachers can download handouts for students. Since most students can't visit us, it allows us to take the park to the students. We also wanted to demonstrate the effects of the war on civilians and the enslaved communities, seeking to bring in other angles of the story that are not generally covered at other battle sites."

The curriculum consists of four elements: the Let's Explore section and three lesson modules discussing soldier, civilian, and slave experiences. If your students are not yet familiar with the Battle of Fredericksburg, I suggest that they start with Let's Explore to gain some background knowledge that they will need to place the lesson modules in their proper context. From there, students can proceed to any of the lesson modules they desire. However, each element is designed to stand on its own. Therefore, if you have specific time constraints or are covering a narrower topic in your classroom, you can pick and choose elements to assign students based on your specific needs. Additionally, all videos featured on the site are available for download. You can use them in your classroom and adapt them to your needs.

Aside from the four main content elements, the virtual classroom consists of two blog features: the Ask a Ranger page and the Virtual Talk Back Wall, both designed to facilitate engagement and critical thinking skills. The Ask a Ranger page is a space for students to ask questions of rangers that might arise over the course of the lesson modules. Students can submit their questions on the main Ask a Ranger page, and rangers will respond in a blog post on the following page. Conversely, the Virtual Talk Back Wall is a space for students to share their thoughts. The park has provided prompt questions that they hope will encourage students to think critically about the information presented and more broadly about the implications and significance of the Civil War.

Teachers nationally have left testimonials like these on the park website:

I am a middle school social studies teacher in Phoenix, AZ. I stumbled across your website while I was searching for virtual field trips. Your site is awesome! I wish there were sites like this for all the National Parks. Thank you so much!

—Sister Claire and my eighth-grade class

You have done a fabulous job on the virtual classroom. I will definitely use the website when we begin our unit on the Civil War! I am very impressed! I plan on sharing it with the rest of the teachers Monday at our PLC meeting.

—Christie, teacher at Chesapeake (VA) Area Schools

I just had a chance to preview the new web-based curriculum . . . it is *extremely* well done!! I was so impressed that I sent the link to all the administrators at Fredericksburg Christian and several of the teachers that I know who teach history (Elem. MS, and HS). I love it when the NPS (and especially this Park) look good to the educators of the area!

—Lee Ann Williams, teacher at Fredericksburg Christian School

Graphic novels are also a great way to introduce students, particularly younger ones, to history. The Cartoon Chronicles of America series, by Stan Mack and Susan Champlain, is a great place to start to locate titles for teaching. *Fight for Freedom* is about the Civil War in and around Fredericksburg and Spotsylvania. The authors have developed a teaching website, stanmack.com, that includes lesson ideas. Jennifer Underwood, a fifth-grade teacher at Hollymead Elementary School in Charlottesville, Virginia, has used the book with great success, saying, "This graphic novel invites the reader along on a journey. The storyline and images are exciting and age-appropriate. The characters are relatable and truly make you feel as if you are *in* the story. I felt like I was sitting next to Abraham Lincoln in the scene with Sam. I felt like I was at the plantation when Clara Barton arrives. This book just melts you into it from the first to the last page. It is also mostly factual, but the cool part is that it includes a section where the authors describe how certain aspects of the battle can be folded into compelling historical fiction and which parts are fact/actually happened in history. The Civil War is a difficult subject to teach to younger students but this story helps make my job a bit easier."

On the Community at War website (https://www.nps.gov/nr/twhp/wwwlps/lessons/45chatham/45facts1.htm), you will find the story of Charles Sprout, an enslaved man who worked at the Ellwood Plantation, which was near the Wilderness and Chancellorsville units of the park. Sprout did in fact escape and served in the United States Colored Troops during the war. You could have students compare and contrast his actual story with the story of Sam in *Fight for Freedom*, determining similarities and differences between both interpretations. This will also add a sense of gravitas to reading the graphic novel.

JOSEPH PIERCE

Like so much of history itself the Journey is full of surprises. Take the tale of Joseph Pierce. Chances are, you have never heard of Joseph Pierce (see Figure 4.8). He certainly

FIGURE 4.8

Joseph Pierce

won't be found inside the covers of a United States history textbook. But his unique story is instructive for all Americans.

I first learned of Joseph Pierce many years ago on a field trip to Gettysburg. We had wrapped up our day and were just about ready to head home. I was wandering the halls of the old NPS visitor center when one of my parent chaperones, fired up with enthusiasm, caught up with me and said, "Mr. Percoco, I have to show you something! Did you know that there was a Chinese person who fought at Gettysburg?" This mother then proceeded to direct me to the Wall of Faces, a tableau of photographs of men from the North and

South who fought at Gettysburg. Pointing to one of the pictures, she said, "Look! This guy here, Joseph Pierce, was from Shanghai." Sure enough, there was a photograph of a man with Asian features, including a pigtail queue, with a label that read "Joseph Pierce, 14th Connecticut." I grabbed a piece of paper and wrote the information down.

The next day I was on the phone speaking with Gettysburg's staff librarian, who assured me that not only was Joseph Pierce Chinese and from Connecticut, but that their records indicated another Union soldier from China at Gettysburg in the Union Army: John Tommy, who served in the Seventy-Second New York Infantry. Tommy was mortally wounded in the Peach Orchard on July 2, 1863. The librarian also gave me contact information for Irving Moy, a gentleman from Connecticut, who is himself of Chinese ancestry and interprets the life of Pierce as a member of the Fourteenth Connecticut Volunteer Infantry reenactment company.

Soon thereafter I was on the phone with Moy, and the next thing I knew, I was on a road trip to visit him at his home in Connecticut, where I was greeted warmly. We went out on a tour of all the Joseph Pierce sites, including his grave in Meriden, Connecticut. It was absolutely fascinating! As a child, Pierce had been sold by his family to a Connecticut seafarer by the name of Amos Peck, for six dollars. Intended to help them recover from some of their personal economic losses incurred during the infamous Opium Wars, the sale was a common practice in China at the time. Peck brought the young boy home with him to Connecticut and raised him as his own. He called him Joe, following the custom of the day in naming little Chinese boys Joe. He gave him the last name of Pierce in honor of Franklin Pierce, then president of the United States.

When the Civil War broke out, Pierce, twenty-one, enlisted as a private in Company F of the Fourteenth Connecticut Infantry that was being mustered together shortly after hostilities broke out in 1861. He rose to the rank of corporal and saw action from Antietam in 1862 until the end of the war at Appomattox in 1865. Most of Pierce's war experience was on land of the Journey. After the war he returned home, joined his local Grand Army of the Republic Lodge, practiced the art of silver engraving, married a white woman, raised a family, and became fully enmeshed in society. Since he lived on the East Coast of the United States, he did not experience the anti-Chinese sentiment legalized by Congress in 1882 in the form of the Chinese Exclusion Act. In the history of the Fourteenth Connecticut, the regiment's historian, Charles D. Page, described the Fourteenth Connecticut's role in repulsing Pickett's Charge on July 3, 1863, writing that Pierce appeared "pig-tail and all, the only Chinese in the Army of the Potomac."

If you want to have some fun with your students using the story of Joseph Pierce, here is what I suggest you do. Write "Joseph Pierce, Fourteenth Connecticut Volunteer Infantry, Union Army" on the board. Next pass out to students some 3-by-5-inch note cards and ask them to write on one side of the card what you have written on the board. Next ask them to flip the card over and ask them to write a description of what they think Pierce looked like. Wait about five minutes for students to complete the task, and then discuss their responses with them. Once you are finished with the discussion, show the photo of Pierce wearing his Union uniform. Then sit back and wait to hear the responses of "No way!" and "Whoa!" coming from your students! I always enjoyed undermining students' preconceived ideas about what they thought they knew, not because it gave me a sense of one-upmanship, but because it brings to bear the understanding of how much we collectively don't know about history. It makes history "cool" and at the same time enlightens them about people of color whom they normally would not associate with the Civil War. I concluded by explaining to them the story of how I came to know about Pierce and how it was an equally epiphany-laden moment for me.

Thanks to the National Parks Service, which for the sesquicentennial of the Civil War developed many public programs about the Civil War under the theme "From Civil War to Civil Rights," several official National Park Service handbooks have been published that explore the history and roles of Latino Americans, Native Americans, and Asian Americans and Pacific Islanders in the Civil War, broadening our ever-growing understanding of this time and place in American history.

CIVIL WAR VODCASTS

The Of the Student, By the Student, For the Student vodcast primer in Appendix 4.1 shows you how to craft a vodcast. I address this in the previous chapter and examine it in greater detail in Chapter 5, but I want to return to that topic once again. Several years ago sixth-grade students from Stonewall Jackson Middle School in Manassas, Virginia, produced a vodcast that explored the role of Irish immigrants at the Battle of Manassas (www.stenhouse.com/immigrantsoldiers). *The Story of Immigrant Soldiers at Manassas* is a gem! What makes it even more poignant is that most of the students who produced this vodcast were either immigrants themselves or children of immigrants; students were from El Salvador, Mexico, Nepal, Guatemala, Morocco, and Argentina. Sixty-three percent of Stonewall Jackson Middle School's population is defined as economically disadvantaged. Interspersed through the film are contemporary students such as Ariadna, from Argentina, explaining, "I'm not Irish and it is not 1861, but my friends and I both know it can be tough to move to a new country. Even though it can be hard to leave family and friends behind, we want to continue to be strong citizens of the United States and stay here." The production of this particular vodcast taps even more personally into the experiences of the students that they bring to bear on the final product. There's a certain sense of historical and personal empathy that you can read when you watch this vodcast, particularly when the following statement scrolls across the screen at the conclusion: "Similar to the motivations of the immigrants in 1861 our families came to the United States eager to take advantage of opportunities it provided. While today we enjoy the freedom the Irish and others spent days fighting for, there are still many challenges as a 'green' member of society, but just as the immigrant soldiers overcame their hardships and fought for their new country, we will never let the American flag fall."

Another vodcast produced by other sixth graders at Stonewall Jackson Middle School is *The Story of James Robinson, Senior*. Robinson was a free black living in Prince William County, Virginia, during the Civil War. The video chronicles his tale of trying to purchase his own parcel of land, enduring the sale of two of his children to slave owners from Louisiana, his pledge to purchase his remaining children, and his attempts to secure damages claims from the federal government for losses on his property as a result of the Civil War. Throughout the video the students display genuine feeling for their characters and bring care and sensitivity to their roles. Both videos, like the other vodcasts various schools have produced, are based entirely upon primary source research and use of historical documents. These students, though younger, are their generation's Ken Burnses. They do not leave a detail untouched, whether it is in writing the script or creating the music, and of course the use of the location makes it even more effective.

Orange County Middle School students, working with staff from Fredericksburg & Spotsylvania National Military Park, also crafted a moving vodcast about the death of Colonel John Patterson of the 102nd Pennsylvania Volunteer Infantry, who was killed in The Wilderness in May 1864. The vodcast looks at not only his death on the field but the long-term repercussions on his family and how his loss led to his family's impoverishment and eventual breakup. Using this vodcast you could tap into the tales of contemporary military lives and how loss affects them today.

GETTYSBURG NATIONAL MILITARY PARK

The most visited Civil War site in the United States is Gettysburg National Military Park in Pennsylvania, which hosts more than 1.3 million visitors a year. Gettysburg was the site of the largest battle of the Civil War and the largest in the Western Hemisphere. Over three days of intense fighting, involving more than 150,000 soldiers, there were more than 55,000 casualties, which included killed, wounded, and missing or captured. The eminent Civil War historian Gabor Borrit called the Battle of Gettysburg "the largest man-made disaster in American history." The National Military Park recognizes not only the honor and the valor of the soldiers who fought there on the first three days of July in 1863, but also the place of Abraham Lincoln's Gettysburg Address, his visit to dedicate the Soldiers' National Cemetery in November 1863, and how his "new birth of freedom" transformed the country.

Since 1998 Barbara Sanders has been the education specialist for the National Park Service at Gettysburg. During her tenure she has assembled a solid slate of educational materials. She has not only helped craft materials that help teachers prep for field trips should they be bringing their students to Gettysburg, but worked hard to make sure these materials are easily transferred into classroom use, since she understands that not every teacher can bring their classes to the park.

Like the Civil War Trust, the education division at Gettysburg National Military Park has a traveling trunk that includes not only tactile objects but lesson plans. These lessons address the issue of emancipation, the Gettysburg Address, and the life of Civil War soldiers who fought at Gettysburg. The lessons are all primary source based and can be found online in PDF format as well. Included with the trunks is a video specifically designed for the trunk program, with clips to play that coordinate with each of the independent learning stations and themes associated with the trunks. Though the trunk program is on the "Life of a Civil War Soldier," each trunk includes an extra station on "Women and the Civil War," "the Medical Corps," and "Lincoln at Gettysburg."

Another program that is run from her office is a blog called *The Gettysburg School Bus*. This teaching tool was developed by one of the park's Teacher-Ranger-Teacher staff members and provides a way of building a community of educators who can post and share ideas about teaching the Civil War and why it remains relevant today. The park has engaged in numerous distance-learning programs as well, including active student engagement with stories about such regiments as the Twentieth Maine and the Fifteenth Alabama of Little Round Top fame.

All of the educational resources of Gettysburg National Military Park can be found at www.nps.gov/gett with a link at the top of the page called "Learn About the Park." Select "Education" and then, under "Parks as Classrooms," select the "Best Field Trip Ever" planning kit for all your field trip and classroom needs. Among the other treasures on this site are eight lesson plans that help students build critical thinking and historical literacy skills framed around leadership, courage, and determination. All lessons engage students with the lives of individuals who experienced some aspect of the Battle of Gettysburg. One of them in particular that your students will really enjoy is the lesson called "Unfinished Work: Creation and Dedication of the Soldiers National Cemetery." Here students work to identify some of the soldiers who were buried in the National Cemetery by looking at letters and objects that provide clues to their identity. However, the best way to incorporate the "Unfinished Work" lesson, if you can, is to bring your students to Gettysburg, where they interact with a ranger in the National Cemetery. Remember, the Civil War Trust can help you here. There are also STEM and art lessons here, including an examination of the agricultural nature of Gettysburg and of medical treatment for wounded soldiers as well as the exploration the public monuments in the park. You could very easily employ the Civil War Trust's IN4 video *Civil War Monuments* if you opt to use this lesson.

If you are fortunate enough to be able to take students to Gettysburg, then I strongly suggest that you use the "Best Field Trip Ever" planning kit. It's a "how-to" document that will help you craft your visit to get the most out of it and includes materials that not only prepare you and your students to maximize your time on the battlefield but also show you how to best use the educational resources in the visitor center. This package includes all of your options—from the film, cyclorama painting, and museum exhibits at the Gettysburg National Military Park Visitor Center to the David Wills House (where Lincoln stayed the night before he delivered the Gettysburg Address) to ranger field programs and licensed battlefield guided tours, and more.

Sanders also organizes sterling professional development programs for teachers. The Days with Documents program is offered every summer and fall, immersing teachers in primary source material about the battle and techniques for effectively incorporating them in the classroom. The Richard Bartol Jr. Educators' Conference in Gettysburg is for educators who teach the Civil War era to middle school students in Pennsylvania, Maryland, West Virginia, Virginia, New York, New Jersey, and Washington, DC, and face challenges in connecting students to the Civil War or lack the necessary tools and approaches to effectively engage their students in Civil War exploration. This professional development opportunity is aimed at Title I schools. The Bartol Educators' Conference selects fifty teachers a year to interact with leading scholars and then examine the battlefield itself.

Sanders fully recognizes the pressure that teachers are under that often discourages them from taking field trips. She understands that these constraints are a combination of lack of funding and fear that instructional time for standardized test preparation will be curtailed. She is hoping to launch a professional development program called Administrators Day where principals, supervisors, administrators, and superintendents can come to Gettysburg and see how field trips can engage students in multiple valuable ways. Field trips are lifelong learning experiences, which students retain. We constantly lament the fact that our students don't know their history. But then we thwart opportunities to get them out and about to engage the past more directly. This is part and parcel of what the Journey is all about—active engagement with the historical environment to take learning to new levels. One of the last years I took students to Gettysburg, I invited our principal along. After we got back to school, he said, "I've been to Gettysburg before, but I didn't get it until today." That's because he saw students engaged in their learning and was inspired by it at the same time he was learning about those three days in July 1863 more intimately.

Like others, Ed Clark, the superintendent of Gettysburg National Military Park, holds a soft spot for the Journey, saying, "The Journey Through Hallowed Ground has provided a tremendous opportunity to Gettysburg National Military Park by helping to showcase the history and heritage of this park. The Journey's innovative education and preservation projects along Route 15 from Gettysburg to Monticello have improved the visitors' experience tremendously and drawn new audiences to the park" (personal communication).

THE COLORS OF COURAGE

One of the "Next Century" goals of the National Park Service Centennial is to get more people of color into our National Parks. I'll never forget on a trip to Gettysburg, when one of my African American students, Cory, said to me, "Mr. Percoco, how come there are no other black people here?" It was a valid question, and at the time, I had no answer. The National Park Service has done a yeoman's task over the past two decades to reinterpret their Civil War parks in a broader context. No longer are sites solely interpreted as places of military activity; now they include themes of race, gender, and other aspects of the social history and effect of the war on various groups.

One of the best books I ever used in my classroom teaching covers just about every human element that is part of the whole story of the Journey. Margaret Creighton's 2005 narrative *The Colors of Courage: Gettysburg's Forgotten History: Immigrants, Women and African Americans in the Civil War's Defining Battle* is not only a great read, but covers a neglected portion of a story that many Americans think they know well. Along with many others, I believe that the Journey taps into the rich and diverse people who shaped America. It was always important for me to recognize the role of those often pushed to the margins of history. Creighton's book resurrects a long-lost tale that completes the Gettysburg saga in ways that hadn't been done before. So taken was I by this book that I promoted it every time I spoke at a Teaching American History grant project event, meanwhile developing the reading guide I used with Cynthia Stout, the social studies specialist from Jefferson County Public Schools in Colorado. The Reading Guide (Appendix 4.2) was actually written for a group of teachers to use while attending a Teaching American History grant project event in Bozeman, Montana. Then I used it with great success in my own classroom. It works really well in helping to bring your students to understand the social history that often overlaps military history, which is unfortunately often neglected. Creighton takes on convention in her book when she addresses Robert E. Lee's use of what she terms "the reverse Underground Railroad." As Lee's army moved into Pennsylvania in June 1863, his forces were rounding up people of color, either free blacks or runaway slaves, and sending them south into slavery. This directly takes on the American myth about the venerated Robert E. Lee, who allegedly opposed slavery but could not draw his sword on his state.

GETTYSBURG ADDRESS READER'S THEATER

In the last chapter I explained the effective use of my creation of the Spirit of American History Players when it comes to employing the reader's theater strategy. One of the most moving moments of my time in the classroom was having students use a reader's theater developed on Lincoln's 1863 Gettysburg Address. You can find it in Appendix 4.3. I always let students volunteer for these activities. In 2009, one of the students who volunteered to read was Pablo, a generally quiet student who came from Honduras. Standing with his peers at the front of the classroom, Pablo breezed through his section of the script. When he was finished, I was stunned! Pablo had never, ever raised his hand for anything and hardly answered questions when called upon, but in this case he really rose to the occasion. After class I pulled him aside to chat. We talked a bit, and I thanked and praised him for his efforts. The next time he was in class I went over to him and, gently leaning on his desk, said quietly, "I really think you need to seriously consider applying to college next year when you are a senior." He simply nodded back with a smile on his face.

One suggestion for when you use the Gettysburg Address reader's theater in your class: project onto the screen behind the students an image of the Gettysburg National Cemetery. This will add a physical feature to the experience and provide some gravitas, making a direct connection to the ground where Lincoln spoke in November 1863. Another option would be to have some students collaborate to develop a PowerPoint slide show about the Battle of Gettysburg using images that relate to the battle at specific points that align with the script of the reader's theater. In this format you could have the students reading the script stand off to the side while the students who developed the PowerPoint project the images. To do this, you will probably need to provide a class period for students to prepare. There is a bonus in this approach, too: without realizing it, all of your students will be immersing themselves in the story of Gettysburg and learning the necessary content about not just the battle and its implications, but the concepts that Lincoln publicly pronounced at Gettysburg.

No matter what approach you take, you can follow up by writing "a new birth of freedom," one of Lincoln's phrases from the speech, on the board and ask students to consider what it meant in 1863 and what it means today in a society that is rapidly changing. Your openness to the question and willingness to lead students in a meaningful conversation and dialogue will elicit genuine remarks. If you are not comfortable with this kind of free-format conversation, you can always have your students respond in a journal entry. This will afford students who may not be comfortable sharing ideas openly to address the question in a more private format. Either way it gets students to study a great public paper from the American canon and place it in a particular context within their own lives. In this way Lincoln's words become more relevant and meaningful to the students rather than relegated to the dustbin of history.

Lincoln, who is the only president with a patent on file (for a device to help river flatboats negotiate river shoals), was fascinated with inventions. During the Civil War he could often be found at the Washington Navy Yard in Washington, DC, trying to learn about the new technology that was being employed in the war effort. But for Lincoln, the greatest invention of humanity was the written word, and he said as much in a speech he delivered at a Wisconsin agricultural fair in the 1850s. Lincoln believed that words gave humans the "ability to communicate with the dead, the absent, and the unborn." In using this approach to teaching the Gettysburg Address you will in effect be giving Lincoln more than his just due; you will be proving him right. One time when I had students write a journal entry about what Lincoln's words meant to them, Betsy wrote, "It's hard to believe that a man from the middle of the nineteenth century is speaking to me, a sixteen-year-old girl, almost 150 years later." Lincoln remains the proverbial American totem. The late Illinois senator Paul Simon once said, "All Americans have to get right with Abraham Lincoln." By exposing to students to the words of Lincoln in this way, you will be not only "getting it right" with Abraham Lincoln, but providing a level of relevancy to his words that continue to echo today.

You can also employ as part of this the Lincoln: 1863 Mobile App developed by the Gettysburg Foundation. This app lets you follow in Lincoln's footsteps on his November 1863 visit to Gettysburg. Using it brings his story and his speech alive a bit differently. It is a free download at the Apple iTunes App Store and can be found at www.GettysburgFoundation.org/Lincoln1863App. Using this app as a primer to the reader's theater you can really set the stage for the bigger story behind Lincoln's journey to deliver the Gettysburg Address.

I want to share with you a powerful story that illuminates Lincoln's Gettysburg Address and took place in the National Cemetery in 2000. In 1999 I had the privilege of being selected for a US State Department Teacher Exchange Program with Russia. For two weeks I lived with a Russian teacher and her family, working with her and her colleagues, to develop various educational programs for her school. In return, the following year I led the Russian teachers who were coming to the United States on a tour of Gettysburg. Some of my former students accompanied us as I demonstrated how I used place-based learning with students at a historic site. Most of these teachers from across Russia were teachers of English and had a strong command of the language. We concluded our visit at the National Cemetery and the site of Lincoln's delivering the Gettysburg Address. What happened there amazed me: a number of the teachers began to cry, saying things like, "We cannot believe that we are here at Gettysburg and where Lincoln spoke those words." I was stunned, but one teacher came over to me and said, "We are so emotional because when we teach our students English, we start with the Gettysburg Address, because Lincoln was such a great writer. His speech helps us show our students how the

English language really works. Being here at this place means a great deal to us, because Lincoln is our model for teaching the English language." I always knew that Lincoln's ten-sentence, 272-word speech illuminated historical literacy, but never considered the fact that it illuminates literacy itself.

I always enjoyed sharing this story with my students, and as I developed various lessons around Lincoln's words, I came to bond with many of the AP Language teachers at West Springfield, because in their curriculum they touch on Lincoln the writer as well. In this case Lincoln made the perfect model for interdisciplinary/cross-curricular instruction.

MOSBY HERITAGE AREA ASSOCIATION

One of the goals of the Journey is to promote the educational uses of local history within the larger framework of American history. The Journey prides itself on modeling its approach with a number of our partners; one such partner who is very skilled in this approach to teaching and learning is the Mosby Heritage Area Association, whose motto is "Preservation Through Education." So, too, is the study of history. As history educators we have an obligation to connect our young people with their immediate environment so that they see how it relates to the larger whole. For example, West Springfield High School, where I taught, was on sixteen acres of the former Ravensworth Plantation, which was a holding of the Lees—one of Virginia's most elite families. That means that enslaved people once traipsed across our campus. And the road on which the school is located, Rolling Road, got its name from the barrels of tobacco and other agricultural produce that were rolled to the Potomac River. When I would share this information with students, I could see the wheels turning inside their heads. It was as if they were imagining seeing enslaved people rolling barrels along what eventually became known as Rolling Road, which many of them drove their cars along. This kind of information makes for a certain sense of immediacy.

John Singleton Mosby is a colorful character from the annals of American history. During the Civil War he led an independent cavalry command attached to Robert E. Lee's army of Northern Virginia. His forces were a nemesis to the Union Army of the Potomac in the eastern theatre of action during the war. His nickname was the Gray Ghost, and his men were known as Mosby's Raiders. After the Civil War he joined the Republican Party, worked hard during the presidency of Ulysses S. Grant for reunification, and served as United States consul to Hong Kong. The area where he employed his tactics during the Civil War is known as the Mosby Heritage Area, much of which is inside the boundaries of the Journey.

Richard Gillespie, former Loudoun County, Virginia, high school history teacher—and one-time Loudoun County Teacher of the Year—is the association's executive director. As their former director of education, he took a lead in crafting many of the school-based, as well as site-based, educational programs. The educational mission of the organization is "to educate about the history and advocate for the preservation of the extraordinary history, culture, and scenery in the Northern Virginia Piedmont for future generations to enjoy." Now in our classrooms we have at our disposal the ability to integrate formal and informal education through numerous platforms, much of it based on evolving technology. The association offers a wealth of resources to schools in the community, annually reaching five thousand students. Not unlike the National Park Service and the Journey, the Mosby Heritage Area Association's educational programs are aimed at developing stewards of the next generation, those future adults to whom custody of this land will be entrusted. Thus much of their educational effort is in shaping these future stewards. Gillespie told me, "These places and stories will help to make classroom studies more relevant to students by being local—featuring places students pass by all the time. Inescapably, they will realize the value of saving historical places and landscapes both here and wherever they ultimately live. It only takes one shining moment for a kid to get turned on to history. That happens best when dealing with historic sites and gripping local stories well told. Let's make the magic happen in your classroom." To help bring home this point, Gillespie sends a letter to all the history teachers who work within the boundaries of the Mosby Heritage Area every year to make them aware of the various programs the association offers.

In a 2014 association newsletter he wrote,

> We have in and about us one of the best-preserved historic landscapes in America. We are also one of the fastest-growing regions in America. This dichotomy makes it important for today's largely suburban or exurban youth to have the historic landscape around them used by their teachers. Learning works best when traditional tools—textbooks, film/video, PowerPoints, primary sources, photos—are supplemented with primary sources and historic sites from right around students' homes. When

American or Virginia history begins to explain the world *right around* your students, you'll see the interest level grow. *Historyland!*

Heritage areas are growing throughout the United States to highlight these historic regions where crucial parts of American history played out and where case studies of American history can be found in abundance. With old roads, old churches, early schools, varieties of historic architecture, old graveyards, battlefields, slavery sites, and industrial sites still standing to illustrate our past, the Mosby Heritage Area of Northern Virginia is a wonderful resource waiting for your use. *Don't be confused*—this Virginia heritage area has a Civil War cavalryman's name, and many historic sites associated with him (John Singleton Mosby—the Gray Ghost), but as a heritage area it has a multiplicity of stories relevant to your teaching . . .

Teachers across the United States should be willing to jump into the fray where they live and follow Gillespie's model. It works!

The Mosby Heritage Area Association website, www.mosbyheritagearea.org, has a number of online lesson plan ideas for upper elementary, middle, and high school students that can be adapted to any region of the country. These lessons not only cover the Civil War era, but also explore issues related to the establishment of the nation, as well as slavery. In particular you will want to check out "It Happened Near Me: Pieces of the Past from Where I Live" (http://mosbyheritagearea.org/it-happened-near-me). Here you will find all kinds of ideas for how you can use your local history to augment the bigger picture of American history. It is a model from which you can launch into a study of your own particular local history.

Joshua Lawrence Chamberlain, who has gained mythic and superstar status from the Civil War, in part because of Michael Shaara's Pulitzer Prize–winning novel, *The Killer Angels*, the Ken Burns series *The Civil War,* and the motion picture *Gettysburg,* delivered a stirring address at the dedication of the Twentieth Maine monument on Little Round Top on the Gettysburg battlefield in 1888. His speech gets to the core of what the Journey is all about. I often had students respond to the meaning of this quote in a journal after our treks to Gettysburg. Based on the materials I have presented in this chapter, you, too, can effectively use this quote with your students in your instruction. It's a great way to bring closure to your Civil War unit. It reads, "In great deeds, something abides. On great fields, something stays. Forms change and pass; bodies disappear; but spirits linger, to consecrate ground for the vision-place of souls . . . generations that know us not and that we know not of, heart-drawn to see where and by whom great things were suffered and done for them, shall come to this deathless field, to ponder and dream; and lo! The shadow of a mighty presence shall wrap them in its bosom, and the power of the vision pass into their souls" (Civil War Trust).

Let these Civil War lessons wrap themselves around your students with the power of the Journey's landscape and vision in a way that passes into their souls.

CHAPTER 5

Quiet on the Set! It's Dwight David Eisenhower

Like Alice Deal Middle School in Washington, DC, Gettysburg Area Middle School, in Gettysburg, Pennsylvania, has embraced its location relative to its history. It borders Culp's Hill at Gettysburg National Military Park, scene of heavy combat during those first three days of July 1863. Given its proximity to the battlefield, Union and Confederate troops more than likely traversed the school's grounds.

Just by walking the halls of the school you can see that there is pride in the local history. Hallways named after famous Pennsylvanians who have a connection to the town memorialize their contributions to history. There's a hall in honor of Pennsylvania congressman and abolitionist Thaddeus Stevens, and a hall in honor of Elizabeth Thorn, the wife of Gettysburg's Evergreen Cemetery caretaker, who helped bury Union dead when she was six months pregnant. There is a hall named after Eddie Plank, the only resident of Gettysburg enshrined in the National Baseball Hall of Fame. Various halls have display boards that address the history of Gettysburg with particular attention to the events of November 19, 1863, and President Abraham Lincoln's delivery of the Gettysburg Address. Facsimiles of documents alongside photographs of Lincoln and others give the school a museum kind of feel. History is palpable here.

Gettysburg is not just the site of the largest battle of the Civil War; it is also home to Eisenhower National Historic Site, the home and farm of the supreme commander of the Allied Forces in Europe during World War II and the thirty-fourth president of the United States, Dwight David Eisenhower. As a junior officer he had been assigned to Gettysburg's Camp Colt, a US Army training post in the years between World War I and World War II.

Eisenhower was born in Texas in 1890, raised in Abilene, Kansas, and attended West Point Academy, graduating in 1915. He was a member of what is called "The Class of Stars," which included among its graduates Omar Bradley and others who would shape the direction of World War II. At West Point he played varsity football, participating in an epic game between the army and the team led by Jim Thorpe of the Carlisle Indian Boarding School. Eisenhower always felt slighted by being passed over for a combat position in Europe during World War I. It continues to amaze people that a man with no combat experience had the skills to lead the Allied coalition in Europe during World War II.

When the war ended, Eisenhower returned to the United States honored as an American hero and given that most unique American tribute—a ticker-tape parade in New York City. But public service remained his forte. In 1948 he accepted the position as president of Columbia University, which he held until he was elected president of the nation in 1952. Two years later he and his wife, Mamie, purchased a piece of property for a home and farm in Gettysburg, a place he had fallen in love with while serving at Camp Colt. There he planned to raise prizewinning cattle. After being wooed by both Democrats and Republicans, Eisenhower opted to throw his hat into the presidential ring as a member of the Grand Old Party (the Republicans) for the 1952 presidential campaign. He ran on the slogan "I Like Ike" and was one of the first presidential candidates to use the new media of television as a means of getting his message out. He defeated his Democratic opponent, Illinois governor Adlai Stevenson, in 1952 and then again in the election of 1956.

During his presidency, Eisenhower enjoyed moments at his home and farm, a short helicopter ride from the White House. He and Mamie spent their time together just relaxing or entertaining important guests such as French President Charles de Gaulle, Indian President Jawaharlal Nehru, and Soviet Premier Nikita Khrushchev, among others. The Eisenhowers really enjoyed playing hosts, and Eisenhower took particular pride is showing off his prize Angus cattle.

Some important events took place at the Eisenhower home and farm. It was here that Eisenhower learned that Gary Francis Powers, the pilot of a downed American U-2 spy plane, had been captured by the Soviet Union in 1960. He also wrestled with the decision over how to make the polio vaccine available to an anxious American public, and struggled with the growing civil rights movement. In 1960, Khrushchev spent several days at the Eisenhower home and farm, which helped to reduce the tension in the Cold War.

Eisenhower has enjoyed a resurgence in popularity among American biographers, who now portray him as being more than the "affable favorite uncle" he'd been labeled since leaving office in 1960. Biographers, particularly Jean Edward Smith and Evan Thomas, view Eisenhower as someone who deliberately gave the impression of being dimmer than he was for political reasons, as a way to keep his detractors guessing.

In this chapter I address specifically how to incorporate the Of the Student, By the Student, For the Student vodcast service-learning project developed by the Journey Through Hallowed Ground in partnership with, in this particular instance, the teachers and administrators of Gettysburg Area Middle School. As an aside, I want to say I always looked forward to teaching about Eisenhower. I knew all kinds of tidbits and used a couple of documents from the National Archives Eisenhower Presidential Library to teach about him.

For instance, when teaching about the D-Day Invasion, I used two documents of Eisenhower's, along with a photograph of Supreme Allied Commander Dwight D. Eisenhower chatting with US Army airborne troops the night of their airborne drop into France launching the D-Day invasion (see Figure 5.1). The first document was Eisenhower's "order of the day," a copy of which was given to every soldier, sailor, and airman involved in the invasion (see Figure 5.2). He also read the order over loudspeakers to the troops before they crossed the English Channel for France. I always asked students to read the document and elicit from it Eisenhower's tone. Students generally used the term *pep talk* when describing it. Then I handed out another document of Eisenhower's: a handwritten piece scribbled out on a single sheet of paper. I used a transcription to read it to students. This was the document Eisenhower would have used to deliver a radio address to the world had the invasion failed, and in it he assumes full responsibility for the failure (see Figure 5.3). The weather in Europe in June 1944 was problematic for the invasion planners. Interestingly the document is dated "July 5, 1944" at the bottom of the page, in his handwriting. In addition to wanting students to see Eisenhower's conviction about his decision to invade France, when the weather was causing the plans to hang in the balance, I wanted them to see how he planned to deal with the possibility that the invasion might fail.

Next I asked students, "What's the deal with the date?" I told them to look seriously at it and think about it. Most of them assumed it was written a month after the invasion took place. "Why would he have waited a month to give this address?" I asked. Some students offered that maybe he needed time to deal with the catastrophe after the fact. So I offered them a clue as a prompt and laid it out this way: "You are the commander of the largest invasion force ever assembled in human history. The fate of the world is in your hands and you know it. How are you going to feel?" I asked. I looked at the puzzled faces of my students and saw the wheels turning. That is when I knew my hook was working. Eventually a student would say he was "scared" or "nervous." Once we came to that consensus as a class, I asked them to consider what Eisenhower might have done in dating the second document. I could see the "aha" moment on their faces as they realized that in his nervousness he had made a simple, human mistake and put down the wrong date.

FIGURE 5.1
Dwight D. Eisenhower speaks with US Army troops at the start of the D-Day Invasion.

Next I would bring a prop into play. Now that we had established that he was nervous the day before the invasion, I asked the students how they thought Eisenhower dealt with the stress of planning this massive operation, which involved delicate dealings with the British and other Allies and often left him feeling like he was walking a tightrope. It was an odd question, so I didn't let them puzzle with it for too long. I reached into my shirt pocket and pulled out a pack of unfiltered Camel cigarettes, showed it to them, and said, "Four packs of unfiltered Camels and forty cups of black coffee a day!" The student response was usually one of disgust and groans. Nevertheless they got the idea.

I liked to deconstruct myths of history with students. I would put on the screen an image of the famous photo taken in the early evening of June 5, 1944, of Eisenhower speaking with the men of the 101st Airborne Division. These paratroopers were going to be dropped late that night over the western flank of the invasion force to secure towns with crucial roads and bridges. In the photograph Eisenhower is speaking with one soldier in particular as others look on, faces smeared in black and camouflage covering their helmets and uniforms. For years the story went that Eisenhower was looking for a soldier who came from his home state of Kansas, and when he found one, he supposedly said, with his right thumb clearly up in the photograph, "Go get em, Kansas!" However, within the last decade the truth has emerged. The Supreme Allied Commander is discussing fly-fishing! So once more, I posed a question to the students about Eisenhower, whom they now know was nervous and feeling the huge weight of responsibility on his shoulders. "Why for heaven's sake would he be talking about fly-fishing on such a momentous occasion?" I asked. Some students viewed this as another way to break the tension for himself and for his troops.

My point once again was to bring attention to Dwight D. Eisenhower as a human being and make him real so that he wasn't just some guy long dead in the past. Using the photograph this way also permitted me to explore with students how myths are created and what that says about us and our history. Certainly there is much more bravado in the statement "Go get 'em, Kansas!" than there is in a conversation about fly-fishing. People expect the heroic from people they perceive as giants of history during epic or iconic moments. It's part of our nature as human beings to believe that something has to be a certain way. The photograph exercise, as with the pack of Camels I showed, took Eisenhower a bit off of his pedestal without being too iconoclastic in the process. It humanized him. One of the things I really wanted my students to know about all the people we studied were their human qualities. It's important that students see the nuanced

SUPREME HEADQUARTERS
ALLIED EXPEDITIONARY FORCE

Soldiers, Sailors and Airmen of the Allied Expeditionary Force!

You are about to embark upon the Great Crusade, toward which we have striven these many months. The eyes of the world are upon you. The hopes and prayers of liberty-loving people everywhere march with you. In company with our brave Allies and brothers-in-arms on other Fronts, you will bring about the destruction of the German war machine, the elimination of Nazi tyranny over the oppressed peoples of Europe, and security for ourselves in a free world.

Your task will not be an easy one. Your enemy is well trained, well equipped and battle-hardened. He will fight savagely.

But this is the year 1944 ! Much has happened since the Nazi triumphs of 1940-41. The United Nations have inflicted upon the Germans great defeats, in open battle, man-to-man. Our air offensive has seriously reduced their strength in the air and their capacity to wage war on the ground. Our Home Fronts have given us an overwhelming superiority in weapons and munitions of war, and placed at our disposal great reserves of trained fighting men. The tide has turned ! The free men of the world are marching together to Victory !

I have full confidence in your courage, devotion to duty and skill in battle. We will accept nothing less than full Victory !

Good Luck ! And let us all beseech the blessing of Almighty God upon this great and noble undertaking.

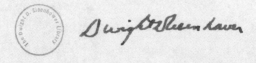

FIGURE 5.2

Eisenhower's "order of the day"

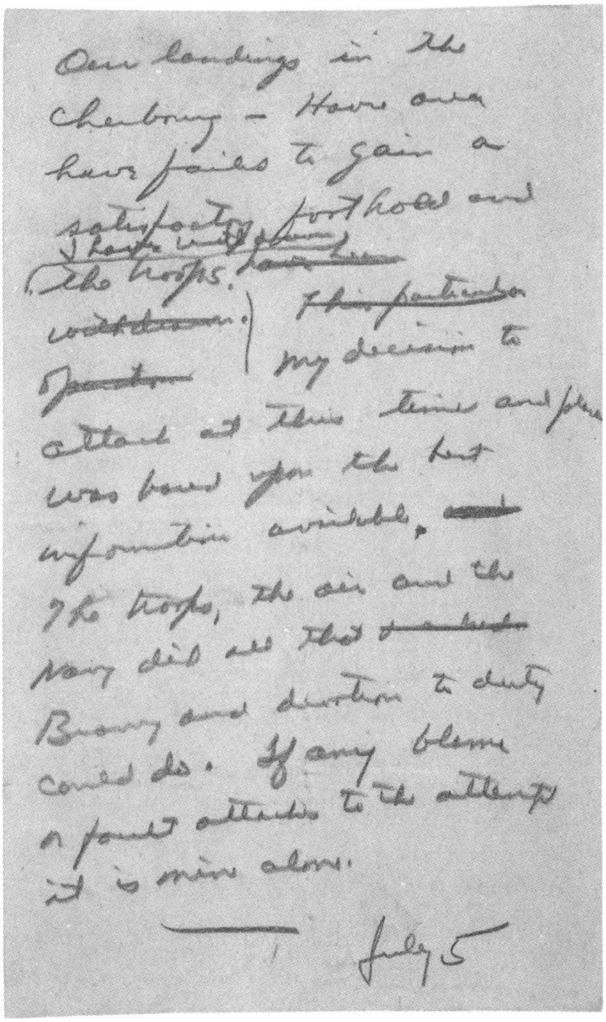
Our landings in the Cherbourg - Havre area have failed to gain a satisfactory foothold and I have withdrawn the troops. My decision to attack at this time and place was based upon the best information available. The troops, the air and the Navy did all that bravery and devotion to duty could do. If any blame or fault attaches to the attempt it is mine alone.

July 5

FIGURE 5.3
The document Eisenhower would have used to deliver a radio address had the D-Day Invasion failed

and shaded sides of people. We share a common humanity as agents for good as well as agents for ill. I worked hard to not put people on a pedestal. It also permitted students to make their own evaluations of the varying characters of history.

The other Eisenhower document I loved to use with students was one written to the president by four girls from Montana who were upset because Elvis Presley's being drafted into the US Army meant he would have to receive a GI haircut. It's a terrific letter for a variety of reasons. First of all it illustrates a piece of social history from the 1950s; it also reflects that the Eisenhower Presidential Library, part of the National Archives and Records Administration (NARA), thought it was an important enough document to keep for the Eisenhower collection. NARA keeps only a small fraction of documents of those they receive. And it was a fun document to use with students, because they could relate to it since it was written by teenagers. Because it was kind of goofy, the students thought it was a hoot.

The Vodcast

As I have alluded to in earlier chapters, Of the Student, By the Student, For the Student is a hallmark program of the Journey Through Hallowed Ground. Here I want to discuss in detail how the project works and how you can employ the same strategy for engaging your students in local history as a mirror of national events. Candidly, it does take a good chunk of time, but if you approach it with the right attitude and are willing to give it a shot, you and your students will be the beneficiaries of an exceptional teaching and learning tool in which we have technology at our disposal. It's also a lot of fun, and what teacher and what student doesn't want to have fun at school?

Careful planning and time taken up front will minimize problems and issues as you proceed. This includes bringing into your school the public historians from your selected historic site with whom you and your students will be working. For this project it was National Park Service Rangers Ahna Wilson and John Joyce. You will need to meet with them several times before launching the project to make sure everyone is on board and working toward the same goals.

Here is a quick glance at the time line we used to get the project rolling. Since the project takes up a good part of the school year, you have to lay the groundwork early. Jessie Aucoin, director of Educational Programs for the Journey, Ahna Wilson, National Park Service Ranger and site manager of Eisenhower National Historic Site, and I first met with staff and administration of the Gettysburg Area Middle School in October. This provided an opportunity for us to get together, get to know one another, lay out expectations, discuss roles and responsibilities, and flesh out a sense of direction. After our initial meeting, students completed and submitted applications, with parental approval to participate. The Journey asks for students to apply so we can determine which ones are the best fit for a project. For example, it helps to know who demonstrates enthusiasm or may be able to bring prior knowledge to the project. For this particular project students were pulled out of class, and the application process provided an opportunity to ensure that those who could handle the extra course load were involved.

As part of the application process, and as an opportunity to see the kind of work they would be creating, interested students watched a vodcast made by students at the school several years earlier. Two weeks later we returned to the school to sort out which students would work together. Once the students were selected by school staff, Aucoin and I met with them. This gave us an opportunity to give them an overview of the project and talk with them about what it means to make a film. I suggest you Google "award-winning short films" to demonstrate to students what makes a good brief film.

We introduced the topic of Eisenhower and then held a class discussion on the art of scriptwriting and what makes a good story. I gave a ten-minute PowerPoint presentation on Eisenhower's life to provide background and context.

Before we approached the school, we went over the basic requirements of the project with the National Park Service. Once the Journey received the nod from the school to proceed, Aucoin and I met with Wilson. Ed Clark, superintendent of the site, whom you met in the previous chapter, was very much in favor of creating vodcasts for the Eisenhower unit of the park. We held a series of meetings with different players to determine each partner's role and responsibility in the process.

Aucoin and I also met with Professor Michael Birkner, Eisenhower Scholar at Gettysburg College, to speak with him about various ideas. The key was to make sure that the events the student groups decided to re-create for the camera were germane to what took place at the farm. By the time we meet with Birkner, we had selected the following topics on Eisenhower: civil rights; and the Cold War, which included two subtopics—the U-2 incident and Khrushchev's visit to the farm in 1960. Birkner suggested we include the story of Eisenhower and his decision to inoculate young Americans with the polio vaccine. Aucoin and I loved the idea, because it was an obvious way to integrate STEM into the project. At the meeting I furiously took notes on possible sources and started going back through my mind to find lessons I had in my teacher toolbox that I could use.

All vodcasts must be based on primary source work so that students can construct their own interpretation of history. Using primary sources gives students the chance to be their own historians, and creating vodcasts forces them to use the actual words from history in their creation, thereby giving the vodcasts a certain sense of gravitas. They need to use secondary sources for context, but the bulk of their work needs to be primary source based.

Birkner suggested some good secondary sources, including the recent biography *Eisenhower in War and Peace* by Jean Edward Smith; *Mayday* by Michael Beschloss, about the U-2 incident; *A Matter of Justice: Eisenhower and the Beginning of the Civil Rights Movement,* and *Eisenhower 1956: The President's Year of Crisis: Suez and the Brink of War,* both by David Nichols, the former of which examines the Little Rock crisis of 1957 and the latter the Suez crisis when Egypt nationalized the Suez Canal; and finally, *Polio: An American Story* by David Oshinsky, a Pulitzer Prize winner in history. The meeting with Birkner proved to be a game changer, because it gave us a better sense of focus.

We next discussed with Wilson the potential topics from which the students would pick: Eisenhower and polio, Eisenhower and civil rights, the Suez crisis, the Cold War, and Eisenhower and leadership. One of the important components of the Of, By, For project is the relevance of the topic selected by students. They are required to make connections to America today not only as they craft their story, but in how they tell it. The five topics selected each offered a window into American life today through the prism of the 1950s while exploring Eisenhower as a leader. We continue to struggle with issues of civil rights, the Middle East remains a region in conflict in which the United States continues to play a role, parents today wrestle with issues around vaccinations of their children, and once more we find tension with Russia.

The next task was to assemble primary source document packets for the students to use as they draft their scripts and create their storyboards. The next day I reached out to the education staff of the Eisenhower Presidential Library in Abilene, Kansas, to determine what documents they might have that we could include. Pam Sanfilippo, education specialist at the library, provided me with a vital link to the daily log kept by Eisenhower's secretary, Ann Whitman, which gave us dates tied to certain events. At home I went through a box of commercially produced Eisenhower Document Teaching Kits created by the National Archives, called *Peace and Prosperity, 1953-1961*, and published by ABC CLIO. From these we were able to pull a number of documents.

Within two weeks Aucoin and I had assembled five packs of documents related to the selected topics. I had also gone out and purchased a copy of Oshinsky's book because it was a story about which I knew very little. Since the school library at Gettysburg Area Middle School did not have any of the secondary sources Birkner recommended, I went to my public library system in Northern Virginia and checked out all the books on his list for the students to use.

Shortly thereafter, students participated in what we called Immersion Day, when they visited the site to get a sense of the place where they would be filming and further fleshed out the life of their subject. The tour of the Eisenhower home was led by NPS Ranger John Joyce. When the tour concluded, we gathered in Eisenhower's barn, gave the students their primary source packets, and spoke with them about personal connections to the site. It is here that we learned that many of the students' families had personal stories connected to the Eisenhowers when they lived in Gettysburg. The students recalled how family stories included members of their family bumping into the Eisenhowers while they were in town shopping or at church services. Suddenly history no longer seemed remote but rather like real life.

The following week we were back in the classroom to meet with the students. Our purpose was to go over with them with a fine-tooth comb the stories that, based on all they had learned, they thought they could best tell in a vodcast. Next, the groups picked the topics for their vodcasts, based on what they had examined in the primary sources they reviewed.

Once you determine a historic site in your area with which to collaborate, you need to get your administration and colleagues on board with the project. A simple phone call to staff at your selected historic site can get the ball rolling. At Gettysburg Area Middle School, the Journey worked with Principal Elwood "Woody" Strait. Strait thought the project was a good idea for his students and teachers, and when we approached him about doing a vodcast with the National Park Service at Eisenhower National Historic site, it took little convincing. "The middle school is excited by the opportunities [the] Journey has provided our students," he told me when we filmed. "The conversations between parents and their children, the history of the Eisenhower era and the academics involved in the project, have created an environment primed for learning."

Principal Strait reached out to several teachers on his staff and asked them to work collaboratively with us and the NPS. The lead teacher for this project was Gifted Specialist Jennifer Riddlemoser. Also on board for the project were Karen Briant, a gifted specialist; Carol Kessel, chairwoman of the school's social studies department; and Alisha Sanders, a civics teacher. What is crucial for you to know is that even though there were only four teachers from the school working on this project, the whole school needs to be engaged, because students may be pulled from regular school activities to participate or may need assistance from technology teachers. In this case the school selected a pool of fifteen students to work on the project.

Relevance to contemporary issues is a key component of the Of, By, For project, and all the adults involved should continue to remind the students about the relevance, since they may not have picked up on this nuance of the program goals. Unless students are really tuned in to current events, they are not necessarily going to be aware of it, so this is the one rare moment during the process when you as a teacher may need to revert to a more didactic role.

Before having the students decide on their topics, they break into two groups of approximately seven students each. Once they do this, they have to decide who will be the director, who will be the screen and storyboard writer, who will be the historian, who will work on props and costumes, and who will be the camera/audio person. You need to monitor this carefully, because stronger students will naturally seek the positions of producer or director, and that leaves open a chance for group domination. It is critical to the process that everyone work together on some component of the project. Since there are five jobs that are assigned to specific students and about seven students per group, the remaining two assist the task leader in their role.

For fun, we asked the students to pick a name for their group. They chose their names randomly. One group chose to be the Narwhals, and the others chose to be known as the Michelin People of America. Once the groups were selected, I showed a brief, ten-minute PowerPoint presentation that provided some context about Eisenhower and his life. Then we let the students tell us about their choice of topics based on the packets of primary source documents we'd presented to them. Once the topics were selected, they researched characters to define roles to help shape the script, determined what costumes and props they needed, and began to develop their storyboard. To help them develop the storyboard, we gave them a template of frame-by-frame shots and told them they could use stick figures to illustrate their story. Before any filming could commence, these factors had to be in place. This process took several weeks of class time before filming began.

FILMING DAYS

For two intense days everyone involved in the project gathered at the Eisenhower home, which has been staged by the Park Service to appear as it looked in 1967. Everything in the home is original, so the students would be working with and filming actual historical artifacts. Eisenhower died in 1969, and his wife, Mamie, lived in the home until her death a decade later, after which the house was turned over to the National Park Service for care and interpretation. Joining us on the first day of filming was "Woody" Strait, who was very excited about the opportunity. He told me he wished he had had the opportunity to learn history this way and that he fully endorsed project-based learning. His enthusiasm was evident in his voice, and his body language exuded it as well.

An extensive agenda (see Appendix 5.1) was written for everyone that began at 7:00 a.m., the moment students arrived at school, and lasted until 2:00 p.m., when they would depart from the Eisenhower home to return to school. It was important that everyone follow the agenda as closely as possible.

On the first day students planned to shoot four scenes at five locations in the house. Riddlemoser encouraged the students to get their scripts out and review them. The script for the Day 1 filming, by the group doing the film on the Cold War and Soviet Premier

Khrushchev's visit, was principally the work of José and was vetted by Riddlemoser, Briant, Wilson, Joyce, and Aucoin.

When the students arrived at the site in the morning, they were energized and ready to go. Some of them had dressed before the visit, but a "green room" was set up in the site's reception center for the remaining students to change into the costumes they had assembled, based in part on the visual primary sources used. Since the project involved fifteen students, not all of them would be filmed at the same time, so the expectation was laid out and space was provided for students to work on other schoolwork when not involved in the filming process. Since students are being pulled frequently from other classes, it's important to ensure that teachers not part of the process have their work with students respected as well.

Scenes are not necessarily filmed in the order in which they appear in the final production, but rather in the order that makes most logistical sense for the site. After all the filming was completed, students edited the film back at school using Adobe Premiere Pro. The student producer for Day 1, Luke, took the lead when he encouraged his peers to be as sharp as possible, helped coordinate the day's activities, and tried to keep the group on schedule. It was important to remember that filming was taking place on a public site where visitors might show up for tours, so everyone had to be organized to the point that if a break had to occur, they could pick up filming where they left off as soon as a tour was finished.

Luke also had to coordinate with Grace, who was in charge of props, to make sure that all the props the students had assembled worked correctly. Students would not be handling any of the original artifacts at the site; they created their own props to use so they wouldn't damage the historical integrity of the objects in the home. Whereas Luke was the producer, Lily was the director, and they had to carefully coordinate and orchestrate the whole process. Aucoin served as an über-director to doubly ensure that everyone stayed on task, and worked carefully amidst the historical objects in the room.

If you are interested in having your school make a vodcast, I suggest that you recruit and work closely with someone from a local university's theater department or a community theater.

Additionally, people from the Journey are eager to help schools across the country engage students and interested teachers to create their own Of, By, For vodcasts. The Journey can provide advice and guidance, and offer the kind of enthusiastic support needed to pull off such a large-scale project.

The first scene to be filmed was in the sunroom, where Eisenhower was to greet Khrushchev and introduce him to his family. There were multiple takes from a variety of angles, including close-ups, but before any shot could be filmed, the student working the camera had to move to properly frame the shot. Once the camera was in place, the students made a dry run without filming to make sure everyone knew what to say based on the script and where to stand during the filming. It is important to note that the actors selected to be in the film were not from the core group of students who were working on the project from its inception. They were other students selected by teachers, and a number of them had worked on the school's theater productions.

Once the dry run was finished to everyone's satisfaction, filming commenced. Luke shouted, "Quiet on the set!" followed by Lily, who shouted, "Camera, ready?" Logan, the student on the camera, replied, "Camera, ready!" Next Lily shouted, "Sound, ready?" The student operating the audio apparatus, Josh, responded after a quick check tapping the microphone, "Sound, ready!" Then Luke shouted, "Action." Standing close by with a copy of the script in his hand was José, the scriptwriter, who made sure students didn't deviate from the carefully planned script (Appendix 5.2), which included student placement.

Filming this short scene took at least an hour after multiple takes. Students were expected to capture a minimum of two "good" takes. The final production would run three to five minutes, but it took many hours to complete. There was an aura of Hollywood authenticity to the whole process. What was very clear was that throughout this production, students were learning not just history, but life skills as well, including how to manage people, how to work under a time line, and organizational planning.

In the first scene Zach as Eisenhower welcomed Khrushchev, portrayed by Evan, who invoked a Russian accent. As the real Eisenhower and Khrushchev did in this same room in 1959, Zach and Evan, channeling the respective world leaders, discussed not only Eisenhower's hobby of oil painting, but the real tensions of the world at that time, specifically the crisis over West Berlin and the proliferation of nuclear armaments. It was very cool to see all of this unfolding in the exact spot where the conversation actually took place. It was the best kind of use of a public history setting in an educational sense for school-age students.

Lily asked for more shots, urging Zach and Evan not to rush their lines. Aucoin, Riddlemoser, and Briant stood on the sidelines, serving as cheerleaders, encouraging the students with remarks such as "That was really great!" or "Nicely done!" They didn't intrude too much into the process, because one of the goals is to get the students to do the actual work, although Aucoin sometimes checked in with Lily to make sure she was comfortable with what had just been filmed.

After the scene with just Eisenhower and Khrushchev, another scene was filmed with Eisenhower introducing his son, daughter-in-law, and grandchildren to the Soviet premier. It was a tough scene to film, because the grandchildren had to behave like grandchildren actually teasing one another or posturing for their grandfather's favor. This took longer than expected because there was some natural and good-natured giggling among the eighth graders as they tried to get the film shot. But the students also encouraged each other to contain their giggles, and the atmosphere was filled with mutual support. It was a serious but lighthearted feeling.

Once numerous takes, including close-ups, had been made, the sound person, who uses a boom device, needed to record ambient sound, which is sound in the room with no dialogue. Ambient noise or sound needs to be recorded to be part of the essence of the film, permitting students to layer the film with dialogue in case there are missed cues during the editing process.

The third scene was shot outside at the Eisenhower farm's cattle barn, with Angus cattle serving as live props in the background. Here Eisenhower and Khrushchev discussed Eisenhower's passion for raising prizewinning cattle and the president offered the Soviet premier one of his cows as a gift.

During the half-hour lunch break I took an opportunity to chat with the students about their experiences. For Lily, "It's interesting to learn history this way because we have to figure out what it looks like and we have to do it as a team."

Logan said he liked it "because we are not being lectured to. It involves us in our learning."

Zach told me, "When you do hands-on work, you get a feel for how people in history felt."

José said, "This is a much more engaging way to learn history as opposed to relying on textbooks."

For Luke it was all about collaboration: "Everyone has a direct responsibility to the project," he said.

Grace said she enjoyed the process "because you get to work with your friends while you still learn."

The last scene filmed on Day 1 was of Eisenhower playing chess with Khrushchev. Purely without input from adults, the students set up the chess game scene so that

Khrushchev was using the black pieces and Eisenhower the white as a metaphor of good versus evil. The whole scene was imagined by José as a greater metaphor for the political games that were taking place during the Cold War. There is no evidence the two leaders played chess when they met, but the National Park Service was supportive of using artistic license to make the point.

What became most obvious watching the filming unfold was how well personal, one-on-one high-stakes diplomacy works. Even though it was an official state visit, the tenor of the Cold War was reduced when the leaders saw each other as human beings, and in such a moment of rapprochement, the people they led were also duly humanized. This was not lost on the students, who indicated to me during our conversation that history became less of an abstraction and more reality based. It's also a reminder of what historian David McCullough has argued for many years: that history is always someone else's present moment.

I returned to Eisenhower National Historic Site the next day when the second set of students filmed the vodcast on Eisenhower's role in endorsing the national vaccination program against polio (www.stenhouse.com/diseasednation). The day's filming had a bit of a twist because the students in this group wanted to tell the broad story of the effect of polio on the nation, and that required a different approach than had been used on Day 1.

On this day four scenes were shot at seven locations at the home. The drill ran much like the day before, with the same kind of energy and enthusiasm from the students. And much like the day before, the devil was in the details: once again, camera angles had to be framed within certain parameters, lighting had to be carefully considered, and all the moving parts had to come together to make a seamless whole. Again, spacing was crucial, because everyone was working inside a space that is a historic home, and there were limits to what could be done within those constraints. But there was a good lesson in that, too, because it made everyone sensitive to not just the historic space, but the objects that occupied the space as well.

The day was cold, rainy, and raw, with stronger storms predicted for later in the day. That forced the students' hands a bit, and they collectively decided to film the outside shots first. The script called for a scene of a family at a cemetery, mourning the loss of their child to polio. Students had created a faux tombstone, and there was little dialogue. The rain and the black umbrellas everyone held during the filming added to the somber atmosphere needed for such a story. Back inside the house the students used the Eisenhowers' kitchen as a set for Dr. Jonas Salk's kitchen, where he vaccinated his family against polio to prove he thought the vaccine he had created was safe.

What was so relevant about this particular episode in American history that the students wanted to depict was that it got to the heart of the question of socialized medicine. Eisenhower bucked his party, the Republicans, to ensure that all Americans were vaccinated against what was believed to be a scourge and a public health crisis. This also got to the argument that some families have raised about inoculating or not inoculating their children against the flu or other medical conditions that are problematic for our society.

Filming went as well as it had the day before, with all of the students behaving professionally and responsibly.

Because this was a civics enrichment project, students were reminded that there would be a premiere of the film before school ended so that parents, Park Service staff, other faculty members, and students could see the great work produced by the student filmmakers and historians.

Once again, at lunch, I chatted informally with the students about what this all meant to them and what they were deriving from the project. Sydney, the camera operator, told me, "It is fun, because as a camera person you have to be there for every scene, so you get to see all of it being put together."

Owen, who played Eisenhower, said, "Working with primary source documents is very cool. You get to see real history."

The director, Soren, related that "It is so much better learning history this way because it is hands-on and you can apply your ideas and construct your view of history through your eyes."

Kalynn, the scriptwriter, had a background in creative writing and told me that she had had to learn to write a whole new way. "It's hard to write historic action and dialogue," she said, "but even though it is very different, I am glad to see it all come to life now that we are filming."

The scene of Eisenhower giving Salk a special presidential honor for his role in finding a cure for polio was both poignant and interesting. Owen committed to memory the exact words Eisenhower spoke at the April 26, 1955, White House ceremony. It was a lengthy series of remarks, and even though it took a fair number of takes, it was as if Owen were actually channeling Eisenhower, complete with the president's nuances. All the other students were very supportive and encouraging of Owen, demonstrating the collaborative nature of the project. It was very clear that the students believed they all had a stake in the vodcast.

The scene was based on an actual photograph of the event, which the students use to help them frame the scene. The students studied the photograph and then posed Owen and Luke, as Salk, just as the men looked in the photograph. Since the scene was filmed in an all-purpose room in a Park Service outbuilding, it was a bit easier for the students to work in the space. A podium from the Park Service was used; affixed to it was a faux Eisenhower Presidential Seal. Students made or procured the vast majority of props, but calls for help were made to the National Park Service when needed, which resulted in a podium that the students would never have been able to re-create effectively.

With both filming days in the books, it was a wrap. There would be a few minor scenes filmed back at school, but the next task was to edit the film and add music.

The equipment the students used was provided by the school's instructional technology department and consisted of a high-end digital camera (high end for a hobbyist, that is) and basic boom microphones. However, should you opt to try out this program at your school, you don't have to get fancy with equipment. Current smartphones will permit you to replicate what I have written about here, and the software for editing is not cost prohibitive.

I heartily encourage you to take the risk and try this. It is well worth it. You may encounter some resistance from your colleagues, particularly given that to complete the various components of Of, By, For you will be pulling students away from other teachers' instructional time on occasion. But the winds in education may be shifting a bit, too, as the push for standardized testing may be waning. After two decades in which standardized testing as a political tool has held sway, the voices of sanity may finally be prevailing—voices not just of teachers, but of parents and incredibly bored students. I think it is fair to say that it is not that young people don't like history; they just don't like the way that it is taught. The Of, By, For project is rich in many ways, and everyone involved in it—teachers, parents, wise school administrators, and the students themselves—see the value in it. During the two days I watched, students were joyful and smiling—but so were all the adults involved in the project, from Principal Strait to National Park Service rangers and the teachers. Since it is such fun for everyone, it proves that learning need not be drudgery but can be playful, which is not only important but also immensely refreshing.

At the end of the two days of filming I was able to chat with Riddlemoser and Briant to ascertain their thoughts about the project and working with the Journey. Riddlemoser told me, "It has been quite an honor working with the Journey Through Hallowed Ground Of the Student, By the Student, For the Student service-learning project this year. My eighth-grade students have had nothing but positive feedback and comments throughout the entire experience. Students have been actively engaged in higher-order thinking, cooperative learning, opportunities to connect content to real-life experiences, social interactions, and real-life work experience in the filming process. All students played an integral role in allowing the history to come to life in the final product of the movie. My students had the opportunity to explore the life and presidency of Dwight D. Eisenhower. They began by visiting his farm, led by an amazing National Park Service guide. They also explored history through primary source documents. JTHG Director of Educational Programs Jessie Aucoin created an atmosphere of respect, excitement, and student leadership within the walls of my classroom. Many students have voiced their desire to continue exploring history and moviemaking as a result of this experience. Providing opportunities for students to have real-world experiences while connecting history is an invaluable part of this process."

Briant affirmed Riddlemoser's sentiments, saying the "Journey Through Hallowed Ground has provided a wonderful experience for the students of Gettysburg Area Middle School. As an educator, I love that the students have been able to draw upon their own strengths and interests to become actively engaged in history. As historians, scriptwriters, art designers, directors, producers, camera crew, and sound engineers, the students learned to come together as a team to research and create an exciting final product. The entire journey has been a learning process that has brought history from their own community alive for the students."

With history being all around us, I encourage you to reach out to your local, state, and national historic sites. The Journey is here to help you do that. We are more than happy to help you from Waterford, Virginia, as much as we can despite what may be great physical distances. Just think how cool it would be if we could engage historic sites that recognize and commemorate the wide sweep of American history, from the native peoples who built cliff dwellings in the American Southwest to the battlefields of the American Revolution. There are inner-city historic sites to choose from as well, such as those found in Chicago, New Orleans, Baltimore, Philadelphia, and Boston, as well as sites of conscience such as the Manzanar National Historic Site in California, which is dedicated to those Japanese American citizens detained in relocation centers. With such a wealth of resources at our disposal, it makes perfect sense to try to use these places as more than just nice places to visit with our students but to engage them directly with the young people who crave a more authentic and dynamic approach to learning about our past.

At the completion of the project two premiers are held: one during an assembly at the school on its awards day and one for parents and friends at the park. This provides an opportunity for the students to showcase their efforts to a wider audience. Classmates and parents alike cheer at the conclusion of the vodcasts *A Diseased Nation* and *The Visit*.

If you are looking for ways to teach outside the box and are willing to work, take risks, and take the necessary steps to create an Of the Student, By the Student, For the Student vodcast, you will be giving your students a marvelous and unforgettable learning experience that will be of real value to them as learners and of service to whatever historic site you choose to partner with.

CHAPTER 6

Historic Preservation and Justified Optimism

T he ramshackle white clapboard structure, eighteen by thirty feet and twenty feet tall, sits forty yards off the road. It's an unassuming building in an abandoned lot. People drive by it every day thinking that this nondescript building, with its peeling paint and "Private Property" sign affixed to it, is of little significance. As you approach it, you drive past well-manicured lawns on which stand modern suburban Northern Virginia homes and strip malls populated by pizza restaurants and other small businesses. Nearby is a bike trail that abuts the route of the former Washington & Old Dominion Railroad, now a Northern Virginia Regional Park. One has to cross the tracks when approaching the building from the south.

The building is clearly sinking, too, and the foundation of native blue fieldstones plowed from local farms is in serious need of being shored up. Tree stumps embedded like clogged arteries can be found along the perimeter of the foundation. On the rear of the structure a shadow appears as part of the clapboard, indicating the location of a woodpile at one time.

Stepping inside the building you are immediately struck by the slack in the floor, the result of loose floor joists. Old electrical wires dangle from the ceilings like tentacles of some creature trying to pry its way inside. The musty odor is pungent, too. The vent for the potbellied stove is still visible above the chalkboard, to which your eye is drawn, which offers a distinct clue about the building's purpose. It was a one-room schoolhouse that could hold sixteen desks—with several students assigned to each—and space for a teacher's desk. It appears that there was a kitchen of some sort inside, too. All in all, it is a tiny, cramped space.

I step out of the gloom onto the front steps on which a modern rail post from Home Depot finds itself supporting a small porch. I am greeted by several students from LSG in Ashburn, Virginia. These students, ranging from sixth grade to high school, are working collaboratively to save and preserve this building, the historic Ashburn Colored School. For two school years now, these junior historic preservationists have been doing the hard but necessary work to save a parcel of the past that has been long forgotten—not just the building itself, but the people who attended the school as well.

Like the famous American architect Daniel Burnham, who once said, "Make no little plans," these students have big dreams and high hopes for their efforts to save the school that was built in 1892. The building closed in the late 1950s when another school was constructed to accommodate black students in Loudoun County. Under the leadership of Sharon Knipmeyer, project manager, and Jana Shafagoj, the director of Preservation and Education for Morven Park, a historic house property in Leesburg, Virginia, and Journey Through Hallowed Ground partner, the school and Morven Park have joined forces to save a small but important slice of American history. Also engaged in the project is a local restoration firm headed by Jane Covington, who will help with the myriad needs of restoring a historic building. The plan is to get the necessary work done to secure the building's status on the National Register of Historic Places. But it's the students who are doing all the legwork to see this come to fruition.

A key and enthusiastic supporter of the project is Deep Sran, the founder of the LSG, who believes with his whole heart and soul that "history is justified optimism," a way of looking at the past that permits us to see the progress that has been made over time as a prism through which to view our present. On this balmy March day, Sran joins us to meet with the students and the contractor, David Ratcliff, who will do the heavy construction lifting based on the research conducted by the students.

In 2015, Sran bought the lot on which the school stands, which was once part of the local African American community's Zion Baptist Church. A new state-of-the-art building will be built on the lot adjacent to the Old School. The Old School will be a centerpiece on the property and preserved as a museum. Sran tells me, "We couldn't let the old building fall down."

To help them in their preservation efforts, the students have formed a 501(c)3 nonprofit called the Framers Project, named after the framers of the United States Constitution, who are the mascots of the school. The students launched a Kickstarter campaign and created a crowd-funding site that initially raised $5,000 toward the estimated $100,000 needed to restore the building. Bringing in the local community, students also got area restaurants to help by dedicating portions of their receipts to the preservation project.

For the 2014–2015 school year the Framers Project was a class of seven students in eighth grade who were devoted to the restoration. Conducting intensive research at Leesburg's Thomas Balch Library, which is dedicated to local history, students uncovered the land plat and other key primary source documents that provided clues about the look and feel of the building in the mid-twentieth century. They also discovered the names of students who attended the school, and have been able to interview either the students themselves or family members of the school's alumni.

In the 2015–2016 school year the students continued their labors as part of an extracurricular activity. They met weekly and traded off between working on-site and fund-raising.

LSG

LSG was established in 2008. Founder Deep Sran grew up and went to school on the north side of the Potomac River in Montgomery County, Maryland, where he had a typical public school education rooted more in STEM than in the humanities.

After attending the University of Maryland and earning doctoral and law degrees, Sran decided he wanted to create the ideal kind of school where all the stakeholders love what they do, be they students or teachers. Sran believed that his high school learning experience lacked in the humanities and that as a result his education was at some level shallow. His dream of his kind of school dates to his freshman year at the University of Maryland. For a short period after graduation he taught in a charter school, but he really wanted to create a school run by teachers.

The school is accredited by the Southern States Association, but outside of those students who opt to take an Advanced Placement curriculum, there is no standardized testing. Math and science are not ignored but don't form the nucleus of the educational framework. It's a place where students are encouraged to think deeply and broadly. As plans are drawn up for the new building, teachers and students will play a formative role in what that building will look like.

The widely diverse students who attend LSG are in grades 6–12. In some but not all ways, it reflects a Montessori School approach as students of varying grades are mixed in a variety of classes such as the elective Empathy in Literature. Forty-one students who come from a fifteen-mile radius attend the school, and class sizes are generally between ten and fourteen students. At the LSG, students read the classics, such as Plato's *Republic*. The students who attend the school are thoughtful, curious, and driven. They go on to some of the most prestigious colleges and universities in the United States, as demonstrated by the many university pennants that hang from the ceiling, including ones from Cornell, William & Mary, Baylor, and Pepperdine, among others.

Like law students, each student has his or her own space, and classrooms frame the sides of the main area. On the walls of the school are quotes such as this one from Aristotle: "We are what we repeatedly do. Excellence, therefore, is not an act, but a habit." Or from Winston Churchill: "If you are going through Hell, keep going." And from Benjamin Franklin, "He that is good for making excuses is seldom good for anything else." From Ernest Renan, "The simplest schoolboy is now familiar with truths for which Archimedes would have sacrificed his life." Along one wall in Sran's office are the words "You are not a delicate flower!" Sran's students are pushed to get the best out of themselves as human beings, and student humanity remains central to the school's mission.

Currently the school resides in a nondescript office space in an industrial park. Yet inside that space you can feel the energy and dynamism at play as students and teachers alike collaborate in a lab setting. Most of the learning is individualized and inquiry based. Yet there is no feel of pretention. The atmosphere is loose and relaxed. This is clearly a school where contemporary issues are at the forefront of learning, creating dynamic citizens. For example, there is a class that examines the current struggles in the Middle East, particularly the civil war in Syria.

Meeting the Student Preservationists

For two days I have the opportunity to meet with the current set of students to discuss the Framers Project. My curiosity is not only about why they are doing what they are doing, but how they are doing it. Over lunch we hold a conversation.

Shailee, an eighth grader, tells me that "the work on the old school represents all the untold stories that are concealed and hidden in plain sight. The school is important to

African American history," she says earnestly. "I've lived near it but always thought it was a shed."

Gwyneth, an eleventh grader, explains, "It is important for people to see something and do something about it. This is an important part of local history that we just can't pass off to others to take care of. If you see something that needs to be done, you should do something."

Katie, another eighth grader, claims she wanted to be involved "to help restore a little-known part of Northern Virginia that has an important tie to African American history. I want to help people to get informed of the community's role in the past."

Karmran, who is in tenth grade, gets to the nub of what this book and the Journey Through Hallowed Ground Partnership is all about. "All history," he asserts, "is local. Larger events in American history, like the oppression of blacks, have a local flavor to them."

For Taz, in sixth grade, it's crucial that he model something different for his peers. "This project is important to me," he explains, "because most of my peers want to play video games, and this shows that there is cool stuff to do besides playing video games. Besides, history is everywhere!"

Collectively there is a singular energy and synergy at work among the students. With great animation they tell me about how they interviewed eighty-four-year-old Yvonne Neal, a former student of the Old School, at a local diner. Neal was able to tell the students about her teacher and give them a visual recollection of the interior space. This helped shape their views of what the space should look like when reopened. Neal shared anecdotes about the average school day, with the biggest takeaway from their interview being her admonition that life is about loving other people. Neal would have to walk past the white school every day to attend class and was taunted by her white peers, but it was important for her not to hate the haters. For Gwyneth, "It was important to see the efforts these black students took to see that they got a good education. The smaller stories from someone helped to see history through the eyes of someone who lived through it."

The students are also learning as they move forward about the serious racial history in Virginia. They have learned that black schools were not equal to white schools and that Virginia perpetuated the problem with massive resistance after 1954's *Brown v. Board of Education of Topeka*. Black students were always on the short end of the stick, inheriting used textbooks and school supplies.

The students continue to dig through records and, with the help of the Black History Committee of the Thomas Balch Library, are looking for more names of people to interview.

With regard to the research Katie notes, "It provided insight into the process of gathering facts while working with little documentation. We really had to find firsthand accounts of what the building looked like."

Gwyneth explains, "The scope of information you obtain by working on a site, particularly when you dedicate time to a site, is a big payoff. Because I have invested time in this site, I want to see it work out."

Acquiring life skills, the students have learned how to analyze buildings, how to conduct oral history interviews, and how to immerse themselves in primary source research. For the five students who opted to join the extracurricular component of the Framers Project, the dividends continue to pay out.

Sharon Knipmeyer is amazed at the progress the students have made and just enjoys being around a group of students who are so dedicated and committed to a cause. Knipmeyer tells me that "the students have learned about archaeology by digging test pits at the site and studying the stratigraphy (examining the layers of soil—a *very* STEM activity) and the students have learned about the human barriers to preservation that are put up by bureaucracies. Right now our immediate fund-raising goal is to raise $20,000 for shoring up the foundation. We see this as a multiyear project." In the end all the final decisions on the building and its preservation will be made by the students themselves. It will be their particular legacy that they leave behind collectively. Gwyneth was quoted in a *Washington Post* news story about the project: "It's up to [a few students] to figure out what it should look like in the end. That's a lot of pressure."

The next day I meet with the students at the Old School to shadow them. The archaeology test pits made by the students early in the process are still visible. Sran joins them, and they discuss the need to make sure that any objects found during the restoration and preservation efforts are respected and interpreted. With great scrutiny the students look over the building, taking careful note of some of the problems such as the bowing walls and how in just a short period of time they have noticed that the structure has shifted a bit. I watch, amazed, as the youthful conservationists engage in conversation. Ideas drawn on notepads will be translated into their final plans. In examining the peeling paint they are careful, because it contains lead. When the final work is done on the school, it will not be physically done by the students but by professionals.

The plot of land on which the Old School sits, and on which the new school will be built, was owned by Harry Saville, who still lives in his home adjacent to the lot. It was his wife's dream to restore the home. Now he's a widower watching the process unfold.

The Role of Morven Park

Journey Through Hallowed Ground partner Morven Park has taken a serious lead in helping the students with their project. The project fits into the strategic plan of organization, which includes reaching out to schools and other members of the local community to assist in various preservation projects. It is powerful proof of the logic of school and community partnerships. Jana Shafagoj explains, "As a preservationist, I feel very strongly about historic buildings. I really wanted to make sure the students were empowered in their work. After last year's research phase, this year I am getting the students to focus on the actual building and grounds to take the next steps to restore and conserve. It is the rehabilitation phase of the project." Continuing, Shafagoj explains, "The students inspire me. They want to figure the building out. They wanted to see what secrets were hidden in the building. I want them to be history detectives. Regardless of age they are at the same place. I just needed to help them see a collective context.

"It is important to me, the long-term goals of the project," she opines, "and I am glad that they are conserving the resource and putting the building into use. I want to let the kids take the lead and have them wrestle with how the building should look when it is finally restored. Should it look like it did when it opened or when it closed? They need to be the ones who interpret the site. They have to deal with the same issues preservationists struggle with all the time. For example, do they keep the original floor or do they replace it? They have come to see that money plays a role in these decisions, too. There are no easy answers," she tells me, "and no right answers either. All I want them to do in the end is provide a logical argument and methodology for their approach."

But there is another agenda here as well for Shafagoj. "Too often we lose our African American resources. This is important, particularly as the kids make connections with former students or family members of students who went to school here. This is a great thing the school is doing for the entire Loudoun County community."

Morven Park operates a Center for Civic Impact, which is a lesson plan platform. On this K–12 site you will see that voice matters. The focus of the center is civic engagement, and it makes history relevant to the present. A preservation-based curriculum called Understanding the World Around Us helps students understand the built environment.

This portal gets students to look at the world in their immediate view and understand the role and function of architecture. Part of the site's purpose is to get students to understand not only construction, but how buildings create social space, by analyzing them. For example, in a home, public space and private space are defined by the stairway. On this site students consider how architecture tells you that you are in a certain space. In historic homes you learn how to determine the functions of various spaces. You have to think about why there are different spaces for visitors, servants, and bathrooms.

What You Can Do in Your School for Historic Preservation

Once again I want you to use this material as a platform of encouragement. Look around your community at places people have ignored. Get curious. Let your students get curious. Then run with your curiosity and see where it leads you. When I was teaching, I always used "places" as platforms for teaching, be they historic homes or cemeteries. These places have something to say to us. Why do you think there is the old saying, "If these walls could talk . . ."

In the classroom I used a film produced by the National Trust for Historic Preservation called *A Living Part*, which explained the mission of the National Trust not only at the sites it administers, but also through various projects related to the sustainability of economic factors for communities. At no cost the National Trust sent me back issues of their magazine *Preservation* that I used with my students to write article abstracts about various National Trust projects.

If you have an old cemetery in your community, pull together a group of students to help restore it. It's a great service-learning opportunity. Cemeteries have records of the people buried there, and obituaries provide a lot of information, too. Some historic cemeteries around the country are doing fund-raising projects whereby they bring to life the people who are buried in them. Often they host public performances where people in costume portray the lives of people buried in a particular location. Many cemeteries also now have ceremonial events on or near certain anniversary dates related to the cemetery graves, when they light the cemetery with candle luminarias. Many of the National Cemeteries across the United States do this near Memorial Day.

If you want to get your students engaged in a fun and meaningful service-learning project, then seriously consider something like what the LSG students are doing. You will open many doors for your students, and it will directly affect not only the community in which they live but the rest of their lives as well.

Playing Well in Peoria

started this book with the notion of "gumption" and ended on a note of "justified optimism." There is space for both of them in your classroom.

A sign reading "Enter the school of your life" was affixed to my classroom door during the last couple of my years at West Springfield High School. It was a riff on some words I had read by Thomas Merton, the twentieth-century American monastic and writer. School is a place where life unfolds, and the students in front of us every day are having an experience. There is no better way to have a history experience than by either "doing it" or being somewhere that history happened. David McCullough argues in his book *1776* that the greatest teachers George Washington ever had were his "experiences." Our experiences mold us and shape us. In a variety of ways, we are the sum of our experiences, both individually and as a nation.

There is the American idiom from the age of vaudeville, "How does it play in Peoria?" I sometimes get teased about this since it often appears that most American history took place east of the Mississippi River. So, I decided to test the idiom in a phone interview with Robert Killion, curator of the Peoria Historical Society in Peoria, Illinois. Killion believes it is important for schools and public history institutions to form bonds. "I want to partner with local schools as much as possible," he tells me. "There are all kinds of opportunities for our organization to help schools engage with students and teachers."

In 1854, Abraham Lincoln gave an important speech in Peoria, in which he famously said, "I was losing interest in politics, when the repeal of the Missouri Compromise roused my interests again." Here is a local story that had national implications. It put Lincoln on the road to the White House.

Teachers in Peoria could consider making a vodcast, like I have discussed in this book, about that story. Peoria's District 150, a school district with many students of color and many who are on free and reduced-price lunch, could—with a bit of funding and under the leadership of an inspired group of teachers and administrators—make this happen. And if there is anything that the Broadway show *Hamilton* has demonstrated, white characters from American history don't have to always be played by white actors or actresses.

Killion desperately wants to work with local teachers. The Peoria Riverfront Museum, a partner of the Peoria Historical Society and an affiliate of the Smithsonian, has published a catalog through the Smithsonian titled *Places of Invention,* which uses case studies to examine innovations all over the United States. In Peoria, teachers have a terrific resource on which to lean. Consider reading the catalog yourself for inspiration.

The winds of the last twenty years of standardized testing may finally be waning, which provides hope for teachers. In April 2016, as part of its centennial celebration, the National Park Service held an education summit, "Learning from the Outside In." Among the goals of the event were to celebrate the National Park Service's 100-year commitment to enhancing America's civic, cultural, and scientific literacy and its pledge to continue supporting these goals in its second century; to help policy makers, and the public at large, understand the importance of an expanded learning landscape, one that equally values and supports the learning that goes on in and out of school; to reshape the definition of public education in America as an education ecosystem that includes lifelong learning in a variety of settings; and to initiate the defining of a collaborative vision for the National Park Service and partner agencies, institutions, and organizations that help reenvision and reshape public education in twenty-first-century America. Building a shared understanding of what it means to make education a kind of ecosystem—discussing the challenges and opportunities facing a national redefinition of the lifelong learning landscape while developing an initial set of action plans for coordinating activities and outcomes in support of making that landscape more cohesive, synergistic, and functional—is at the core of what the National Park Service wants to see happen as we move through the twenty-first century.

In 1968, Thomas Merton had an epiphany on the corner of Fourth and Walnut in Louisville, Kentucky, which he wrote about in his book *Conjectures of a Guilty Bystander.*

The Commonwealth of Kentucky thought Merton's writing was so important that they later raised a state historic marker on the spot. Essentially Merton relates how, in that moment, he fell in love with all of humanity. He ends his epiphany with the statement, "There is no way of telling people that they are all walking around shining like the sun."

If you are reading this book, I presume you want to be in your own way Mertonesque. You want to be a good teacher, you want, in your work, to bring the best out of your students, yourself, and your colleagues. I hope you can use the ideas in this book to help transform your students into deeper thinkers, and I hope you are able to use the Journey Through Hallowed Ground to help take yourself and your students on journeys that neither of you will ever forget.

Afterword

rue to form, Jim Percoco has written another useful teacher resource book, this one designed to bring historic sites into the classroom. In the process, he convincingly builds a case for the importance of location, in addition to time, as a crucial element in teaching and learning history. Jim's teaching philosophy, "an active, hands-on, integrated approach to the subject," is articulated in such a way that teachers anywhere can replicate his lessons in their own curricula. Tying his lessons to content related to the Journey Through Hallowed Ground, Jim offers teachers a refreshing way to teach American history while embracing all that our national parks have to offer.

The lessons in *Take the Journey* are focused on the Journey Through Hallowed Ground National Heritage Area, an area along the East Coast. Teachers within the boundaries of the area or in surrounding environs can employ the lessons and take their students on field trips to various sites. But it is important to point out that, in this era when we have seen numerous schools cut funding for field trips, teachers still can teach their students about the importance of place by using the documents and visuals of the lessons. The same can be said for teachers outside the Heritage Area. Wherever they may teach—in states around the country, in international and Department of Defense schools overseas—teachers will have the means to teach standard and required parts of the American history curriculum (e.g., colonial and early American or Civil

War history) in a way that will excite their students, even if they cannot see the sites up close and personal.

What is probably most useful for teachers well outside of the Heritage Area is the modeling that is evident in Jim's lessons. The lesson methodology is replicable to other eras and historic places. This is true, in fact, of all of Jim's helpful books and lessons. His work serves as a model for teacher use regardless of topic, content, or place. He notes, in Chapter 1, that although his lesson on the Racial Integrity Act of 1924 "is in many ways a piece of local history, it has national implications." This is a good example of how a teacher in, say, Arizona could use the same lesson formula but focus on a local example while tying the topic to a national movement. "Think globally, act locally" certainly applies here.

Jim also makes the case for teaching difficult topics and how to approach them with students. Jim has never been one to shy away from controversial topics. He warns against showing bias and urges teachers to allow students to work through difficult themes by allowing them to ask questions and draw their own conclusions after they conduct their own research. If Jim shows any bias himself, it is his emphasis on student-centered teaching via teacher-student partnerships. This is particularly evident in Chapter 1, in which he outlines both a physical (i.e., actually going to a site) and a pedagogical approach.

What permeates all of the lessons in *Take the Journey*, as well as all of Jim's work, is teaching history in such a way that allows "young people [to] make informed choices as they read and reflect on our history." In so doing, students take ownership of their learning and show a greater interest in finding out more. When taught in this way, students are likely to "like" history. National History Day (NHD) and "History Clubs and their proliferation are living proof" of that.

Teachers who are interested in encouraging their students to go further with their projects can involve the students in the National History Day program. Like Jim's mission, NHD is designed to improve the way in which history is taught and learned by making the past come alive. NHD invites students in sixth through twelfth grades to choose a topic in history related to an annual theme, and conduct extensive research before presenting their material in creative formats. Past themes have included *Taking a Stand in History, Triumph & Tragedy in History, Innovation in History,* and *Leadership & Legacy in History,* among others. Students dig deeply into primary materials at archives and museums, conduct oral history interviews, and use critical thinking skills to draw conclusions about their topic's impact in history. They then develop presentations in the form of original papers, table-top exhibits, documentaries, performances, or websites. This type of approach is very similar to the Of the Student, By the Student, For the Student vodcast project, explained in a step-by-step approach in Chapter 5.

Teachers who *Take the Journey* will take their students down a road of discovery and find the path fascinating and fun. To continue the journey on their own, students can become more deeply involved in their topics after the classroom lesson is over by engaging in NHD.

Cathy Gorn
Executive director, National History Day

Appendixes

Eugenics in Relation to the New Family (entire pamphlet)

EUGENICS

in relation to

The New Family

and the law on

Racial Integrity

Including a paper read before the
American Public Health Association

Second Edition

Issued by the

BUREAU OF VITAL STATISTICS
STATE BOARD OF HEALTH
RICHMOND, VA.

Richmond:
Davis Bottom, Supt. Public Printing
1924

INTRODUCTION

THE VIRGINIA BUREAU OF VITAL STATISTICS, as a part of its duties is endeavoring so far as its means will permit to make a genetic and racial study of the population in order that it may inform law makers and others regarding existing dangers and their remedies, and that it may so far as it is able with the instruments already in its hands, combat these dangers, hoping for more effective means in the future.

But our chief hope is that the public may speedily become aroused to the danger and be led to unite in an effort to remove it.

To aid that purpose, this, the fourth of the New Family series of booklets, is sent out with the hope that it will be read by the young people of our schools and colleges, and by others who are, or will be, our leaders in thought.

It contains, besides a brief reference to the subject of eugenics, a paper read before the American Public Health Association, with a copy of the 1924 act of the

1

Virginia legislature, known as the "Racial Integrity" law.

All are invited to request the Bureau of Vital Statistics to mail without cost the other booklets, "The New Family," "Feeding the New Family," and "Bread for the New Family."

Second Edition

Owing to the unusual demand for this booklet by high schools, colleges, physicians, dentists, ministers and others, the first edition of 35,000 was exhausted within a few weeks and this second edition of 30,000 is issued.

Virginia teachers are specially requested to ask for their quota for older pupils.

A number of teachers of biology and sociology in other states, chiefly in the North, have requested them for their classes. Hundreds of letters of approval have been received.

W. A. PLECKER, M. D.,
State Registrar.

Richmond, Va.,
708 State Office Building,
March, 1925.

2

EUGENICS

Eugenics is the science of improving stock whether human or animal.

That there is a growing interest in this subject is shown by the frequent inquiries addressed to those of us who are supposed to be familiar with it, by thoughtful young persons as well as by those of more mature years.

When we consider the immense importance of the question of establishing a new family by marriage, the desire for such information should be supplied, and, when not sought, should be offered to the young by teachers, health officials and others whose duty it is to guide their thoughts and studies.

It is with that duty in mind that this booklet is prepared and it is hoped that all who can profit by this knowledge themselves or who can pass it on to others will spare the time necessary to read and consider carefully the pages that follow.

The principles of eugenics as we know them now are primarily few and simple and may be easily grasped by even superficial thinkers, but if developed to their limit may demand the deepest study and the research of the ablest minds.

Eugenics may be wisely applied by the young man or young woman when consid-

3

ering marriage, the greatest and most important of human relations, or it may be applied by statesmen, law makers and others who are responsible for the future of the State and welfare of the race.

As these objects are dependent upon the composition of the individual families, it is necessary that those who have the preservation and improvement of the most valuable race stocks as their chief purpose, should guide the thoughts and actions of the young into the proper channels.

The science of eugenics is based upon the principle that like begets like and that qualities and traits of various kinds either good or bad are passed on from parent to child, though we cannot always predict the exact result.

Applying the observations made upon animal life and man, we will find that a certain characteristic of mind as well as of body is dominant and perpetuates its kind with a great degree of regularity.

If two white hens are mated to a black male, one will have chicks all black, the male being dominant as to color, while the other will raise all or nearly all white ones, the female being dominant. If she is not wholly dominant some of her chicks will be black.

Exactly this condition exists when white and black human beings are mated. The black may appear to be bred out of the family, but according to the rule of reversion

4

a black child will appear though both parents may seem white and neither be conscious of any black blood on either side.

Many deformities, such as harelip, club-foot, six fingers and other characteristics as color of eyes, hair and skin, are thus passed on from parent to child, but will not show in every offspring unless both parents have by inheritance the same peculiarity.

While it is therefore always undesirable to marry into a family any member of which is a physical or mental defective, the danger is greatly increased when this trait exists on both sides.

That is why intermarriage of family connections for generations may develop a certain defect until it becomes almost constant.

In the same manner a desirable characteristic may be developed when there are no harmful ones to offset it, and intermarriage of cousins may be free from objection.

In making practical application of the principles of heredity within the same race there is nothing that may be more certainly foreseen than the disastrous results of feeble-minded individuals being permitted to marry or bear children.

As such persons are apt to be attractive only to those of the same type, their children are almost sure to be of the same or worse kind.

5

Insanity, tendency to crime, and immorality are also almost surely transmitted to their children, especially when, as is frequently the case, both parents are of the same class.

We have in various parts of our State family groups of this kind. In one county are people bearing two or three family names, all closely related and of white and black racial mixture. These furnish nearly all of the criminals, moonshiners and women of low morals for the county. As other families do not intermarry with them, the only foreign strains introduced are out of wedlock, and this is all too frequent.

The worst forms of undesirables born amongst us are those when parents are of different races.

Stockbreeders have learned that the offspring of greatly different breeds are inferior to either parent, and that it is not wise to perpetuate such strains. This is likewise true with man.

The variation in races is not simply a matter of color of skin, eyes, and hair and facial and bodily contour, but goes through every cell of the body.

The mental and moral characteristics of a black man cannot even under the best environments and educational advantages become the same as those of a white man. But even if the negro's attainments should be considerable, these could not be transmitted to his offspring since personally ac-

6

quired qualities are not inheritable. Neither can the descendants of the union of the two races if left to their own resources, be expected to develop or maintain the highest type of civilization.

Virginia has therefore acted wisely when through her legislature she has declared that no white person shall intermarry with one containing a trace of any other than white blood.

It is a deplorable fact that while Virginia is making this attempt at race preservation, the District of Columbia and nineteen northern States permit the free intermarriage of the races, the situation being the worst in the northwest.

Dr. Frederick L. Hoffman, in Eugenics in Race and State, Volume II, 1923, quotes Professor A. E. Jenks, of the University of Minnesota, who with an assistant made a study of the racial intermixture by marriage in St. Paul—Minneapolis. Professor Jenks, describing a club says: "This club is known as the 'Manassas Club' and has about 200 members in the twin cities, its only rule for eligibility being that the negro seeking admission have a white wife."

The only objection raised to this horrible situation, says Professor Jenks, "is raised by the black women, whose chief objection is that such marriages deprive a black girl of the opportunity of marrying a worthy black man."

But the author adds:

7

"The white women associated with this society do not constitute a social loss to the white population, for they are a worthless and degraded set of human beings, mostly Swedish or German, or otherwise foreign born."

Prevention of Race Deterioration

This is the greatest problem that confronts our Nation and is one that will not be satisfactorily answered till the young people in our high schools and colleges are taught to realize its enormity, and be ready to meet the situation when they enter upon the active duties of life.

As each young man and young woman is the prospective head of a new family each one should use his or her highest reasoning faculties, when selecting a life mate.

See by careful investigation that you are not marrying into a family containing members who are hereditarily defective physically, mentally, or morally. Remember that the 200,000 feeble-minded persons in the United States furnish one-fourth of our criminals, forty per cent of our abandoned women, and half of the inmates of our almshouses.

If every intelligent young person will follow this advice and will live in accordance with the known principles of good health outlined in the other of the New Family booklets, we may expect in the next generation to have in our State a large

8

body of Virginians strong in body, mind and character, capable of overcoming difficulties at home, and of influencing the Nation to push to a successful finish the reforms necessary to fit us to fill the place as leader of the nations of the world.

At present the most urgent task before us is to suppress the shameful intermixture of the races which has been going on practically unchecked and which will mean our future downfall if not controlled permanently and effectually.

The new Racial Integrity law will stop the greater part of the legal intermixture by marriage, but only a more wholesome mode of thought and conduct on the part of our young men can stop the intermixture now going on out of wedlock.

To attain this result there can be but one standard of morals for the young man and his sister.

When the time comes that our young women demand this, we will be on the real road to race preservation.

Let the young men who read this realize that the future purity of our race is in their keeping, and that the joining of themselves to females of a lower race and fathering children who shall be a curse and a menace to our State and civilization is a crime against society, and against the purity and integrity of their future homes and the happiness of their future loved ones and of themselves.

9

For those who cannot be reached by the appeal of duty, the State should step in and declare such an act a crime, worthy of the same punishment meted out to a thief or robber.

When the organ peals out the wedding march and the betrothed couple marches slowly up the aisle, the person of romantic turn of mind will wonder if love is the crowning motive of this union.

The practical man of affairs will estimate as to the bridegroom's financial standing and ability to maintain a family. The society woman will wish to know if they are social equals and into what class will they fit. The patriotic scientist who loves his State and longs to see her peopled with the best possible stock, will revolve in his mind as to their fitness physically, mentally and spiritually to become the heads of another one of the State's families. He will wonder whether or not they will be prompted by selfish motives only, caring naught for more than their own comfort and pleasure, or will they be willing to perform their part in the world and leave two sturdy descendants to fill their own places, two more to replace the natural loss by death and to make up for the neighboring couple which has none, these being the four children needed to each family merely to maintain the present population. Then he knows that there must still be some extra ones coming from this family or from some others, who must furnish the natural increase which the State expects to maintain, and he secretly hopes that the splendid couple standing at the altar will not disappoint him.

That our choicest young people may not be lacking in the stamina and courage to measure up to the expectations of this thoughtful man, is the earnest hope of the writer.

The one thing of which we may be sure is that the feeble-minded, paupers and the otherwise undesirables, will do more than their part, in imposing their kind as a burden upon the State.

In one large community of negro-Indian-white intermixture, they have practiced close inbreeding for generations until many undesirable traits have become accentuated. Illiteracy and immorality are general, but families of ten and twelve children are the rule.

With families two or three times the size of those of the white people amongst whom they live, they are by mere natural increase crowding out the more desirable population, and are becoming a serious problem in the part of the State in which they live.

10

11

VIRGINIA'S ATTEMPT TO ADJUST THE COLOR PROBLEM*

By W. A. PLECKER, *State Registrar of Vital Statistics, Richmond, Virginia.*

The landing of English colonists on Jamestown Island in Virginia in 1607, marked the inauguration of perhaps the most important undertaking in the history of mankind. It meant that Anglo-Saxon civilization was no longer to be confined to the British Isles, but that a new land surpassing in area and resources the rest of the white world, was then being claimed for English speaking people, ultimately to become the greatest nation the sun had ever shone upon.

While the Cavaliers and Scotch of Virginia, the Puritans of Massachusetts, the Dutch of New York, the Quakers and Germans of Pennsylvania, or the Huguenots of the South never perhaps in their wildest dreams imagined what their little colonies would within three centuries become, they did know that they were bringing to America the best that the world could then offer.

They came, not as did the Spanish and Portuguese adventurers of the southern continent, without their women, bent only on conquest and the gaining of wealth and power; but they came bringing their families, the Bible, and high ideals of religious and civic freedom.

They came to make homes, to create a nation, and to found a civilization of the highest type, not to mix their blood with the savages of the land, not to originate a mongrel population combining the worst traits of both conquerors and conquered, with the subsequent mixture of a third still lower element transported from Africa, as was done by the men from the Hispanic Peninsula.

These hardy pioneers defending themselves against the cunning savages of the land, set earnestly to the task of building their humble habitations clearing the forests, and planting their crops.

Thus far all was well until that fateful day in 1619, when a Dutch trader landed twenty negroes and sold them to the settlers, who hoped by means of slave labor to clear the land and develop the colony more quickly.

Few paused to consider the enormity of the mistake until it was too late. From this small beginning developed the great slave traffic which continued until 1808, when the importation of slaves into America was stopped. But there were already enough negroes in the land to constitute them the great American problem.

In the past a grave misapprehension ob-

*Read before the American Public Health Association, at Detroit, October 23, 1924.

12

13

tained and indeed still persists conerning the negro problem. Jefferson, Madison, Lincoln, Webster and other far seeing statesmen knew that the problem was not slavery, but the presence of the negro in what should be a white man's land.

They knew that the only solution of the problem was the return of the negro to his native home. But for Lincoln's tragic death, his colonization scheme might have become a reality.

Let us consider the problem as it really exists.

Two races as materially divergent as the negro in morals, mental powers, and cultural fitness, cannot live in close contact without injury to the higher, amounting in many cases to absolute ruin. The lower never has been and cannot be, raised to the level of the higher.

This statement is not an opinion based on sentiment or prejudice, but is an indubitable scientific fact. Recently published ethnological studies of history lead to this conclusion, as do the psychologic tests of negro and negroid groups, especially the U. S. Army tests made under the World War draft. It is evident that in the hybrid mixture the traits of the more primitive will dominate those of the more specialized or civilized race. It is equally obvious that these culturally destructive characters are hereditary, carried in the germ plasm, and hence cannot be influenced by environ-

14

mental factors such as improved economic, social and educational opportunities. On the contrary, such opportunities often accelerate the inevitable decadence. Dr. A. H. Estabrook, in a recent study for the Carnegie Institute, of a mixed group in Virginia, many of whom are so slightly negroid as to be able to pass for white, says: "School studies and observations of some adults indicate the group as a whole to be of poor mentality, much below the average, probably D or D— on the basis of the army intelligence tests. There is an early adolescence with low moral code, high incidence of licentiousness and twenty-one per cent of illegitimacy in the group."

Not only do the most enlightened modern authorities recognize negro inferiority and the danger of amalgamation, but leading Americans in the past also, until the issue was confused by being thrown into politics, saw clearly the possibility of disaster to our institutions and culture. Surely no one could maintain that Abraham Lincoln was influenced by race prejudice or unfriendly motives toward the negro. Even in the heat of the political discussion of slavery he saw clearly. Hear what he said at Charleston, Illinois, September 18, 1858: "I will say then, that I am not, nor ever have been, in favor of bringing about in any way the political and social equality of the white and black races—that I am not, nor ever have been, in favor of mak-

15

ing voters or jurors of negroes, nor of qualifying them to hold office, nor to intermarry with white people; and I will say in addition to this that there is a physical difference between the white and black races which I believe will forever forbid the two races living together on terms of social and political equality. And inasmuch as they cannot so live, while they do remain together, there must be the position of superior and inferior, and I, as much as any other man, am in favor of having the superior position assigned to the white man."

When two races live together there is but one possible outcome, and that is the amalgamation of the races. The result of this will be the elimination of the higher type, the one on which progress depends. In the mixture the lower race loses its native good qualities which may be utilized and developed in the presence of a dominant race.

The mongrels are superior in mental power to the lower race. They are more cunning and more capable, but they lack the creative power of the higher race, and cannot sustain a lasting civilization that will rank with the best of the world.

History affords many examples.

Egypt in the day of her greatness was white. But the white Pharaohs began to extend their dominion south into the negro land, and to bring back multitudes of cap-

16

tives for laborers and soldiers, special mention being made also in their records that women in large numbers were included.

Interbreeding with these negroes began and continued through many centuries until the country became largely negroid.

The climax was finally reached when one of the Pharaohs took to himself a negro wife, his mulatto son, Taharka, succeeding to the throne. The color line had vanished and with it Egypt's greatness.

Assyrian invaders met with no effective resistance. From that day to this Egypt has been a mongrel nation, incapable of initiative, and now dependent upon foreign protection and leadership.

India affords a parallel example. Four thousand years ago the invasion of India by Aryans occurred. These came into contact with a mixed population of white-yellow-black composition.

The conquerors attempted to prevent their own amalgamation with the natives by establishing a rigorous caste system which was not, like the present one, based upon occupation but on color. This system failed and though caste is still in force in India, the reason for it no longer exists.

Modern South Africa is a melancholy example of what may occur when the intermixture, which inevitably results, is hastened by fanatical religious teaching and misguided legal interference from the mother country. Major E. S. Cox, who

17

spent years in that region and other countries studying race conditions, gives a graphic account in his book, "White America,"* of the struggle made by the determined colonists against the imposition. They lost out, and the population of Cape Colony province is today largely mixed, showing how quickly this condition results when the natural process is speeded up by negrophilism and by the law.

Let us return now to our own country, and, as we are considering Virginia, to that State in particular.

There are about 12,000,000 negroes of various degrees of admixture in the Union today. Of the population of Virginia, nearly one-third is classed as negro, but many of these people are negroid, some being near-white, some having actually succeeded in getting across into the white class.

The mixed negroes are nearly all the result of illegitimate intercourse. The well known moral laxity, resulting from close contact of a civilized with a primitive race, makes illegitimate intermixture an easy matter. This is illustrated by the fact that the illegitimate birth-rate of Virginia negroes is thirty-two times that of Rhode Island, while the District of Columbia rate is thirty-seven times, and that of Maryland is forty-six times the Rhode Island rate.

In the days when slavery was still a

*White America Society, Richmond, Va.

18

blight upon our State, it was quite a common occurrence for young white men or bachelor slave owners to father children born to the negro servants.

The history as related to me of at least one colony of people known as "Issue" or "Free Issue," which have now spread over several counties is that they originated in part in that manner.

It was considered undesirable to retain these mulattoes on the place, bearing the family name, and a number from one county were given their freedom and colonized in a distant county. These intermarried amongst themselves and with some people of Indian-negro-white descent, and received an additional infusion of white blood, either illegitimately or by actual marriage with low-grade whites.*

At present these people are claiming to be white, or Indian, and under the former law, when a person with one-sixteenth negro blood could be declared white, they were able in some instances to establish their claim legally.

These mixed breeds are not classed as white by the people of the community, and will not associate with the genuine negroes. Five hundred or more in number, they thus constitute a class of their own, and a serious problem in that county and others to which they migrate.

If refused classification as white, they claim to be Indian, and as such, have been

*See Appendix.

19

accepted in the birth reports to avoid listing them as white.

In a recent test case, the court, upon evidence submitted from our birth records reaching back to 1853, and from the testimony of old residents, decided that these people under the new "Racial Integrity" law, cannot be permitted to intermarry with whites.

Another large colony which extends over into North Carolina probably has a similar origin. We have also compromised with these, and accept certificates as Indians, which indicates to us that they are not white.

In another county are about forty descendants of an illegitimate mating of a negro man and white woman, four generations back. All of these have been succeeding in being classed as white, though under the new law our office has supplied clerks who issue marriage licenses, school authorities, Commonwealth's attorneys, physicians and local registrars with a complete family tree, with the injunction to class them as colored in the future.

Similar conditions exist in other localities, though not yet so far advanced. A case was recently discovered where a white man married a mulatto woman (probably in another State), and now has nine children, four of them being reported to our office as white. Investigation revealed the fact that two other women bearing the same

20

family name had mated with white men and were raising large families of children.

Another man whose birth was reported in 1878, both parents being registered as colored, had the court declare him a white man under the one-sixteenth law, married a white woman, and has four children reported as white by physicians.

The question of their color was referred to our office by the school authorities when the facts were discovered, and the white school advised not to receive them, under the new law, though they engaged a lawyer to assist them.

These examples illustrate the fact that even in Virginia, where the question of race and birth receive as much attention as anywhere in the country, the process of amalgamation is nevertheless going on, and in some localities is well advanced. Complete ruin can probably be held off for several centuries longer, but we have no reason to hope that we shall prove the one and only example in the history of the world, of two races living together without amalgamation.

In Mexico, much of South America and the West Indies, the process is practically complete, the mixture being Spanish or Portuguese, Indian and negro.

Some portions of southern Europe have undergone a similar admixture.

Immigrants from these lands to this country while really negroid, are classed as white.

21

Several South American countries, or portions of them, still retain a considerable degree of race purity, which is being maintained by European immigration.

The immigration law recently passed by our Congress will stop the legal admission of Mongolians and will check much of the negroid immigration from elsewhere in the old world, but does not prevent negro and negroid immigration from other parts of the western hemisphere. It is estimated that there are today from 500,000 to 750,000 Mexicans in the State of Texas alone, and that Mexicans compose more than half of the population of Arizona.

We come now to the question of solution of the problem.

There is but one absolute solution which is acceptable and feasible, and that the one advocated by Lincoln and other far seeing statesmen of the past, the separation of the races by gradual repatriation of the colored races. This measure is still possible, but the longer it is deferred the greater the task.

In the life time of some now living, we may expect the present twelve million colored population to increase to twenty or possibly thirty millions, and perhaps to one hundred millions during the next century, to say nothing of the prolific Mongolians who are already firmly established upon our western coast.

With this large population of people of

22

low ideals, and low standard of living, the white laboring population will be to that extent crowded out.

The white birth rate will be diminished by the presence of this low grade competition, and by the great effort of securing the means of maintaining a family up to the desired standard. This situation is said to exist already in the New England States, where the native American stock is decreasing in the presence of the more prolific new comers with low standards of living.

Those who advocate birth control and who are now besieging Congress to let down the bars for the free distribution of their teachings by mail, are already successfully reaching our native born intelligent, American stock, whose birth rate, even without such advice, is declining at a woeful rate.

They are failing utterly, and will always fail to reach the uneducated, the feeble-minded, the morons, the negroes, criminals and undesirables, who do not read and hear, and if they did, would not have foresight, self-denial, or fortitude to practice the methods advocated.

It is no small part of the duty of physicians and health workers to create a more healthy sentiment amongst our better people in reference to their duty to society in doing their part in raising families of healthy children, who can aid in maintaining our American civilization,

23

Laws are needed to prevent the increase of feeble-minded, morons and criminals by segregation or sterilization. These are the classes who do much toward furnishing us with our race problem.

Virginia has made the first serious attempt to stay or postpone the evil day when this is no longer a white man's country. Her recently enacted law "for the preservation of racial integrity" is, in the words of Major E. S. Cox, "the most perfect expression of the white ideal, and the most important eugenical effort that has been made during the past 4,000 years." Of course this law will not prevent the illegitimate mixture of the races, although a law requiring the father to share with the mother the responsibility of the birth would have a deterring effect. When more than one man is involved, all should be held equally responsible in sharing the cost, as is the case in Norway.

But it is possible to stop the legal intermixture, and that Virginia has attempted to do in the above mentioned law, which defines a white person as one with "no trace whatsoever of blood other than Caucasian," and makes it a felony punishable by confinement for one year in the penitentiary to make a wilfully false statement as to color.

Clerks are not to grant licenses for white persons to marry those with any trace of colored blood. It is needless to call attention to the sad plight of a white person who is thus imposed upon or of a white woman who under such circumstances would give birth to a child of marked negro characteristics, as will occur from time to time under Mendel's law.

This law places upon the office of the Bureau of Vital Statistics much additional work but we believe it will be a strong factor in preventing the intermarriage of the races and in preventing persons of negro descent from passing themselves off as white.

We are greatly encouraged by the interest and co-operation of physicians, local registrars, clerks, school authorities, the general public, and even the midwives. Our success during the first four months of the law in securing more accurate statements as to color on our birth certificates and in correcting previously existing errors is far beyond our expectation.

The States which now permit free intermarriage of the races, as listed in "American Marriage Laws," Russell Sage Foundation, New York, 1919, are: Connecticut, District of Columbia, Illinois, Iowa, Kansas, Maine, Michigan, Massachusetts, Minnesota, New Hampshire, New Jersey, New Mexico, New York, Ohio, Rhode Island, Pennsylvania, Vermont, Washington, Wisconsin and Wyoming. The most urgent need is the speedy adoption by these States and the District of Columbia of a law for-

24

25

bidding the intermarriage of the white and colored races.

We are all interested in reducing the death rate from preventable diseases, and of increasing our birth rates.

Is that, however, the only thought that may occupy the mind of health workers? Is it not of greater importance to the welfare of the State to give some thought to the quality and value of its future citizens, than to lavish all of its energies and money upon prolonging the lives and increasing the number of the unfit, who are already increasing far more rapidly than the more desirable?

The white race in this land is the foundation upon which rests its civilization, and is responsible for the leading position which we occupy amongst the nations of the world. Is it not, therefore, just and right that this race decide for itself what its composition shall be, and attempt, as Virginia has, to maintain its purity?

This is working no hardship and no injustice upon the other races, for the same effort tends at the same time to maintain the purity of their races as well.

That the mongrel races are liable to perpetuate the undesirable qualities of their constituent stocks, is abundantly demonstrated by a study of the larger and older of the mongrel groups in Virginia, as well as upon a study on a far larger scale in various other parts of the world.

26

The colored races therefore should be equally zealous in preventing both the legal and illegal admixture of the races.

We are glad to say that the true negro of Virginia is beginning to appreciate this point and is agreeing to the wisdom of this movement. Our chief trouble is with some of the near-white who are desirous of changing from the colored to the white class.

By firm adherence to the standard which has been set, we believe that it is possible within a reasonable time to secure through our office, an adjustment of the larger number of racial differences, and by constantly securing correction of our vital statistic records, and by stopping all further legal and much of the illegitimate intermixture, at least to hold the situation in check until Lincoln's real remedy can be adopted.

This, however, is but the beginning and our efforts will be of less avail until every State in the Union joins in the move to secure the best marriage laws possible, and a wholesome public sentiment on this, the most important of all questions confronting us as a nation.

Four hundred years ago there were nations whose ships sailed the waters of the world and whose armies and navies made England tremble with fear. They claimed continents as their own, they grew rich upon their vast trade in slaves, selling in a day thousands of them from one block.

27

These slaves have disappeared, not by transportation, but by assimilation.

Today families of the old type are rare, and these peoples are scarcely thought of in the councils of nations.

Today the eyes of the world are turned with envy upon us, and millions crave the privilege of landing upon our shores.

We are now engaged in a struggle more titanic, and of far more importance than that with the Central Powers, from which we have recently emerged.

Many scarcely know that the struggle which means the life or death of our civilization is now in progress, and are giving it no thought.

What odds will it make in the year 2500 or 3000 to the few Caucasic remnants of our present day Americans, when they look around upon the half billion brown skinned descendants of the races now occupying our land, whether the typhoid death rate of 1924 was one, or one hundred, per 100,000?

What they find in that day will depend upon how we of today think and act. The very existence of our race in that time is dependent upon the thought and action of us today. Let us then accept our responsibility and meet its demands with wisdom and courage.

Let us turn a deaf ear to those who would interpret Christian brotherhood to mean racial equality.

28

AN ACT TO PRESERVE RACIAL INTEGRITY

1. Be it enacted by the General Assembly of Virginia, That the State Registrar of Vital Statistics may as soon as practicable after the taking effect of this act, prepare a form whereon the racial composition of any individual, as Caucasian, negro, Mongolian, American Indian, Asiatic Indian, Malay, or any mixture thereof, or any other non-Caucasic strains, and if there be any mixture, then the racial composition of the parents and other ancestors, in so far as ascertainable, so as to show in what generation such mixture occurred, may be certified by such individual, which form shall be known as a registration certificate. The State Registrar may supply to each local registrar a sufficient number of such forms for the purposes of this act; each local registrar may personally or, by deputy, as soon as possible after receiving said forms, have made thereon in duplicate a certificate of the racial composition as aforesaid, of each person resident in his district, who so desires, born before June fourteenth, nineteen hundred and twelve, which certificate shall be made over the signature of said person, or in the case of children under fourteen years of age, over the signature of a parent, guardian, or other person

29

standing in *loco parentis*. One of said certificates for each person thus registering in every district shall be forwarded to the State Registrar for his files; the other shall be kept on file by the local registrar.

Every local registrar may, as soon as practicable, have such registration certificate made by or for each person in his district who so desires, born before June fourteen, nineteen hundred and twelve, for whom he has not on file a registration certificate, or a birth certificate.

2. It shall be a felony for any person wilfully or knowingly to make a registration certificate false as to color or race. The wilful making of a false registration or birth certificate shall be punished by confinement in the penitentiary for one year.

3. For each registration certificate properly made and returned to the State Registrar, the local registrar returning the same shall be entitled to a fee of twenty-five cents, to be paid by the registrant. Application for registration and for transcript may be made direct to the State Registrar, who may retain the fee for expenses of his office.

4. No marriage license shall be granted until the clerk or deputy clerk has reasonable assurance that the statements as to color of both man and woman are correct.

If there is reasonable cause to disbelieve that applicants are of pure white race, when that fact is stated, the clerk or deputy clerk

30

shall withhold the granting of the license until satisfactory proof is produced that both applicants are "white persons" as provided for in this act.

The clerk or deputy clerk shall use the same care to assure himself that both applicants are colored, when that fact is claimed.

5. It shall hereafter be unlawful for any white person in this State to marry any save a white person, or a person with no other admixture of blood than white and American Indian. For the purpose of this act, the term "white person" shall apply only to the person who has no trace whatsoever of any blood other than Caucasian; but persons who have one-sixteenth or less of the blood of the American Indian and have no other non-Caucasic blood shall be deemed to be white persons. All laws heretofore passed and now in effect regarding the intermarriage of white and colored persons shall apply to marriages prohibited by this act.

6. For carrying out the purposes of this act and to provide the necessary clerical assistance, postage and other expenses of the State Registrar of Vital Statistics, twenty per cent of the fees received by local registrars under this act shall be paid to the State Bureau of Vital Statistics, which may be expended by the said bureau for the purposes of this act.

31

7. All acts or parts of acts inconsistent with this act are, to the extent of such inconsistency, hereby repealed.

APPENDIX

Howe, in his history of Virginia, written in 1845, says: "There is the remnant of the Mattaponi tribe of Indians, now dwindled down to only fifteen or twenty souls. Further up on the Pamunkey, at what is called Indian Town, are about 100 descendants of the Pamunkeys. Their Indian character is nearly extinct, by intermixing with the whites and negroes." (Pages 349-350.)

The new history of Virginia, by Philip Alexander Bruce, LL. B., LL. D., of the University of Virginia, makes the same statement: "By this date, 1736, war, disease, and intemperance, had reduced the Indian tribes to very thin ranks. The Pamunkeys on York River could only show a roll of ten families. This was the remnant of Powhatan's powerful kingdom. (Vol. I, page 334.)

Alexander Francis Chamberlain, A. M., Ph. D., Assistant Professor of Anthropology. Clark University, Worcester, Massachusetts, in his article, Indians, North American, in the Encyclopaedia Britannica, Eleventh Edition, Vol. 14, pages 460, 464, says of the Chickahominy Indians: "No pure bloods left. Considerable negro admixture," and of the Pamunkeys: "All mixed-bloods; some negro mixture."

Page 468, he says: "In some regions considerable intermixture between negroes and Indians (Science, New York, Vol. XVII, 1891, pp. 85-90), has occurred, e. g., among the

Pamunkeys, Mattaponies and some other small Virginia and Carolinian tribes." "It is also thought probable that many of the negroes of the whole lower Atlantic coast and Gulf region may have strains of Indian blood." This probably accounts for the increasing number of negroes who are now writing to our Bureau demanding that the color on their birth certificates and marriage licenses be given as "Indian."

The Amherst-Rockbridge group is the most notable example.

John Garland Pollard, in his pamphlet "The Pamunkey Indians of Virginia," a Smithsonian publication, U. S. Bureau of Ethnology, 1894, says: "There has been considerable intermixture of white blood in the tribe, and not a little of that of the negro, though the laws of the tribe now strictly prohibit marriage to persons of African descent."

The Handbook of American Indians (Bulletin 30), Bureau of American Ethnology, under the heading "Croatan Indians," says: "The theory of descent from the lost colony may be regarded as baseless, but the name itself serves as a convenient label for a people who combine in themselves the blood of the wasted native tribes, the early colonists or forest rovers, the runaway slaves or other negroes, and probably also of stray seamen of the Latin races from coasting vessels in the West Indian or Brazilian trade.

Across the line in South Carolina are found a people, evidently of similar origin, designated "Redbones." In portions of western North Carolina and eastern Tennessee are found the so-called "Melungeons" (probably from French mélange, 'mixed') or "Portuguese," apparently an offshoot from Croatan proper, and in Delaware are found

32

the "Moors." All of these are local designations for peoples of mixed race with an Indian nucleus differing in no way from the present mixed-blood remnants known as Pamunkey, Chickahominy, and Nansemond Indians in Virginia, excepting in the more complete loss of their identity. In general, the physical features and complexion of the persons of this mixed stock incline more to the Indian than to the white or negro."

The same under "Mixed-bloods," says: "The Pamunkey, Chickahominy, Marshpee, Narraganset, and Gay Head remnants have much negro blood, and conversely there is no doubt that many of the broken coast tribes have been completely absorbed into the negro race."

It is believed that the group of mixed people of Halifax county, Virginia, are a part of the North Carolina "Croatans."

In several southwest Virginia counties we are meeting with families of Melungeons who have moved there from western North Carolina or Eastern Tennessee.

As we consider that all of these people are a composite race of negro, white and perhaps Indian mixture, they cannot be registered on birth and death certificates as white, nor can they under the Racial Integrity law be granted licenses to marry white persons.

APPENDIX 1.2
Template for State Historical Markers

Nat Turner's Rebellion: A Historical Marker

You have been commissioned by the state of Virginia Historical Trust to develop a historical marker that will be placed along the roadside adjacent to the area to the area impacted by Nat Turner and his followers. Your task is to develop the inscription for the marker that describes your interpretation of Nat Turner and his actions. Your inscriptions should take into account:

- The specific factors involved in the event
- The various reactions to Nat Turner (artistic, and other)

> ## NAT TURNER
>
> Here, Nat Turner, an African American slave, lead one of the first rebellions and opened the doors to many more. Turner was considered a phrophecy of God and his visions gave him the idea and courage to take on such an impossible task. Although Turner and his followers were killed, they still made an impact on the society and will forever be remembered as heroes.

Why I came to this decision (What documents most impacted your decisions and why?): I decided to portray Turner as a hero because what he did was very courageous. He took on an impossible task and although he did fail it made a big impact. People will always remember Turner as for leading one of the first slave rebellions and thats how he deserves to be remembered, not as insane. People do see Turner as insane because his motives and ideas seem questionable but all along he just wanted freedom and to help his people. cromwell and Gray's sources helped me come to this conclusion because cromwell knows the whole story and Gray was there with Turner interviewing him. Therefore, Nat Turner deserves to be remembered as a hero.

Historical Houses

Historical Houses

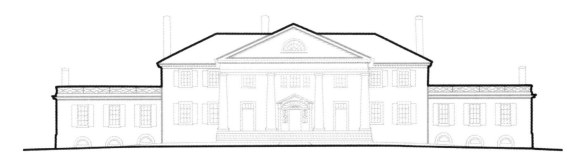

Montpelier

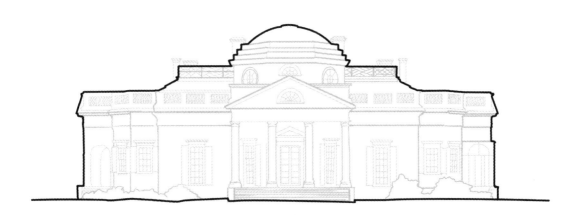

Monticello

Take the Journey: Teaching American History Through Place-Based Learning by James A. Percoco. Copyright © 2017. Stenhouse Publishers.

APPENDIX 2.2

Preamble to the Constitution

By Lorraine Griffith; adapted by Timothy Rasinski
A choral reading for a large group or a reader's theater for seven voices.

R1: The Constitution

R2: of the United States of America.

All: *We the people*

R1: The people:

R2: First the American Indian,

R3: then a flood of European immigrants,

R4: Africans,

R5: Middle Easterners,

R6: Asian peoples,

R7: South Americans

R1–R4: And they keep on coming.

All: *We the people of the United States,*

R1: The United States:

R2: All fifty!

R3: From Portland, Maine, west to San Diego, California,

R4: from Fargo, North Dakota, south to El Paso, Texas,

R5: Alaska and Hawaii

All: *We the people of the United States, in order to form a more perfect Union,*

R6: That Union seemed perfect. All of the colonies became states as well as the territories to the west,

Take the Journey: Teaching American History Through Place-Based Learning by James A. Percoco. Copyright © 2017. Stenhouse Publishers.

R7: until the Southern states seceded because they wanted states' rights.

R1: But the Civil War ended with a more perfect union of states based upon the belief that all Americans deserved the right to life, liberty, and the pursuit of happiness.

All: *We the people of the United States, in order to form a more perfect Union, establish justice,*

R2: Even before the established United States, justice was valued.

R3: John Adams actually defended the British in court after they had attacked and killed colonists during the Boston Massacre. Although he didn't believe in the British cause, he still believed justice was more important than retribution.

R4: Justice was ensured for Americans by following the fairness of John Adams in establishing a court system, beginning with local courthouses and moving up to the Supreme Court in Washington, DC.

All: *We the people of the United States, in order to form a more perfect Union, establish justice, insure domestic tranquility,*

R5: There have been times when our nation's tranquility has been disturbed.

R6: But in spite of Pearl Harbor, December 7, 1941,

R7: and the horror in New York City, Washington, DC, and Pennsylvania, on September 11, 2001,

All: we still live in a stable and peaceful country.

All: *We the people of the United States, in order to form a more perfect Union, establish justice, insure domestic tranquility, provide for the common defense,*

R2: The air force. No one comes close! Soar to new heights in the wild blue yonder!

All: Nothing can stop the US Air Force!

R3: The army. Be all you can be! Be an army of one!

All: Hoo-ahh!

R4: The navy. Welcome aboard;

All: Anchors aweigh! Full speed ahead!

R1: The Coast Guard, protecting America. It's our job every day!

All: Semper Paratus. Always ready.

R5: And the marines. The few, the proud.

All: Semper Fi!

We the people of the United States, in order to form a more perfect Union, establish justice, insure domestic tranquility, provide for the common defense, promote the general welfare,

R7: People's basic needs must be met in a country.

R5: Needs for housing, education, transportation, and health care are overseen by our government system.

R6: Labor laws ensure that people work in safe environments and that they are paid fairly for the work they do.

All: *We the people of the United States, in order to form a more perfect Union, establish justice, insure domestic tranquility, provide for the common defense, promote the general welfare, and secure the blessings of liberty to ourselves.*

R1: Jefferson's promise of life, liberty, and the pursuit of happiness came later for many of the peoples of our nation.

R2: African Americans did not share the rights of whites by law until the Fourteenth Amendment in 1868.

R3: Women did not share in the rights of men to vote or own property until 1920, when the Suffrage Act was ratified.

R4: But people all around the world still look to the United States as the land of liberty for all.

All: *We the people of the United States, in order to form a more perfect Union, establish justice, insure domestic tranquility, provide for the common defense, promote the general welfare, and secure the blessings of liberty to ourselves and our posterity,*

R1: That's you and me!

R2–R3: And our children!

R4–R5: And our children's children.

R6–R7: And their children, too!

All: *We the people of the United States, in order to form a more perfect Union, establish justice, insure domestic tranquility, provide for the common defense, promote the general welfare, and secure the blessings of liberty to ourselves and our posterity, do ordain and establish this Constitution for the United States of America.*

R5: The Constitution of the United States of America has stood the test of time.

R6: Although it was signed on September 17, 1787, it still stands as a ruling document of laws, ensuring the rights and liberties that we still enjoy today.

R7: And so, let us proclaim once again for all the world to hear . . .

R1: The preamble to the Constitution of the United States of America.

R2–R3: We the people of the United States,

R2–R5: in order to form a more perfect Union,

R2–R6: establish justice, insure domestic tranquility,

R2–R7: provide for the common defense, promote the general welfare,

All: *and secure the blessings of liberty, to ourselves and our posterity, do ordain and establish this Constitution for the United States of America.*

Take the Journey: Teaching American History Through Place-Based Learning by James A. Percoco. Copyright © 2017. Stenhouse Publishers.

APPENDIX 2.3
The Declaration of Independence

Adapted by Timothy Rasinski

A reader's theater for six voices: three narrators (N) and three readers of the Declaration of Independence (D)

N1: This is the story

N2: of the birth of the

N1–N3: United States of America.

N2: At one time the United States was made up of colonies of Great Britain. However, people in the colonies began to feel that the king of Great Britain was exerting more control over them than they felt was warranted.

N2–N3: Colonists began to call for the separation of the North American colonies from Great Britain. They began to call for independence.

N3: The king had imposed on the colonies laws and taxes that the colonists felt were unfair.

N1–N3: The king had also ignored petitions, or requests, from the colonies that their grievances be heard.

N1: And so, one by one, the various colonies began to demand independence from Great Britain. By May 1776, eight colonies had decided that they would support independence.

N2: On May 15, 1776, the largest colony, Virginia, resolved that

N2–N3: *"The delegates appointed to represent this colony in General Congress be instructed to propose to that respectable body to declare the United Colonies free and independent states."*

N3: The Continental Congress was the governing body of the thirteen colonies. It met a few weeks later in Philadelphia. On June 7, Richard Henry Lee of Virginia read this resolution to the Continental Congress:

N1: *"Be it resolved: That these United Colonies are, and of right ought to be, free and independent States, that they are absolved from all*

Take the Journey: Teaching American History Through Place-Based Learning by James A. Percoco. Copyright © 2017. Stenhouse Publishers.

allegiance to the British Crown, and that all political connection between them and the State of Great Britain is, and ought to be, totally dissolved."

N2: A committee of five members was then formed to create a written statement of freedom from Great Britain.

N3: The members of the committee consisted of two men from New England: John Adams from Massachusetts and Roger Sherman from Connecticut;

N1: Two representatives from the middle colonies: Robert Livingston of New York and Benjamin Franklin from Pennsylvania;

N2: And one Southerner: Thomas Jefferson from Virginia.

N3: Jefferson was given the primary task of writing the document.

N1: By the end of June, Jefferson had completed his declaration. It was sent to the Continental Congress on July 1.

N2: There was some discussion and revision to the declaration.

N3: And, although the independence that the colonies sought was not totally realized until several years later,

N1: the declaration began a new country whose history is still being written today—our country,

N1–N3: The United States of America.

N2: On July 4, 1776, the declaration was adopted by the Continental Congress. Church bells throughout Philadelphia rang out in celebration as the declaration was read to the people.

D1–D3: *In Congress, July 4, 1776, the unanimous declaration of the 13 United States of America:*

D2: (slowly and deliberately) *When in the course of human events, it becomes necessary for one people to dissolve the political bands which have connected them with another, and to assume among the powers of the earth, the separate and equal station to which the Laws of Nature and of Nature's God entitle them,*

D3: *a decent respect to the opinions of mankind requires that they should declare the causes which impel them to the separation.*

D1: *We hold these truths to be self-evident, that all men are created equal, that they are endowed by their Creator with certain unalienable Rights*

All: *That among these are Life, Liberty, and the pursuit of Happiness.*

D2: *That to secure these rights, Governments are instituted among Men, deriving their just powers from the consent of the governed.*

D1: *That whenever any Form of Government becomes destructive of these ends, it is the Right of the People to alter or abolish it and institute a new Government, laying its foundation on principles and organizing itself in a way that to them shall seem most likely to bring their Safety and Happiness.*

D3: *Prudence, indeed, will dictate that long established governments should not be changed for light and transient causes;*

D2: *But, when a long train of abuses reduces and oppresses the people, it is their right, it is their duty, to throw off such Government, and provide a new government for their future security.*

D1: *Such has been how the Colonies have suffered.*

D2: *And such is now the necessity which forces them to alter their former government.*

D3: *The history of the present King of Great Britain is a history of repeated injuries and taking of rights and liberties, all done to establish an absolute Tyranny over these States . . . .*

D1: *In every stage of these Oppressions, we have petitioned for redress in the most humble terms from the King.*

D2: *Our repeated petitions have been answered only by repeated injury.*

D3: *A Prince whose character is thus marked by acts that define a Tyrant, is unfit to be the ruler of a free people . . .*

D1: *We, therefore, the Representatives of the United States of America, in General Congress, assembled here,*

D2: *Appealing to the Supreme Judge of the world, do, in the Name, and by Authority of the good People of these Colonies, solemnly publish and declare*

D3: *That these United Colonies are, and of Right ought to be Free and Independent States,*

D2: *That they are absolved from all Allegiance to the British Crown,*

D1: *And that all political connection between them and the State of Great Britain, is and ought to be totally dissolved.*

D3: *And that as Free and Independent States, they have full Power to levy War, conclude Peace, contract Alliances, establish Commerce, and to do all other Acts and Things which Independent States may of right do.*

D1: *And for the support of this Declaration, with a firm reliance on the protection of divine Providence, we mutually pledge to each other our Lives, our Fortunes, and our sacred Honor.*

All: This is the story of the birth of the United States of America—our country.

My country, 'tis of thee,
Sweet land of liberty,
Of thee I sing;
Land where my fathers died,
Land of the pilgrims' pride,
From every mountainside,
Let freedom ring!

APPENDIX 2.4

Handout A: Black Panther Party—Ten Point Program

Handout A: Black Panther Party: Ten Point Program, What We Want, What We Believe—October 15, 1966.

Also available online at <http://socialjustice.ccnmtl.columbia.edu/index.php/Black_Panther_Party_::_Ten-Point_Program>.

1. WE WANT FREEDOM. WE WANT POWER TO DETERMINE THE DESTINY OF OUR BLACK COMMUNITY.
We believe that Black people will not be free until we are able to determine our destiny.

2. WE WANT FULL EMPLOYMENT FOR OUR PEOPLE.
We believe that the federal government is responsible and obligated to give every man employment or a guaranteed income. We believe that if the White American businessmen will not give full employment, then the means of production should be taken from the businessmen and placed in the community so that the people of the community can organize and employ all of its people and give a high standard of living.

3. WE WANT AN END TO THE ROBBERY BY THE CAPITALISTS OF OUR BLACK COMMUNITY.
We believe that this racist government has robbed us, and now we are demanding the overdue debt of forty acres and two mules. Forty acres and two mules were promised 100 years ago as restitution for slave labor and mass murder of Black people. We will accept the payment in currency which will be distributed to our many communities. The Germans are now aiding the Jews in Israel for the genocide of the Jewish people. The Germans murdered six million Jews. The American racist has taken part in the slaughter of over fifty million Black people; therefore, we feel that this is a modest demand that we make.

4. WE WANT DECENT HOUSING FIT FOR THE SHELTER OF HUMAN BEINGS.
We believe that if the White Landlords will not give decent housing to our Black community, then the housing and the land should be made into cooperatives so that our community, with government aid, can build and make decent housing for its people.

5. WE WANT EDUCATION FOR OUR PEOPLE THAT EXPOSES THE TRUE NATURE OF THIS DECADENT AMERICAN SOCIETY.
We Want Education That Teaches Us Our True History And Our Role In The Present-Day Society. We believe in an educational system that will give to our people a knowledge of self. If a man does not have knowledge of himself and his position in society and the world, then he has little chance to relate to anything else.

6. WE WANT ALL BLACK MEN TO BE EXEMPT FROM MILITARY SERVICE.
We believe that Black people should not be forced to fight in the military service to defend a racist government that does not protect us. We will not fight and kill other people of color in the world who, like Black people, are being victimized by the White racist government of America. We will protect ourselves from the force and violence of the racist police and the racist military, by whatever means necessary.

7. WE WANT AN IMMEDIATE END TO POLICE BRUTALITY AND MURDER OF BLACK PEOPLE.
We believe we can end police brutality in our Black community by organizing Black self-defense groups that are dedicated to defending our Black community from racist police oppression and brutality. The Second Amendment to the Constitution of the United States gives a right to bear arms. We therefore believe that all Black people should arm themselves for self- defense.

8. WE WANT FREEDOM FOR ALL BLACK MEN HELD IN FEDERAL, STATE, COUNTY AND CITY PRISONS AND JAILS.
We believe that all Black people should be released from the many jails and prisons because they have not received a fair and impartial trial.

9. WE WANT ALL BLACK PEOPLE WHEN BROUGHT TO TRIAL TO BE TRIED IN COURT BY A JURY OF THEIR PEER GROUP OR PEOPLE FROM THEIR BLACK COMMUNITIES, AS DEFINED BY THE CONSTITUTION OF THE UNITED STATES.
We believe that the courts should follow the United States Constitution so that Black people will receive fair trials. The Fourteenth Amendment of the U.S. Constitution gives a man a right to be tried by his peer group. A peer is a person from a similar economic, social, religious, geographical, environmental, historical and racial background. To do this the court will be forced to select a jury from the Black community from which the Black defendant came. We have been, and are being, tried by all-White juries that have no understanding of the "average reasoning man" of the Black community.

10. WE WANT LAND, BREAD, HOUSING, EDUCATION, CLOTHING, JUSTICE AND PEACE.
When, in the course of human events, it becomes necessary for one people to dissolve the political bands which have connected them with another, and to assume, among the powers of the earth, the separate and equal station to which the laws of nature and nature's God entitle them, a decent respect of the opinions of mankind requires that they should declare the causes which impel them to the separation.

We hold these truths to be self-evident, that all men are created equal; that they are endowed by their Creator with certain inalienable rights; that among these are life, liberty, and the pursuit of happiness. That, to secure these rights, governments are instituted among men, deriving their just powers from the consent of the governed; that, whenever any form of government becomes destructive of these ends, it is the right of the people to alter or abolish it, and to institute a new government, laying its foundation on such principles, and organizing its powers in such form, as to them shall seem most likely to effect their safety and happiness. Prudence, indeed, will dictate that governments long established should not be changed for light and transient causes; and, accordingly, all experience hath shown that mankind are more disposed to suffer, while evils are sufferable, than to right themselves by abolishing the forms to which they are accustomed. But, when a long train of abuses and usurpations, pursuing invariably the same object, evinces a design to reduce them under absolute despotism, it is their right, it is their duty, to throw off such government, and to provide new guards for their future security.

Yohuru Williams, "Was Thomas Jefferson a Black Panther?" *OAH Magazine of History*, Vol. 22 (3), July 2008: 37–38, by permission of Oxford University Press.

Handout B: Thomas Jefferson Quotations

Handout B:
Thomas Jefferson Quotations

"The most effectual means of preventing [the perversion of power into tyranny are] to illuminate, as far as practicable, the minds of the people at large, and more especially to give them knowledge of those facts which history exhibits, that possessed thereby of the experience of other ages and countries, they may be enabled to know ambition under all its shapes, and prompt to exert their natural powers to defeat its purposes."

–Thomas Jefferson: Diffusion of Knowledge Bill, 1779.

FE 2:221, Papers 2:526

"Above all things I hope the education of the common people will be attended to convinced that on their good sense we may rely with the most security for the preservation of a due degree of liberty."

–Thomas Jefferson to James Madison, 1787.

Madison Version FE 4:480. Available at <http://etext.virginia.edu/jefferson/quotations/jeff1350.htm>.

"A system of general instruction, which shall reach every description of our citizens from the richest to the poorest, as it was the earliest, so will it be the latest of all the public concerns in which I shall permit myself to take an interest."

–Thomas Jefferson to Joseph C. Cabell, 1818.

FE 10:102. Available at <http://etext.virginia.edu/jefferson/quotations/jeff1350.htm>. Madison Version FE 4:480.

"The earth is given as a common stock for man to labor and live on. If for the encouragement of industry we allow it to be appropriated, we must take care that other employment be provided to those excluded from the appropriation. If we do not, the fundamental right to labor the earth returns to the unemployed... It is not too soon to provide by every possible means that as few as possible shall be without a little portion of land. The small landholders are the most precious part of a state."

–Thomas Jefferson to James Madison, 1785.

ME 19:18, Papers 8:682. Available at <http://etext.virginia.edu/jefferson/quotations/jeff1350.htm>. Madison Version FE 4:480.

Yohuru Williams, "Was Thomas Jefferson a Black Panther?" *OAH Magazine of History*, Vol. 22 (3), July 2008: 37–38, by permission of Oxford University Press.

APPENDIX 2.6
History Time Line Template

Title _____ Date _____ Name _____

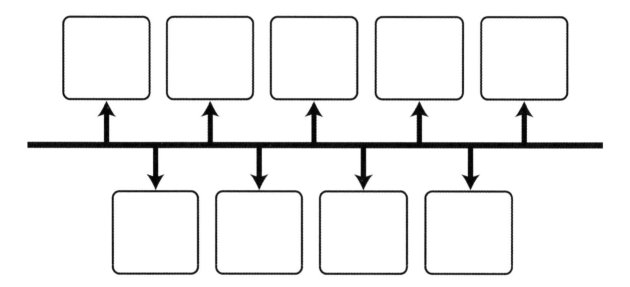

Script for *Ran Away*

Ran away, the mulatto wench Mary. Has a cut on the left arm, a scar on the left shoulder, and two upper teeth missing.

Ran away, a black girl named Mary. Has a scar on her cheek, and the end of one of her toes cut off.

Ran away, my mulatto woman Judy. She has had her right foot broke.

Ran away, Negress Caroline. Had on a collar, with one prong turned down.

Ran away, a black woman, Betsy. Had an iron bar on her right leg.

Ran away, the negress Fanny. Had on an iron band about the neck.

Ran away, a negro woman named Rachael. Has lost all her toes except the large one.

Ran away, a negro girl called Mary. Has a small scar over her eye, a good many teeth missing, the letter A is branded on her check and forehead.

Ran away, a negro woman named Maria. Has a scar on one side of her check, by a cut. Some scars on her back.

Ran away, negro slave Sally. Walks as though crippled in the back.

Ran away, a negro woman and two children. A few days before she went off, I burnt her with a hot iron, on the left side of her face. I tried to make the letter M.

Source: Charles Dickens (1842)

APPENDIX 4.1

Of the Student, By the Student, For the Student Curriculum Resource Guide

By Robin Meyers of the Journey Through Hallowed Ground Partnership

DIRECTORY

OF THE STUDENT, BY THE STUDENT, FOR THE STUDENT

OVERVIEW

The Of, By, For program is a groundbreaking National Service-Learning project created to connect students with the history in their backyard as they preserve it for future generations. How do we accomplish this? We immerse the students in the world of moviemaking. They become the researchers, the directors, the writers, the costume designers, the actors—they re-create history with their own hands, through their eyes, and on the very land where those monumental events occurred.

> I can't believe these soldiers walked this much and were lying on this ground.
>
> —Seventh-Grade Gettysburg Area Middle School Student (in reference to walking ten minutes through mud and shrubbery and witnessing the sheer number of voles that appeared from the ground)

It is after this real-life experience that the students begin to truly understand their movie is more than just a history lesson—it carries a message that runs deep into their heart because they are able to relate it to themselves as a student, as a family member, and as a citizen of their town and America.

> I think, today, we need to be more like the Black Ducks and not let fear stop us from standing up for something we think is important to us.
>
> —Seventh-Grade Gettysburg Area Middle School Student (in reference to the secret fraternity that helped runaway slaves, even when its members knew they could be jailed or even killed for helping out)

The Of, By, For program is a visionary tool to not only educate our future leaders of America, but help them understand the importance of their role in preserving history at a National Park or historic site. The program will plant a seed, and it will raise awareness of resources, attract younger visitors, and enrich the on-site experience. It is essential that this seed continue to be planted in each child—in turn, the reward for the National Parks, historical sites, community, student, and America will grow exponentially today, tomorrow, and for generations to come.

> I can't believe how awesome the Shriver home was. I went back with two of my friends and they thought it was so cool.
>
> —Seventh-Grade Gettysburg Area Middle School Student (the Shriver home is two blocks away from school, and none of the students had ever visited there till they started the Journey project)

THE GETTYSBURG MODEL: A RECIPE FOR SUCCESS

OVERVIEW

The Of, By, For Program began in 2006 with Harpers Ferry National Historical Park (HFNHP) and Harpers Ferry Middle School. A solid foundation was built, and each succeeding year brought a significant improvement to the program. In 2012/2013, a more refined model was created for the Gettysburg Area Middle School and the Gettysburg National Military Park, one that would serve as a guideline for all future National Parks and schools.

THE PHASES

Twelve phases make up the entire project from inception to completion.

PHASE 1—Building Support

PHASE 2—Technological Support

PHASE 3—Project Planning

PHASE 4—Kick-Off Assembly

PHASE 5—Immersion Day

PHASE 6—A Four-Day Pitch Presentation Workshop

PHASE 7—Pre-Production

PHASE 8—Production aka Principal Photography (Filming Day)

PHASE 9—Post-Production

PHASE 10—Marketing/Premiere Prep

PHASE 11—Premiere

PHASE 12—Project Analysis and Review

PHASE 1—BUILDING SUPPORT

Teamwork cannot be stressed enough with the students, but what about teamwork from the adults? The Gettysburg Model proved to be successful because of the supporting cast surrounding the students. The school may seek, but is not limited to, the following support:

- The National Park/Historical Sites
    - Park Rangers
    - Administration
    - Historical Site Owners
- School Administration
    - Principal and Assistant Principal
    - Office Faculty
    - Maintenance/Service Department
- School Faculty
    - Music and Theater Department
    - Technology/Media Department
    - Art and History Department
    - Other Departments
- The Community
    - Businesses (Students having access to props, materials, etc.)
    - Historians
- Partners
    - Local Filmmakers or Documentarians
    - Fund-Raising Partners
- The Parents
    - Parent donations of supplies or items possibly needed for filming day

PHASE 2—TECHNOLOGICAL SUPPORT

Once a strong foundation has been formed from the various parties listed above, the next step will require acquiring the right tools for the students to use. At minimum, the students will need access to the following:

	PC	MAC
Video/Audio Recording Device	Consumer HD video cameras or digital cameras capable of recording 720p (1080p recommended)	Same as PC or an iPAD capable of recording 720p (1080p recommended)
Computer	Any PC desktop or laptop with the following specifications: Monitor—1280x720 ratio or higher (1920x1080 or higher recommended) Hard drive—1 TB or higher Memory—2 GB or higher USB 2.0/3.0 Ports (4 or more) DVD or Blu-Ray Burner Keyboard/Mouse Sound Card Speaker/Headphone Jack	Any Mac desktop or laptop with the following specifications: Monitor—1280x720 ratio or higher (1920x1080 or higher recommended) Hard drive—1 TB or higher Memory—2 GB or higher USB 2.0/3.0 Ports (4 or more) DVD or Blu-Ray Burner Keyboard/Mouse Sound Card Speaker/Headphone Jack
Video Editing Software (FREE)	Movie Maker Free open-source video editing software (Ask your school tech department whether it supports the video file you will be using.) Or	
Video Editing Software (Student Edition Purchase)	Adobe Premiere Student Edition (minimum) *(Purchase of Adobe Creative Suite 6 Master Collection recommended—includes video editing, photo editing, sound editing, DVD burning, web designing, and more)*	Final Cut Pro X or higher (minimum)

PHASE 3—PROJECT PLANNING

Phase 3 will require the research of primary sources. Primary sources include the following:

- Diaries
- Artifacts
- Photographs
- Firsthand accounts
- Actual footage of that event
- And more . . .

The primary sources may be divided up by themes (teams). Here are some examples:

- Team Legacy (Red)
- Team Battlefield (White)
- Team Homefront (Blue)

Each theme will then consist of anywhere from ten to fifteen stories (folders) that will be accompanied by a plethora of primary sources. (*The total number of folders will be dependent on how many students are participating and whether the school thinks there are enough material for the students to choose from.*)

PHASE 4—KICK-OFF ASSEMBLY

OVERVIEW

The kick-off assembly, a one-day event, is designed to get the students excited about the journey they are about to embark on. A grade-level or schoolwide assembly should run approximately 90 minutes, and student participation will be essential.

The school knows their students the best and should cater the assembly to their interests and learning abilities. A few ideas that have been used in the past:

- Musicians
- Storytellers

Take the Journey: Teaching American History Through Place-Based Learning by James A. Percoco. Copyright © 2017. Stenhouse Publishers.

- Historians
- Reenactments

OBJECTIVE

Students' imaginations are bigger than we think, and to capture their interest, we must always strive to exceed their expectations. This will allow the students to get excited about the project that lies ahead.

> If you always do what you always did, you will always get what you always got.

> —Albert Einstein

PHASE 5—IMMERSION DAY

OVERVIEW

Immersion day, a one-day event, will take place on location at the national park or historical site. With the help of the National Park Service and volunteers, several activities and stations can be set up for small student groups to rotate throughout the day. The students will experience and learn various themes such as medicine, life as a soldier, artillery, and more. The students will begin to respect and appreciate the richness of the land and history that surrounds them.

OBJECTIVE

To get the students out and help them discover the history that sits right in their backyard

PHASE 6—A FOUR-DAY PITCH PRESENTATION WORKSHOP

DAY 1 OVERVIEW

1. The researched primary sources, organized by topics, will be presented to all the teams. The students will be asking themselves these questions during the presentation:
   a. Is this a good story?

    b.   Do I think this story can turn into a good movie?

    c.   Why should I care about the story?

2.   Each student will rate the topics according to their interest in the story (sample below):

	BLUE TEAM (HOMEFRONT)—TOPIC SURVEY	1	2	3	4
1	Jennie Wade				x
2	Tillie Pierce			x	
3	Sallie Myers			x	
4	Elizabeth Thorn				x
5	12-Year-Old Civilian—Mary Montfort		x		
6	Harpers Weekly				x
7	Gettysburg College—Black Ducks	x			
8	William Fisher				x
9	The Shriver Family	x			
10	Jeremiah Gage				x
11	Aftermath of the Battle				x
12	Famous Black Families				x

1 = Enjoyed it a lot

2 = Caught my attention

3 = Not as interesting

4 = No interest at all

3.   After rating the topics, each team will make a group decision on which topics they liked most, second most, third most, and so forth.

4.   A "fishbowl" lottery system will be held, and if that team's number is called, they will have the opportunity to come up and select a folder (if their first choice is there, wonderful, and if it's not, then they can select their second choice).

Take the Journey: Teaching American History Through Place-Based Learning by James A. Percoco. Copyright © 2017. Stenhouse Publishers.

5. Once all the teams have selected their stories, they will begin analyzing the material with a critical and in-depth eye. Each student will answer eight questions that will help them initiate a storytelling mind-set (sample below):

---

1. What people and/or objects are shown in the photos or discussed in the primary source(s)? *(e.g., "The real Gettysburg Address written by Abraham Lincoln" or "General Meade and his horse.")*

2. What events are shown in the photos or discussed in the primary source(s)? *(e.g., "Day 3 of the Battle of Gettysburg" and "Pickett's Charge.")*

3. Where is/are the setting(s) of the event based on the primary source(s) you have read? *(e.g., "The home of the Shriver family in Gettysburg, Pennsylvania, on July 1, 1863" and "Andersonville—a prison that held Union soldiers captive.")*

4. If available, who was the author or creator of the primary source, and did the writer or creator of the primary source want the reader to feel or think something specific? *(e.g., "The writer of the source was John Gordon, and he wanted people to see how fair and caring he was and how much he values a human being.")*

5. What emotions or feelings did you draw from the primary source? *(e.g., "I felt hope and inspiration. I felt that if we could figure out how to settle our own differences, we could make the world a more peaceful place to live in.")*

6. What is it about the story that you think movie watchers will care about? *(e.g., "I believe the risks that the Black Ducks made as a secret white college fraternity to help runaway slaves will be what movie watchers really care about.")*

7. What additional information do you need to help tell your story from beginning to end? *(e.g., "We need more photos of Abraham Lincoln and letters by close friends or family that mentions Lincoln being a great leader.")*

8. What do you think is the message of the story, and how does this message relate to you today as a young student? *(e.g., "The message of the story is that 'the war stays with us even after the battle has*

> *ended' and the message of the story relates to me because we often go through hard times—sometimes even tragic moments, and those memories can never be erased from us. It's important to understand how we can help others adjust to the aftermath, so we don't end up having the same fate as the Shriver family.")*

DAY 1 OBJECTIVES

1. Students begin to learn how to work as a team on a unique project that demands absolute teamwork and professionalism.

2. As a team, the students will build a compelling story that they wish to tell.

3. As a team, the students will find a strong message and begin understanding the importance of the message and its modern relevance.

DAY 2 OVERVIEW

1. The faculty will review and reiterate the importance of teamwork and professionalism.

2. Students will then select their role on the team for Days 2–4. (These roles are only for the workshop.) Sample below:

Spokesperson = Student will be in charge of choosing the folder, making sure the team is working on their tasks and progressing in a timely fashion, and will be the main presenter in front of the film panel.

Storyboard Artist = Student 1 will be responsible for coming up with camera shots and descriptions; Student 2 will be responsible for illustrating the camera shots with descriptions.

Screenplay Writer = Student 1 will be responsible for writing the dialogue/narration; Student 2 will be responsible for writing the visuals (describes the scene occurring at the moment); Students 1 and 2 will be responsible for listing audio bits and FX (sounds of footsteps or cannon noise).

Movie Poster Artist = Student will be responsible for illustrating and coming up with a title, tagline, etc.

Researcher = Student 1 will be responsible for going through the primary resources and finding key elements that could benefit the screenplay writer; Student 2 will be responsible for going through the primary resources and finding key elements that could benefit the storyboard and movie poster artist.

SPOKESPERSON _____

STORYBOARD ARTIST _____

STORYBOARD ARTIST _____

SCREENPLAY WRITER _____

SCREENPLAY WRITER _____

MOVIE POSTER ARTIST _____

RESEARCHER _____

RESEARCHER _____

3. Once roles have been selected, the team will review and share their individual answers from the eight-question analysis sheet (filled out on Day 1) to each other.

4. After reviewing the eight-question analysis sheet, the spokesperson will then fill out a four-question team guide sheet (sample below), which will help them determine a specific story and message they want to tell in their movie:

1.   What is the story being told?

2.   What is the message of the story?

3.   Why is the message important to you, and how does the message affect and relate to you today as a student, a citizen of America, and/or you and your family?

4.   How would you like to convey this modern relevance in your movie? *(How will you tell your story?)*

5.   Once the team has determined the direction they want to take for their movie, they will begin working on the following items:

  a.   MOVIE POSTER—The movie poster will require a movie title, a tagline (a short, concise, catchy phrase, such as "You'll believe a man can fly" *[Superman 1978]*), and an illustration that best represents your story.

  b.   SCREENPLAY—The screenplay will be the opening scene of their movie (not the full movie); the screenplay will require dialogue/narration, visuals, and sound (sample below):

NARRATION/DIALOGUE	VISUALS	SOUND
GEORGE SHRIVER (voiceover) I need you to know that I am coming back home . . . I promise **HETTIE SHRIVER (voiceover)** I hope so . . .	**(BLACK SCREEN)**	Start to hear faint cannon noises and the sound of soldiers yelling.
NARRATOR The war began, and after three days the war ended . . .	George and soldiers running away from the Confederates	The only sound heard is a heartbeat starting fast, but then it slowly fades away.
NARRATOR But what the Shrivers did not realize was that the war would stay with them forever. **SADIE** I can't wait for Father to come home.	**DINING ROOM** Hettie and the two daughters, Mollie and Sadie, are setting up the dining table.	No Sound FX

   c. STORYBOARD—The storyboard will be an shot-by-shot illustration of the screenplay's opening scene; the storyboard will require a minimum of five shot descriptions that are accompanied by an illustration for it:

SHOT:	SHOT:	SHOT:
MEDIUM CLOSE-UP of Sadie seeing the battle begin	2-SHOT of Sadie and Mollie fearing for their lives	MEDIUM SHOT of Sadie seeing the soldiers raid her house

DAY 2 OBJECTIVES

1. Create team trust and build a solid foundation for team success.
2. As a team, determine a compelling story to tell, accompanied by a strong message that has great meaning and modern relevance.
3. Complete a movie poster, screenplay, and storyboard.

DAY 3 OVERVIEW

Students will be taught what "the pitch" is, the process of "the pitch," and why "the pitch" is important in the moviemaking business and how it applies to valuable life-skill sets (public speaking, organizational and communication skills, teamwork, professionalism, etc.). The spokesperson, with the support of the team members, will begin rehearsing their "pitch presentation." The spokesperson will have a pitch template they can fill out and use on Day 4. Students will have three to five minutes to do their entire pitch presentation on Day 4. Below are samples of a pitch summary and the pitch template (samples below):

PITCH SUMMARY

Pitching: The Art of Bringing Your Vision to the Screen

Pitching an idea for a film is a very meticulous but very exciting process—it is an art form. Ultimately, you are inspiring someone to help finance *your* project and to help make *your* idea come to life. Regardless of whom you speak to (producer, studio executive, or agent), it is imperative that you spark their interest within the early moments of your pitch. An elevator pitch is a great example of how concise you have to be in an immediate time frame. The idea is that you should be able to convince a producer that your idea is worth their time and money, all in a span of an elevator ride—which one should assume will last, at the very least, thirty seconds.

> "Northern England, 1984. Young Billy Elliot, the son of a poor local miner, decides to start training for a career—in ballet."
>
> **(Billy Elliot)**

Once a producer is hooked on your idea, it is a matter of how creative you choose to be with the rest of your pitch: storyboards, a teaser trailer, posters, line/scene acted out from the script, etc. If you are confident and enthusiastic, it's likely the producer will be, too.

Of, By, For the Student—Pitch/Presentation

A representative from each team will have two to five minutes to pitch their idea in front of a panel of judges (the "producers"). The key will be to hook the judges with a strong introduction and then to transition into a creative presentation of the following:

- (Mandatory) Sample film poster of your project with a movie title and movie tagline
- (Mandatory) Three-page storyboarding (total of five frames) with shot descriptions
- (Mandatory) Opening scene written in screenplay format

- In addition to the three mandatory items listed above, team members may reenact their opening scene while the team spokesperson continues his or her pitch

A few things to note when speaking in front of a panel:

- Maintain eye contact.
- Be aware of your time limit. (It is good to practice beforehand.)
- Articulate your words. (Do not rush through the presentation.)
- Make the story matter to you. (It will be important to focus on how the story relates to you today and how it can affect you today and in the future.)
- Be absolutely professional. (Groups will be automatically disqualified for unprofessionalism.)
- Be confident, breathe, but most important . . . enjoy!

PITCH TEMPLATE

1. GOOD MORNING! My name is . . .

[Introduce yourself and your team members.]

2. This is the story of . . .

"James Maxwell."

3. [Straight-to-the-point description of the movie]

Battle of Gettysburg, 1863; James Maxwell, a Union Army soldier and a husband and father of three, plants a dream for his family, only to have it uprooted by a Confederate soldier—that Confederate is himself.

4. It is very important that this movie gets made. With your support, we can teach other seventh graders and the rest of the world that . . .

". . . a strong family bond is needed for stability—especially in our society today, where we still have war, divorce, and other issues that can split us apart."

5. I present to you, our film, *[team member shows movie poster]*

The Lost Seed Named James Maxwell.

6. We have a great tagline for it: *[team member points to the movie poster tagline]*

"Dreams Can Become the Enemy."

7. We are using primary resources to help tell our story. For example . . . *[team member shows resources]*

"this photo of James Maxwell is the centerpiece for our movie poster. His photo, along with some of his letters, will help us reenact what we think happened to him, and his decision to switch from the Union to the Confederates."

8. This is our storyboard showing part of the opening scene from our screenplay:

- We start with a WS of James Maxwell in the middle of a wheat field,

- then a MS of James Maxwell bending down and digging a hole,

- and we end with a CU of James Maxwell's hand planting seeds in the hole.

9. Lastly, this is the opening scene from our screenplay (can be a reenactment by the team):

- *[team member reading James Maxwell's narration]* I didn't know what the war would be like.

- *[spokesperson reads visuals]* James Maxwell steps out of his house and listens for a noise.

- *[team member makes sounds]* cannon and musket noises far in the distance
- *[team member reading James Maxwell's narration]* But I knew it was coming.
- *[spokesperson reads visuals]* James Maxwell's three children come running out of the woods crying.
- *[team member reading James Maxwell's narration]* But what happened next would change my life.
- *[spokesperson reads visuals]* The three children run past their father to hug their mother, leaving James Maxwell standing alone.

10. [end by restating message of movie/story and how the message has modern relevance]

James Maxwell needed a strong family bond over 150 years ago, we need it today, and we will need it 150 years from now; that is how we bring stability and peace to this world, and this movie, supported by the Journey, will be the first step toward this goal.

THANK YOU!

DAY 3 OBJECTIVES

1. Learn what a pitch is, the process of the pitch, and why it's important.

2. Spokesperson will fill out the pitch template and then rehearse with their team members (making sure to stay within the three-to-five-minute mark).

DAY 4 OVERVIEW

The spokesperson and their team will have three to five minutes to complete their pitch presentation in front of a panel of judges and among their peers. The spokesperson may use their filled-out pitch template. After each pitch, the panel will complete a grading rubric, which will be used to determine the finalists (sample below):

Assignment Requirements

OBJECTIVES	TOTAL POINTS POSSIBLE
PITCH and MESSAGE (50)	
The message and its modern relevance were clearly demonstrated.	/25
The overall pitch was clear and effective.	/10
The team demonstrated great potential (based on the pitch, the message/modern relevance, leadership, team dynamic, and professionalism).	/15
PRIMARY SOURCES (14)	
Are primary sources used correctly/accurately?	/7
Are primary sources used effectively?	/7

MOVIE POSTER, STORYBOARD, SCREENPLAY (6)	
Is there a completed movie poster?	/2
Is there a completed storyboard?	/2
Is there a completed screenplay?	/2

PROFESSIONALISM (30)	
The presentation is conducted maturely and professionally.	/25
The spokesperson's dress attire is professional and appropriate.	/5
OVERALL PRESENTATION SCORE	**/100**

All students will be handed a separate peer review sheet, which will allow them to rate each pitch presentation.

All grading rubrics will be collected at the end. The overall scores will be tallied, which should determine the finalists (other factors in combination with the final score that may determine winners are importance of story for the Park Service or community or the uniqueness of the story (a story that hasn't been told before).

DAY 4 OBJECTIVES

1. Spokesperson and team will present in a professional and mature manner throughout the entire pitch.

2. Students find a way to tell a compelling story with their primary sources.

3. Students are able to convey a strong message and convey how that message relates or is important to them today as a student, a family member, or even as a citizen of their town and America.

4. Students will show accurate and proper use of their primary sources.

5. Students will present their movie poster, screenplay, and storyboard.

6. Have fun!

PHASE 7—PRE-PRODUCTION

OVERVIEW OF ROLES

The finalists will have an opportunity to select new roles *(number of positions created and opened up will be dependent on the number of students per team). (Faculty does not have to use the same position titles listed below, but they are encouraged to inform the students of the actual position titles and descriptions used in the industry.)* The finalists will then move on to the pre-production phase. (Sample roles for winning team members below; **mandatory positions)

> PRODUCER: The producer will oversee the entire film project and be involved throughout all phases of the project from pre-production to post-production; the producer role is very similar to the "spokesperson" role. (Pre-Production, Production)

**DIRECTOR: Oversees the creative aspect of the film; directs the actors' performance. (Pre-Production, Production)

**SCREENPLAY WRITER 1: (Writing Team) The screenplay writer is in charge of laying out the vision of the film in script format; often, writers work closely with the director to better understand their vision of the film. (Pre-Production and Production)

**DIRECTOR OF PHOTOGRAPHY: (Camera Team) The director of photography, often known as the "DP" or "cinematographer," works closely with the director during pre-production to discuss camera shots and angles; the DP will work with a camera operator, and both will take turns operating the video camera on production day. (Pre-Production and Production)

BOOM OPERATOR: (Sound Team) The boom operator, often known as the "boom op," will be in charge of operating the boom microphone to record audio; the boom op will work with a sound utility technician to ensure the audio cable and equipment are handled with absolute care. (Production)

**PRODUCTION DESIGNER: (Art Department) The production designer will work closely with the director, costume designer, and propmaker; they will help research the outfits that will be worn by the actors (soldiers or civilians) and the props (items such as authentic-looking letters or items that would go on a table) that will be created/acquired for the director's vision. (Pre-Production and Production)

**LEAD RESEARCHER: (Research Team) The lead researcher will supervise the research of materials that could aid the director during pre-production and the editor during post-production. (Pre-Production and Post-Production)

FILM EDITOR: (Post-Production Team) The film editor will assemble the various shots into a coherent film; they will work closely with a second film editor (Post-Production) (****MUST BE AVAILABLE TO EDIT AFTER SCHOOL****)

Students who were not on the final selected teams will have an opportunity to sign up for additional important roles (sample roles for nonfinalists; they may sign up for these roles closer to filming day; **mandatory positions):

FIRST ASSISTANT DIRECTOR: The first assistant director, or "first AD," will work with the director to familiarize themselves with the script and shots in case they need to step in as the director; the first AD will also supervise the film crew to make sure everyone remains professional on the set and is on time. (Production)

SCRIPT SUPERVISOR (Writing Team): The script supervisor, better known as the "script supe" (pronounced "soup"), will be in charge of breaking down the screenplay and will keep track of scenes that need to be or have already been shot by the director. (Pre-Production and Production)

CAMERA OPERATOR: (Camera Team) The camera operator, or "cam op," will take turns with the director of photography to record footage onto a video camera; The cam op will also be in charge of handling and carrying the video equipment professionally and with great care. (Production)

SOUND UTILITY TECHNICIAN: (Sound Team) The sound utility technician will work closely with the boom operator; they will be in charge of handling and carrying the audio cables/equipment professionally and with great care. (Production)

COSTUME DESIGNER: (Art Department) The costume designer will use research done by the production designer to acquire, or possibly help create, wardrobe or other materials that need to be sewn together (a sewing team will be assembled); the costume designer will also assist with wardrobe on production days. (Pre-Production and Production)

**PROPMAKER: (Art Department) The propmaker will use research done by the production designer to acquire, or possibly help create, props needed for the set or the actors; the propmaker will also assist with setting up props on production days. (Pre-Production and Post-Production)

ASSISTANT RESEARCHER: (Research Team) The assistant researcher will assist with research on materials needed for the director and the screenplay writer and material that may be requested by the post-production team (Pre-Production)

Students who were not on the final selected teams will also have an opportunity to sign up as actors/actresses right before filming day.

Take the Journey: Teaching American History Through Place-Based Learning by James A. Percoco. Copyright © 2017. Stenhouse Publishers.

OVERVIEW OF PRE-PRODUCTION CALENDAR

The ten stages can be completed around the school schedule (ranging anywhere from one to two months, depending on the scale of the project/story):

Stage 1—Finding a message; what is the modern relevance of that message?

Stage 2—Write the screenplay; Draft 1 reviewed.

Stage 3—Continue writing the screenplay; Draft 2 reviewed.

Stage 4—Finalize the screenplay; Final Draft reviewed.

Stage 5—Location scouting based on the scenes from all the screenplays.

Stage 6—Practice framing shots with camera/practice recording audio (if applicable).

Stage 7—Acquire/create props and wardrobe.

Stage 8—Complete casting call; finalize all filming day preparation.

Stage 9—Create camera shot list (great way to keep the students' vision organized).

Stage 10—Script rehearsal/organize all production items one or two days before filming day.

OBJECTIVES OF PRE-PRODUCTION

1. Continue building teamwork, organizational, and communication skills.

2. Prepare everything needed for filming day (screenplay, actors, camera shot list, props, wardrobe, cameras, audio equipment, etc.).

3. Students will build a network with the available faculty resources (librarian, sewing instructor, art teacher, history teacher, etc.).

PHASE 8—PRODUCTION aka PRINCIPAL PHOTOGRAPHY

OVERVIEW OF FILMING DAY

Be sure to have *all* of the following:

- All the actors scheduled to be filmed that day
- The screenplay (you will need extra copies)
- Camera shot list
- The students who have a role for filming day (director, camera operator, etc.)
- Wardrobe and props
- Video camera (or video recording device)
- Extra video camera batteries (always helpful to have these)
- Audio recording equipment (if applicable)
- Bottled water (trash bag required)

IT'S FILMING DAY! Faculty, administration, and any support received from park services, historians, or local volunteers will guide the students to their filming locations. The students will begin to work their magic by filming everything they listed on the camera shot list and ensuring everything from the screenplay is being recorded (dialogue, action, emotions, etc.).

It is highly recommended that a faculty member monitor what is being recorded on the camera to assist with any composition adjustments. A student should never have just one take for one shot. Even if the student is very satisfied with the first shot, a safety shot is required; if the student is unsatisfied with the first five shots and is happy with the sixth shot, they should do a seventh shot for safety. Faculty will make sure the students are getting all their shots within the allotted time for filming. *(Note: time will go by very fast, so it is imperative that the students be organized, communicating, and listening at all times; this will help them move swiftly from shot to shot and location to location.)*

OBJECTIVES OF PRODUCTION

1. Have fun!

2. Use all the skill sets learned from the four-day workshop and pre-production phases (teamwork, organizational and communication skills, professionalism, etc.).

3. Build time management and prioritization skills.

PHASE 9—POST-PRODUCTION

OVERVIEW OF POST-PRODUCTION

Before the start of post-production, faculty is advised to select editors based on several factors: technical prowess, absolute patience, creativity, focus, organization, someone who is open to new ideas and works well with others. It is recommended that the person in the editor position work closely with the language arts instructor, history instructor, and/or an instructor who handles the technical side of the editing program.

The music supervisor will be required to have great musical insight and the ability to play instruments *or* have a passion for music and be able to seek other students with the ability to sing or play instruments. It is recommended that the person in the music supervisor position work closely with the school music instructor.

The positions for Phase 9 are as follows:

Editor (1–2)

Music Supervisor (x1)

1. The students will begin to edit their recorded video and audio.

2. They will also apply visual FX and insert sound FX.

3. They will be encouraged to compose their own music or to play copyright-free music pieces (such as classical music that is over 100 years old and in the public domain).

OBJECTIVES OF POST-PRODUCTION

1. The students will strive to create a coherent and compelling movie from beginning to end.

2. The students will build a strong network with various school instructors (*those who will best be able to assist the students with the technical side of editing and the storytelling*).

PHASE 10—MARKETING/PREMIERE PREP

OVERVIEW OF PREMIERE PREP

Faculty and administration will coordinate to premiere the student vodcasts at a location of their choice (school, local theater, etc.). The family, friends, the entire school, all volunteers, park services, historians, and local businesses are encouraged to attend the movie premiere.

OVERVIEW OF MARKETING (OPTIONAL)

The students will have an opportunity to market their "product." The students may create artwork (movie posters, art paintings, sculptures, etc.) and social media sites to promote their film and school. The students may also want to consider holding a fund-raiser by selling their artwork to help fund their movie premiere venue or equipment that may be required for the upcoming class.

OBJECTIVES OF MARKETING/PREMIERE PREP

1. To teach students the concept of marketing and how to raise money to support their vision

2. To bring the community together and show support for the future leaders of America

PHASE 11—PREMIERE

OVERVIEW OF PREMIERE

It is time for the students to show the results of their hard work and dedication!

(optional)

The school may consider forming a panel with students and faculty members to participate in a Q&A session after the movie screening. The school may also consider holding a reception afterward.

OBJECTIVES OF PREMIERE

1. The students get to relax and enjoy!

2. The students should share their enthusiasm with family and friends and share all the things they have learned over the course of the entire project.

PHASE 12—PROJECT ANALYSIS AND REVIEW

OVERVIEW

Phase 12 is an opportunity to bring all participants of the projects (faculty, administration, park services, select students, etc.) together to analyze and review all aspects of the project they just completed.

Together, everyone will come to a consensus on what worked, what didn't, and what could strengthen all phases of the project. The OBF (Of, By, For) Curriculum Resource Guide can be overwhelming, but it is up to the school to adjust their lesson plans and this guide in ways they think work best for their students and all those who are participating as leaders.

OBJECTIVES

1. The school will bring all leaders together to build upon their success with the students.

2. The school will adjust their lesson plans accordingly, based on the analysis and review of the completed project.

3. Be ready for the next set of students!

Take the Journey: Teaching American History Through Place-Based Learning by James A. Percoco. Copyright © 2017. Stenhouse Publishers.

APPENDIX 4.2
Guiding Questions for *The Colors of Courage*

Please answer the following questions in several complete sentences. Please type your responses.

PART 1

- After reading the book, what more might be added to the vignettes of the "Principal Characters: spring and summer, 1863" found in the prologue?

- What attitudes did free blacks, immigrants, and white women have toward one another at the advent of the battle?

- When Margaret Creighton tells the story of Sadie Bushman [page 43] she, in essence, is presenting a biography of the common experience of a schoolgirl in the summer of 1863. What historical evidence does the author use to construct her biography of Sadie?

- Before the Battle of Gettysburg, what was the African American experience? Please comment on the "continuum of danger" [page 50] and the "other underground railroad" [page 51].

- What was the influence of the AME church in the lives of free blacks and in understanding the society in which they lived for African Americans in Gettysburg during this time?

PART 2

- What were the various experiences of the townspeople who stayed in the borough during the battle? How did those experiences compare with their encounters with Southern and Northern troops as they prepared for battle?

- How did the experiences of white and black women differ in Gettysburg in the period before, during, and after the battle?

- Creighton talks about "boundaries," "arenas," and "perimeters" [page 98] in relation to each of the groups she has chosen to study. What is the significance of each of these terms to the Battle of Gettysburg?

- How does the immigrant experience reflect the attitude of "native-born" Americans in the mid-nineteenth century?

- In the aftermath of the battle, how did the work of whites differ from that of blacks (both men and women)?

PART 3

- How could you tell the "story" of the aftermath of the Battle of Gettysburg in terms of
  - the physical environment?
  - economic opportunity?
  - how the lives of each of the "studied" groups changed?
- What do artifacts [page 156] found on bodies tell about the lives of those who possessed them?

- Keeping in mind Tom Connors's advice to "Embed complex concepts in concrete stories. Choose stories with meaning for your narrative," which stories will you select to tell to help students understand the significance of Gettysburg? The Civil War? Life in a mid-nineteenth-century town?

- The story of Gettysburg changed over time. Trace the changes and connect them to national events and attitudes that influenced the different ways the story was told.

- Historian Phillip Shaw Paludan argues that "History challenges memory to make what we think and believe about our nation reflect actual experience. At times history does not make us feel good." In that context, why do you think the story of Gettysburg evolved in our national memory the way it did despite what really happened to women, African Americans, and immigrants who participated in this event?

Take the Journey: Teaching American History Through Place-Based Learning by James A. Percoco. Copyright © 2017. Stenhouse Publishers.

Gettysburg and Mr. Lincoln's Speech

Gettysburg and Mr. Lincoln's Speech

By Timothy Rasinski

A reader's theater for five voices

Narrator 1: The Civil War was a tragic time in America. It pitted the Southern states against the Northern states.

Narrator 2: It also pitted brother against brother and friend against friend.

Northern Soldier: I fight to end slavery and to make our country whole again— although we may come from many states, we are one nation and always will be one nation.

Southern Soldier: I fight against the Northerners who try to impose their will on the South, telling us that we have to put an end to slavery, telling us that we cannot live our lives the way that we wish.

Narrator 1: The war was a bloody one. More American soldiers died in the Civil War than in any other war involving the United States.

Narrator 2: Through the first few years of the Civil War, the Southern, or Confederate, army, under General Robert E. Lee, won battle after battle against the North.

Southern Soldier: One of us Rebels can whip the tar out of ten Yankees!

Northern Soldier: We are good soldiers and we're ready to fight. Our generals, however, are no match for the Confederate generals—Robert E. Lee and Stonewall Jackson.

Narrator 1: In 1863, General Lee felt strong enough to invade Pennsylvania, an important Northern state. By taking the war to the North, Lee thought that he could convince the North to give up its attempt to reunite the states and end slavery.

Narrator 2: At this time, the Union army was under the command of General George Meade. He knew that the army had to stop the Confederates. The armies met during the first three days of July 1863 in a small Pennsylvania town called . . .

All: GETTYSBURG!

81

Take the Journey: Teaching American History Through Place-Based Learning by James A. Percoco. Copyright © 2017. Stenhouse Publishers.

Gettysburg and Mr. Lincoln's Speech *(cont.)*

Narrator 1: For three days, under the hot summer sun the two huge armies struggled.

Southern Soldier: Long live the Confederacy!

Northern Soldier: Union forever! Rally 'round the flag, boys!

Narrator 2: The battle swung back and forth over those blistering hot days. It finally ended in a failed attempt by the Confederates to break through the line of Union soldiers.

Southern Soldier: We called it Pickett's Charge. It was a disaster. Thousands of gray-clad soldiers were cut down in the murderous fire coming from the Yankee lines.

Narrator 1: Pickett's Charge failed, and Lee knew he had lost the battle. He knew he had to withdraw his army to Virginia—his home state and friendlier territory.

Narrator 2: And so Lee moved his battered and defeated army from Pennsylvania on July fourth. He had to leave so quickly that many of the dead and wounded Southern soldiers were left lying on the battlefield.

Southern Soldier: We didn't want to leave our fallen brothers lying on Northern soil. But we had to retreat south or risk being annihilated by the victorious Yankees.

Narrator 1: The next day, Meade's army followed Lee out of Pennsylvania, hoping to catch up with him and complete the destruction of the Southern army. He also left many of his dead lying on the battlefield. All told, nearly 50,000 soldiers, Northern and Southern were killed, wounded, or missing at Gettysburg.

Northern Soldier: We tasted sweet victory at last. Now, we wanted to finally put an end to this bloody war. We had to chase the enemy wherever he went.

Narrator 2: But for the people living in Gettysburg, the battle was far from over. When the few thousand residents of Gettysburg returned to their homes, they were greeted by the sight and stench of death.

Take the Journey: Teaching American History Through Place-Based Learning by James A. Percoco. Copyright © 2017. Stenhouse Publishers.

Gettysburg and Mr. Lincoln's Speech *(cont.)*

Narrator 1: Imagine the scene—thousands of dead soldiers and animals lying out in the middle of the battlefield and in shallow graves under the broiling July sun. Something had to be done quickly to prevent the spread of disease from all the dead and decaying bodies.

Narrator 2: In previous battles, bodies of dead soldiers were sent to their hometowns for burial.

Narrator 1: But this was not possible at Gettysburg. There were simply too many dead and not enough workers to prepare the bodies for transport home. It would take too long.

Narrator 2: The governor of Pennsylvania then made an important decision: the dead soldiers would be buried in a new cemetery in Gettysburg. Burying the bodies in Gettysburg could be accomplished quickly. The threat from the spread of disease would be averted. All the Northern states were asked to contribute money for the cemetery for the Gettysburg dead.

Northern Soldier: And so, from July to November, in the year 1863, workers gathered the bodies of our fallen comrades and buried them in the new cemetery.

Southern Soldier: Even some of our Southern martyrs were buried at Gettysburg.

Narrator 1: By November, the cemetery was finished. By November, the country understood just how important the Battle of Gettysburg was. No more would the Confederate army threaten the Northern states. The Confederacy had reached its high mark and was now in decline.

Narrator 2: Thus, it was decided that a dedication for the cemetery should take place to honor those Northern soldiers who made the ultimate sacrifice at Gettysburg.

Narrator 1: Dignitaries from around the country were invited. President Lincoln came. The greatest orator, or speechmaker, of the day, Edward Everett, was also asked to give a grand speech. He spoke for over two hours.

83

Gettysburg and Mr. Lincoln's Speech *(cont.)*

Narrator 2: Those who came to the dedication were tired and wanted to go home by the time Everett had finished his long speech.

Narrator 1: But then, it was President Lincoln's turn to make a few brief remarks.

Narrator 2: Slowly, and so very deliberately, President Lincoln stood up and made his way to the podium. Quietly, he faced the crowd of public dignitaries and ordinary citizens standing in front of him. Somberly, he looked over the countless rows of dead soldiers behind him. And, in just 272 words, Mr. Lincoln helped all of us, those living in 1863 and those of us alive today, understand what is special about our country and why it could not be broken up into free and slave, Union and Confederate, North and South.

(Pause for effect.)

Lincoln: *Four score and seven years ago, our fathers brought forth on this continent, a new nation, conceived in liberty, and dedicated to the proposition that all men are created equal.*

Narrator 1: Lincoln uses words from the Declaration of Independence to remind us why the United States was founded in the first place.

Lincoln: *Now we are engaged in a great civil war, testing whether that nation, or any nation so conceived and so dedicated, can long endure. We are met on a great battlefield of that war. We have come to dedicate a portion of that field, as a final resting place for those who here gave their lives that the nation might live. It is altogether fitting and proper that we should do this.*

But in a larger sense, we cannot dedicate, we cannot consecrate, we cannot hallow this ground. The brave men, living and dead, who struggled here, have consecrated it, far beyond our poor power to add or detract.

Narrator 2: Although the dedication at which Lincoln was speaking was meant to make this land special, Lincoln knew, and he told the audience, that the brave soldiers who fought here that summer had made it much more special through their actions than by anything Lincoln could say or do.

84

Gettysburg and Mr. Lincoln's Speech *(cont.)*

Lincoln: *The world will little note nor long remember what we say here. But it can never forget what they did here. It is for us the living, rather, to be dedicated here to the unfinished work which they who fought here have thus far so nobly advanced. It is rather for us to be here dedicated to the great task remaining before us. That from these honored dead we take increased devotion to that cause for which they gave the last full measure of devotion.*

Narrator 1: Although the soldiers who died here saved the Union, much fighting and hard work still need to be done before the nation can be whole again.

Narrator 2: Lincoln realized that the United States was a grand and never-before-tried experiment for all the world to see—Can a government created by its citizens and run by its citizens truly work? The world was watching and waiting to find out.

Lincoln: *That we here highly resolve that these dead shall not have died in vain. That this nation, under God, shall have a new birth of freedom. And that . . .*

All: *Government of the people, by the people, for the people, shall not perish from the earth.*

Background Information

President Lincoln delivered the Gettysburg Address on November 19, 1863. The battlefield was to become a national cemetery. This was its dedication ceremony.

85

"Khrushchev" Group: Filming Agenda

TIME	SCENE	SHOOT LOCATION	ACTORS	PROPS
8:25–10:30 am	Scene 2	Sunroom	• Eisenhower • Khrushchev • Barbara • John • Barbara Anne • David • Susan • Mary Jean	Lapel pins
10:30–11:00 am	Scene 2	House exterior	• Eisenhower • Khrushchev • Secret Service Agents	
11:00 am–noon	Scene 3	Cow enclosure	• Eisenhower • Khrushchev • Secret Service Agents • Cows	
noon–12:30 pm	Lunch Break			
12:30–1:00 pm	Scene 4	Eisenhower office	• Eisenhower	• Pen • Notebook • "Brass" nameplates for notebook • Chair (provided by NPS) • Desk (provided by NPS)
1:00–1:45 pm	Scene 5	Den	• Eisenhower • Khrushchev	• Chess pieces • Chess table (provided by NPS) • Chairs (provided by NPS) • Blankets to cover chairs

Khrushchev Script ALL ROLES: Opening Scene

(Montage of symbols, signs, and sounds of the Cold War.)

[Bomb sirens, planes flying, others.]

(Close-up of chess pieces moving across a chessboard.)

Narrator: The Cold War was a time of fear for many Americans. Dwight David Eisenhower, the president of the United States at the time, had the difficult job of navigating the tension of the Cold War. It was during this time that his excellent leadership and strong foreign policy shined through for all to see. One of his shrewdest moves in the ongoing Cold War chess game and one of the greatest acts of political negotiation that he put into action was to invite America's most feared and hated enemy Nikita Khrushchev to his farm in Gettysburg, Pennsylvania, on September 26, 1959. With this visit, both Khrushchev, the leader of the opposing Soviet Union, and Eisenhower truly gave meaning to the saying "Keep your friends close and your enemies closer."

Scene 2

(Khrushchev and Eisenhower in sunroom. Secret Service people stand in the background.)

Khrushchev: This painting is impressive.

Eisenhower: Thank you.

(Awkward pause.)

Eisenhower: The Cold War is the most pressing issue of our time, and as you know, our two countries are at the center of it all. The people from both our countries have become worried. Nuclear weapons are being multiplied by the minute and people are on . . . edge. Disarmament is needed, but first we need to work out our differences over West Berlin.

(Grandkids, John, and Barbara come through the door.)

Grandkids: Grandpa!

John: David! Susan! Come now, say hello to Mr. Khrushchev.

(They walk toward Eisenhower and Khrushchev. The kids are hugging their parents' waists and holding hands with them.)

Barbara: Barbara Anne, Mary Jean, you say hello, too.

Eisenhower: Ah, hello! Mr. Khrushchev, meet my son John, his wife,

Barbara, and their children.

(John and Khrushchev shake hands. Barbara and Khrushchev exchange polite smiles.)

John: Pleased to meet you. The name's John Eisenhower.

(Children start play-fighting. John and Barbara go to break it up.)

Khrushchev: Some children you have there.

John: Yeah, they're a handful.

Barbara: *(Laughing.)* You're right about that.

Eisenhower: They take after their father.

David: So . . . You speak a different language?

Khrushchev: I speak a language called Russian, or as my people call it, Russkiy.

Mary Jean: Please, sir, can you tell us some words in Russian?

Khrushchev: Sure. I can tell you what each of your names mean in

Russkiy. David, your Russian name means "beloved" or "friend," and Susan . . . Susan . . . Well, I don't know what your name is in Russian.

Susan: *(Confused.)* Hey! But . . .

David: *(Smirks.)*

Khrushchev: Mary Jean, how we define your name in Russian is "rebellion," "bitter," and "gift from God." Barbara Anne, yours is "foreign grace."

Barbara Anne: That explains a lot!

Mary Jean: Heyyy!

John: Barbara Anne . . .

Khrushchev: I have special presents for you children from Moscow.

Barbara Anne: Oh boy!

(Khrushchev hands children red lapel pins.)

David: What are these?

Khrushchev: These are pins of the Union of Soviet Socialist Republics.

(Children stare in awe at pins, with adults in the background.)

[Remove camera focus off the children and Khrushchev and refocus on the adults.]
(John, Barbara, and Eisenhower look scared/concerned.)
[Music gets louder, higher, drops next scene.]

Scene 3
[Opens to Eisenhower and Khrushchev at the barn, looking at the cows.]
(Secret Service people standing in background.)

Eisenhower: I've been raising cattle here since shortly after I bought this house in 1950, after I finished my military career.

Khrushchev: You seem to be treating these steers quite well. Have

you bred any prize winners from your herd?

Eisenhower: I've had a few prize-winning cattle. Ankonian 3551 was my first winner . . . . How'd you like one of my heifers as a gift? *(Continues with cows while volume fades)*

Scene 4
(Eisenhower writing in his office.)
[Eisenhower voiceover, reading from his reflection of the Khrushchev visit.]

Final Scene

(Eisenhower walks back into the den and moves chess piece to stalemate with Khrushchev's side in a checkmate.)

[Cut to more scenes of the Cold War.]

Narrator: And so it was that two Cold War enemies got to know each other at a farm in Gettysburg and parted ways agreeing to end tensions over Berlin and to meet again at a summit to further discuss peace. Khrushchev even invited Eisenhower to come visit him in the Soviet Union. But eight months later, the bond that was created that day was lost. An American U2 spy plane was shot down and recovered by Soviet forces, along with the pilot. The United States originally tried to pass off the U2 as a harmless weather research plane, but Soviet analysts saw through the ruse. Khrushchev, angered at the recent development, walked out of the Paris Summit, a meeting of many powerful nations scheduled as a result of Khrushchev's successful visit to Eisenhower's farm, where peace and demilitarization treaties were to be put into action. The silence between the USSR and America resumed, continuing for another thirty years. However, the meeting of these leaders in Gettysburg had lasting positive effects for the two nations. The people of both nations began to tolerate each other a little more. The shroud of mystery around the people of the Soviet Union was peeled back little by little, slowly revealing more commonalities in humanity than differences in beliefs. In his farewell address to the nation, Eisenhower said, *(Narrator's voice begins to read quote, fading into Eisenhower's voice, who continues reading.)* "in the goodness of time, all peoples will come to live together in a peace guaranteed by the binding force of mutual respect and love." His lasting message is a goal of prosperity for peoples of all nations, races, and ethnicities to reach for all future generations.

Selected Bibliography

General Resources

Cockburn, Andrew. 2009. *Journey Through Hallowed Ground: Birthplace of the American Ideal.* Washington, DC: National Geographic.

Glass, Brent. 2016. *50 Great American Places: Essential Historic Sites Across the U.S.* New York: Simon and Schuster.

Lee, Deborah A. 2009. *Honoring Their Paths: African American Contributions Along the Journey Through Hallowed Ground.* Waterford, VA: Journey Through Hallowed Ground.

Lillard, David Edwin. 2006. *The Journey Through Hallowed Ground: The Official Guide to Where America Happened.* Sterling, VA: Capital Books.

Percoco, James A. 1998. *A Passion for the Past: Creative Teaching of US History.* Portsmouth, NH: Heinemann.

———. 2001. *Divided We Stand: Teaching About Conflict in US History.* Portsmouth, NH: Heinemann.

———. 2008. *Summers with Lincoln: Looking for the Man in the Monuments.* New York: Fordham.

Rasinski, Timothy, and Lorraine Griffith. 2007. *Building Fluency Through Practice and Performance.* Huntington Beach, CA: Shell Education.

Chapter 1

Brimhall, Melanie R., Carole Nash, and Karenne Wood, eds. 2006. *Beyond Jamestown: Virginia Indians Past and Present.* Charlottesville: Virginia Foundation for the Humanities.

Brooks, James F., ed. 2002. *Confounding the Color Line: The Indian-Black Experience in North America.* Lincoln: University of Nebraska Press.

Coleman, Arica. 2013. *That the Blood Stay Pure: African Americans, Native Americans, and the Predicament of Race and Identity in Virginia.* Bloomington: Indiana University Press.

Commonwealth of Virginia, Bureau of Vital Statistics. 1924. *Eugenics in Relation to the New Family and the Law on Racial Integrity.* Richmond, VA: Bureau of Vital Statistics, State Board of Health.

Dorr, Gregory Michael. 2008. *Segregation's Science: Eugenics and Society in Virginia*. Charlottesville: University of Virginia Press.

Egloff, Keith, and Deborah Woodward. 2006. *First People: The Early Indians of Virginia*. Charlottesville: University of Virginia Press.

Gould, Stephen Jay. July 1984. "Carrie Buck's Daughter." *Natural History*. Reprinted in Gould's *The Flamingo's Smile*, 1985. New York: Norton.

Lombardo, Paul A. 2010. *Three Generations, No Imbeciles: Eugenics, the Supreme Court, and* Buck v. Bell. Baltimore: Johns Hopkins University Press.

Smith, David. 1992. *The Eugenic Assault on America: Scenes in Red, White, and Black*. Fairfax, VA: George Mason University Press.

Smith, Karla. 2003. *Virginia Native Peoples*. Chicago: Heinemann Library.

Tayac, Gabrielle, ed. 2009. *Indivisible: African-Native American Lives in the Americas*. Washington, DC: Smithsonian.

Whitlock, Rosemary Clark. 2009. *The Monacan Indian Nation of Virginia: The Drums of Life*. Tuscaloosa: University of Alabama Press.

Wood, Karenne. 2009. *The Virginia Indian Heritage Trail*. Charlottesville: Virginia Foundation for the Humanities.

Chapter 2

Adams, Henry. 1909. *History of the United States of America During the First Administration of Thomas Jefferson*. New York: Charles Scribner's Sons.

Adams, John Quincy. 1839. *The Jubilee of the Constitution: A Discourse*. New York: Samuel Colman.

Bigler, Philip, and Annie Lorsbach. 2009. *Liberty and Learning: The Essential James Madison*. Harrisonburg, VA: James Madison Center.

Brookhiser, Richard. 2013. *James Madison*. New York: Basic Books.

Burstein, Andrew, and Nancy Isenberg, 2010. *Madison and Jefferson*. New York: Random House.

Cheney, Lynne. 2015. *James Madison: A Life Reconsidered*. New York: Penguin.

Ellis, Joseph. 1998. *American Sphinx: The Character of Thomas Jefferson*. New York: Vintage.

———. 2001. *Founding Brothers: The Revolutionary Generation*. New York: Knopf.

Gordon-Reed, Annette. 2008. *The Hemingses of Monticello: An American Family*. New York: W. W. Norton.

Gordon-Reed, Annette, and Peter Onuf. 2015. *"Most Blessed of the Patriarchs": Thomas Jefferson and the Empire of Imagination*. New York: Liveright.

Hickey, Donald R. 2012. *The War of 1812: A Forgotten Conflict*. Urbana: University of Illinois Press.

——, ed. 2013. *War of 1812: Writings from America's Second War of Independence.* New York: Library of America.

Kass, Amy A., Leon R. Kass, and Diana Schaub, eds. 2011. "*Federalist* No. 10." In *What So Proudly We Hail: The American Soul in Story, Speech, and Song.* Wilmington, DE: ISI Books. http://www.whatsoproudlywehail.org/wp-content/uploads/2013/03/Publius_-Federalist-No.-10.pdf?2db700.

Mattern, David B., ed. 1997. *James Madison's "Advice to my Country."* Charlottesville: University Press of Virginia.

Meacham, Jon. 2012. *Thomas Jefferson: The Art of Power.* New York: Random House.

Miller, Brandon Marie. 2011. *Thomas Jefferson for Kids: His Life and Times with 21 Activities.* Chicago: Chicago Review Press.

O'Connor, Sandra Day, and John Glenn. 2015. "Teaching Better Civics for Better Citizens." *The Wall Street Journal,* May 12. http://www.wsj.com/articles/teaching-better-civics-for-better-citizens-1431471803.

Onuf, Peter S. 2000. *Jefferson's Empire: The Language of American Nationhood.* Charlottesville: University Press of Virginia.

Ragosta, John. 2013. *Religious Freedom: Jefferson's Legacy, America's Creed.* Charlottesville: University Press of Virginia.

Schwartzman, Paul. 2016. "Why Some Whites Are Waking Up to Racism." *Washington Post,* August 3. https://www.washingtonpost.com/local/social-issues/why-some-whites-are-waking-up-to-racism/2016/08/03/5f2c2386-5051-11e6-aa14-e0c1087f7583_story.html?utm_term=.1ad10bbfa7df.

Stewart, David O. 2015. *Madison's Gift: Five Partnerships That Built America.* New York: Simon and Schuster.

Wills, Garry. 2015. *James Madison.* New York: Times Books.

Chapter 3

Bordewich, Fergus M. 2005. *Bound for Canaan: The Underground Railroad and the War for the Soul of America.* New York: Amistad.

Dickens, Charles. 1842. *American Notes for General Circulation.* London: Chapman and Hall.

Douglass, Frederick, and Henry Louis Gates, ed. 1994. *Frederick Douglass: Autobiographies: Narrative of the Life of Frederick Douglass, Frederick Douglass, an American Slave/My Bondage and My Freedom/Life and Times of Frederick Douglass.* New York: Library of America.

Du Bois, W. E. B. 1996. *The Souls of Black Folk.* New York: Modern Library.

Earle, Jonathan. 2008. *John Brown's Raid on Harpers Ferry: A Brief History with Documents.* New York: Bedford/St. Martins.

Horowitz, Tony. 2011. *Midnight Rising: John Brown and the Raid That Started the Civil War.* New York: Henry Holt.

The Journey Through Hallowed Ground. 2009. Excerpt from Robert G. Stanton speech. https://www.hallowedground.org/Education/Of-the-Student-By-the-Student-For-the-Student-Service-Learning-Projects/Harpers-Ferry-1859-2009.

McBride, James. 2013. *The Good Lord Bird.* New York: Riverhead Books.

McFeeley, William S. 1991. *Fredrick Douglass.* New York: W. W. Norton.

Moore, Jacqueline. 2003. *Booker T. Washington, W. E. B. Du Bois, and the Struggle for Racial Uplift.* New York: Rowman and Littlefield.

Norrell, Robert J. 2009. *Up from History: The Life of Booker T. Washington.* Cambridge, MA: Belknap Press of Harvard University Press.

Reynolds, David. 2005. *John Brown: Abolitionist.* New York: Knopf.

Washington, Booker T. 1995. *Up from Slavery.* New York: Dover.

Chapter 4

Adelman, Garry, ed. 2011. *The Civil War 150: An Essential To-Do List for the 150th Anniversary.* Guilford, CT: Lyons Press.

Civil War Trust. n.d. "Reflecting on the 150th Anniversary of the Civil War." http://www.civilwar.org/150th-anniversary/message-from-jim-lighthizer.html?referrer=https://www.google.com/#.

Hennessy, John. 2015. *The First Battle of Manassas: An End of Innocence.* Harrisburg, PA: Stackpole Books.

McPherson, James. 2002. *Antietam: The Battle That Changed the Course of the Civil War.* New York: Oxford.

———. 1988. *Battle Cry of Freedom: The Civil War Era.* New York: Oxford.

———. 1997. *For Cause and Comrades.* New York: Oxford.

———. 2015. *The War That Forged a Nation: Why the Civil War Still Matters.* New York: Oxford.

O'Reilly, Francis A. 2006. *The Fredericksburg Campaign: Winter War on the Rappahannock.* Shreveport: Louisiana State University Press.

Rable, George C. 2002. *Fredericksburg! Fredericksburg!* Raleigh: University of North Carolina Press.

Sears, Stephen W. 1993. *Antietam: Landscape Turned Red.* New York: Ticknor and Fields.

———. 1996. *Chancellorsville.* New York: Houghton Mifflin.

———. 2003. *Gettysburg.* New York: Houghton Mifflin.

Shively, Carol A., ed. 2015. *Asians and Pacific Islanders and the Civil War.* Washington, DC: National Park Service.

Tucker, Glenn. 1995. *High Tide at Gettysburg: The Campaign in Pennsylvania.* Gettysburg, PA: Stan Clark Military Books.

Twain, Mark, and Charles Dudley Warner. 1873. *The Gilded Age: A Tale of Today.* Hartford, CT: American.

Chapter 5

Ambrose, Stephen. 1991. *Eisenhower: Soldier and President.* New York: Simon and Schuster.

Beschloss, Michael. 1988. *Mayday: Eisenhower, Khrushchev, and the U-2 Affair.* New York: Harper and Row.

Eisenhower, David. 2011. *Going Home to Glory: A Memoir of Life with Dwight Eisenhower.* New York: Simon and Schuster.

Eisenhower, Dwight D. 1963. *The White House Years: Mandate for Change, 1953–1956.* New York: Doubleday.

———. 1965. *The White House Years: Waging Peace, 1956-1961.* New York: Doubleday.

Oshinsky, David M. 2005. *Polio: An American Story, The Crusade That Mobilized the Nation Against the 20th Century's Most Feared Disease.* New York: Oxford.

Smith, Jean Edward. 2012. *Eisenhower in War and Peace.* New York: Random House.

Chapter 6

Bluestone, Daniel. 2010. *Buildings, Landscapes, and Memory: Case Studies in Historic Preservation.* New York: W. W. Norton.

Kaufman, Ned. 2009. *Place, Race, and Slavery: Essays on the Past and Future of Historic Preservation.* Abingdon, UK: Routledge.

Tomlan, Michael A. 2014. *Historic Preservation: Caring for Our Expanding Legacy.* New York: Springer.

Tyler, Norman, and Ted J. Ligbel. 2009. *Historic Preservation: An Introduction to Its History, Principles, and Practice.* New York: W. W. Norton.

Index